Battles for the Standard

Modern Economic and Social History Series

General Editor: Derek H. Aldcroft

Titles in this series include:

Battles for the Standard

Bimetallism and the spread of the gold standard
in the nineteenth century

TED WILSON

Ashgate

Aldershot • Burlington USA • Singapore • Sydney

© 2000 Ted Wilson.

All rights reserved. No part of this publication may be reproduced, stored in a retrieval system, or transmitted in any form or by any means, electronic, mechanical, photocopied, recorded, or otherwise without the prior permission of the publisher.

The author has asserted his right under the Copyright, Designs and Patents Act, 1988, to be identified as the author of this work.

Published by

Ashgate Publishing Ltd
Gower House, Croft Road,
Aldershot, Hampshire GU11 3HR
UK

Ashgate Publishing Company
131 Main Street
Burlington, VT 05401–5600
USA

Ashgate website: http://www.ashgate.com

ISBN 1 85928 436 1

British Library Cataloguing-in-Publication Data
Wilson, Ted, 1946–
    Battles for the Standard: Bimetallism and the Spread of the Gold Standard
    in the Nineteenth Century. — (Modern Economic and Social History)
    1. Bimetallism—History—19th century.   2. Gold standard—History—19th
    century.   I. Title
    332.4'23'09034
MK

US Library of Congress Cataloging-in-Publication Data
The Library of Congress control number is pre-assigned as: 00–105497

This volume is printed on acid-free paper.

Typeset by Manton Typesetters, Louth, Lincolnshire and printed in Great Britain by TJ International Ltd., Padstow, Cornwall.

Contents

To Jan, Linz and Em.

Modern Economic and Social History Series
General Editor's Preface

Economic and social history has been a flourishing subject of scholarly study during recent decades. Not only has the volume of literature increased enormously but the range of interest in time, space and subject matter has broadened considerably so that today there are many sub-branches of the subject which have developed considerable status in their own right.

One of the aims of this new series is to encourage the publication of scholarly monographs on any aspect of modern economic and social history. The geographical coverage is world-wide and contributions on non-British themes will be especially welcome. While emphasis will be placed on works embodying original research, it is also intended that the series should provide the opportunity to publish studies of a more general and thematic nature which offer a reappraisal or critical analysis of major issues of debate.

Derek H. Aldcroft

Manchester Metropolitan University

Acknowledgements

I would like to acknowledge the help of my colleagues John Hassan, Terry Wyke, Neville Kirk, John Wilson, Derek Aldcroft and Audrey Kaye for reading various sections of the work and making valued recommendations. I would like to thank Peter Cain for first suggesting the topic many years ago.

Preface

The aim of this book is to trace the development of bimetallism in the nineteenth century, before and during the period when the gold standard was expanding after about 1870. A major contention of the book is that the worldwide orthodoxy in the earlier nineteenth century consisted in bimetallism in its many variants, and that the international gold standard arrived as much out of default as by any deliberate course of actions either by states or individuals. The reason why the world, to use Kindleberger's phrase, 'stepped on to the gold standard' after 1870, was essentially because of the many problems, some of them seemingly not understood at the time, which prevented the introduction of a statutory, international, bimetallic standard. Different states, because of their different economic histories and prospects, had widely differing views of the possibilities of introducing a bimetallic standard. In order to understand why this was so, it is necessary to examine briefly the cases of the major countries involved in the creation of the international gold standard in the nineteenth century: Britain, France, Germany, the United States, and India. By the 1870s there was a pressing need for a monetary regime which would enable countries around the world to trade more effectively with each other and hence a system ultimately emerged in the last quarter of the nineteenth century, despite the fact that the age also saw the development of resurgent nationalism and competitive imperialism. Yet most of experts and statesmen in the countries concerned were not in favour of standardisation based upon the gold standard and in some, notably in the United States, there was a rampant opposition to it. Though for much of the time the American government went along with the British, there was considerable friction between the two states which is still not fully understood. European governments appreciated the need for greater standardisation, especially the French, who have perhaps wrongly been seen as over-zealous bimetallists. The wider perception in Europe was that standardisation could only arrive if both the precious metals were to be included. The German decision to go on to the gold standard in 1872 was primarily to emulate Britain and to ease the path towards industrialisation, though even there there was much opposition to gold monometallism. India was eventually forced on to the gold standard by the British government but only at the very end of the nineteenth century and only after much debate and in-fighting both in Britain and in the sub-continent. Nevertheless India provides a good example of a peripheral economy during the age of the international gold standard and it was the problems associated with the Indian exchanges which led directly to study of the system and ultimately the devising of the gold exchange standard, the predominant form of the interwar period. Ironically the development of a bimetallic movement in Britain partly stemmed from the realisation that India could not remain on silver and maintain its position as an important trading partner of Europe's.

Various arguments have been advanced in recent years to explain the spread of the gold standard. For example, Redish [1992] has argued that technological developments allowed monometallic systems such as the gold standard to become established by producing token coinage which could not easily be counterfeited. This book will seek to show that if this was the case, it was not understood at the time and therefore cannot be advanced to explain the spread of the system, as Redish does. Contemporay perceptions of the technical possibilities were at variance with Redish's account. Gallarotti (1994) has argued that there was a general international drift towards the gold standard after 1873 which he characterises in terms of 'chain gangs' pulling towards British practice: states were panicked into adopting a gold system because of fears about the future of silver as a monetary commodity. This book is generally sympathetic towards this point of view though it differs in detail from Gallarotti. It seeks to show, however, that although there was such a drift the reasons for moving towards gold differed widely between countries, and that therefore there is still a need for deeper consideration of the special factors in each case.

The book also focuses upon the 'Great Debate' (the term used by Francis Walker, a contemporary American economist) at the end of the nineteenth century. The main aim here is to show that the call for international bimetallism, made in many centres, was always a futile one because of the great diversity in the understanding of what was required to bring it about. In fact no ground rules were ever laid down, no agreed definitions came forward, no international organisation to focus support for a single system was ever set up. There was a vast difference between what I have called 'unilateralism' and 'internationalism' (i.e. between those who thought that international bimetallism could be brought about by a succession of individual countries joining a system, and those who thought that only international concert could succeed). Similarly there was a huge gap between 'low-ratio bimetallism' which was supported by the American silverites (and was tantamount to inflationary silverism) and the 'high-ratio bimetallism' of the more sober academicians in many countries who sought monetary stability rather than inflation. These variations have never been brought out and there is therefore a need for an international study of the kind attempted in this book. For obvious reasons there is much interest at the present time in what we might call monetary regime transformation and it is hoped that such a book will give cause to compare the spread of the gold standard in the late nineteenth century, when in many ways conditions were not good for international agreement, with the attempt to rationalise European regimes under a single currency approximately a hundred years later.

CHAPTER ONE

Gold, silver and money

Bimetallism is the name given to a monetary system in which both gold and silver are on precisely the same footing as regards mintage and legal tender.

(*Chambers Encyclopaedia*, 1908; entry on bimetallism by Professor J. S. Nicholson)

The functions of money

As economists have long recognized, money has three distinct functions. It acts as a medium of exchange, which allows the process of exchange itself to be separated into the two distinct acts of buying and selling, enabling producers to find the most suitable outlet for their goods, and encouraging specialization. It acts as a measure of value, providing a system of units in which the relative values of different objects can be expressed, massively simplifying the task of establishing, for example, how many light bulbs should be proffered for a ton of coal, or how many video games for a ten-speed bicycle. And it also serves as a store of wealth, facilitating saving, which would be almost impossible under a system of barter, and allowing wealth to be set aside for future contingencies. Only with money can capital formation take place, raising productivity and thus the general standard of living.

Money is defined largely in terms of its functions, so it follows that anything which acts as money, that is to say, which provides all of the three functions outlined above, is money, regardless of what it consists of in itself. 'Money is as money does', in other words. But to understand money further it is necessary to introduce the concept of liquidity. Liquidity is defined by the economist as the ability to turn wealth into any form without loss or delay. Using this concept, we can define money as anything, any substance at all, that confers liquidity on its holder. To act as money, a substance, or a commodity, must be generally acceptable in exchange for other goods and services of all kinds, and it must also be acceptable in the settlement of debts. Thus the basic requirement of money is that it must confer complete liquidity on whoever holds it (Nevin, 1964).

Historically, a wide variety of substances, or commodities, has been used as money. Certain kinds of polished stones, animal teeth, most kinds of metal and, famously, sea-shells and beads made from shells, such as the 'wampum' of the North American Indians, have all functioned as money from time to time. Even in recent times, cigarettes have performed some of the functions of money, in prisoner-of-war camps or even in civil society in postwar Germany, for example, when conventional forms of money have been unavailable. But in recent centuries, gold and silver, for reasons which will become apparent, have become the most widely acceptable commodities to be used as money. Until the last fifty years or so, it was only in times of war, or similar dire circumstances when the availability of the two precious metals was jeopardized for some reason, that the authorities in most countries were prepared to move their currencies away from 'convertibility' with gold or silver or gold and silver. It was only in the second half of the twentieth century that developed nations moved decisively away from what we may call 'commodity convertibility' of this kind. This is thanks to the virtual perfection of the techniques of finance and banking, which have at last allowed countries to use the cheaper option of 'paper money', whose value is not fixed by convertibility into a commodity of known value. Of course, gold is still used as a store of wealth by governments, institutions and individuals around the world, though in 2000 even this residual function seems to have been under threat.

The precious metals

Monetary systems based almost entirely on inconvertible paper, sometimes called 'fiat moneys', are, then, quite rare in economic history until the modern period and were nearly always temporary expedients resorted to only in times of war. An international monetary system based largely on fiat-paper money, such as we have today, is a truly recent phenomenon.

Gold and silver functioned as money because both commodities enjoyed great popularity and were in constant demand in all communities, from relatively primitive societies to the most advanced of civilizations. And as well as being used as money, they have always been popular for use in such items as ornaments, jewellery and ritual vessels, to the chagrin of certain economists, as we shall see. So it is not surprising that any money which consisted of gold and silver, or was convertible into gold and silver, should have enjoyed great confidence. Both precious metals fulfilled, in slightly different ways, the four basic requirements of 'money commodities': portability, homogeneity, divisibility and durability. Other likely substances simply do not fit the bill for various reasons. Lead is not sufficiently portable to be used efficiently as money (try

picking up a piece of lead of only 2" cube); diamonds are not sufficiently homogeneous, valuable though they often are; cowry-shells are
scarce enough in some (inland) territories but are not sufficiently divis-
ible to act as money in some of its requirements, and cows (still used as
money, especially for marriage dowries, in some parts of the world
today) are scarcely to be considered durable and might even die (giving
up some of their value) before a transaction has been completed.

Of the two great money metals, silver is perhaps closest to the ideal
of a money commodity. It is not as portable as gold, that is, its value-to-
weight ratio is not as high, but one might argue that gold is too
portable, that a gold coin embodies too much value to be used in most
transactions. Gold and silver enjoy both homogeneity and divisibility in
equal degree. Silver is less durable than gold in the sense that it corrodes
on exposure to air, whereas gold does not corrode at all (hence its use
as a dental filler and as a coating on electrical contacts). But silver is
more durable in the sense that it is a harder element not requiring so
many additives as gold to improve its torsional stability and resistance
to marking. Both metals have a high value in relation to their weight,
and furthermore this value is not much threatened by the appearance of
massive new supplies of either commodity. The annual output of the
world's gold and silver mines, even during the great gold rushes of the
nineteenth century, has always been small relative to the total stock of
the metals in existence.

It is for these reasons that these two particular precious metals have
performed as money through most of the modern period. Gold was
always the more valuable metal for the simple reason that far less of it
was mined and far less of it existed in usable form above ground. At
times this gave way to the *auri sacra fames*, the 'accursed hunger for
gold' remarked upon down the ages, which caused European princes
such as Frederick the Great of Prussia and Augustus of Poland to seek
artificial ways of producing the yellow metal. Alchemists who were
reckless enough to claim to possess the 'philosopher's stone' might well
find themselves imprisoned in remote castles until they gave up their
secrets. Sometimes the prince would provide them with a well-equipped
laboratory to assist their efforts, and in at least one instance this kind of
investment proved fruitful. Johann Böttger in Saxony discovered the
'arcanum' (the secret recipe) for porcelain manufacture in the early
eighteenth century at Meissen near Dresden, and thus provided his
monarch with the 'white gold' which hitherto only the Chinese had
been able to produce (see, for example, Gleeson, 1999).

We now know that the only way to change one element into another
is by harnessing vast amounts of nuclear energy and showering it with
neutrons in a nuclear reactor, but had Johann Böttger or any of his

rivals succeeded in performing the transmutation (surely the most unlikely of all counterfactual hypotheses), gold would have been destroyed
both as a unit of measure and as a store of value. The mere knowledge
that some German prince could produce limitless amounts of the substance without having to pay privateers to steal it from Spanish galleons
(the English method) would have left silver as the only candidate for a
monetary commodity, at least until a method of manufacturing it, too,
was found.

Of course, the philosopher's stone was never found, and thus mon-
archs and states always had the choice of using one or both of the two
great precious metals to give validity to their currencies. The choice lay
between a gold standard, a silver standard, or a bimetallic standard
which, as Professor Nicholson, a noted nineteenth-century proponent
of bimetallism, explained, 'used both gold and silver on the same footing as regards mintage and legal tender'.[1]

Commodity money and fiat money

In Britain, as in many other countries in the nineteenth century, both
gold and silver coins were in circulation. This did not necessarily mean,
however, that they were on bimetallic currency systems. The silver coins
used in Britain were in fact only 'token coins', and were legal tender
only up to the value of forty shillings. The value of the silver contained
in such coins was below the nominal, or face, value of the coin. Thus,
for example, the silver in twenty shillings was not worth as much as the
gold in a sovereign. A gold sovereign was what we call a 'full-bodied'
coin, where the face value of the coin was more or less equal to its
intrinsic value. In practice the face value would tend to be slightly
higher than the intrinsic value because a small fee, called a seigniorage,
was charged by the mint for converting bullion into coin.

This distinction between 'full-bodied' and 'token' coins is not merely
of passing interest. There was, as Professor Nicholson went on to
explain, a fundamental conceptual difference between *standard* gold
coin and *token* silver coin. A significant increase in the world's supply
of gold, by new discoveries for example, would result in an increase in
the amount of gold brought to the mints of the world. To countries
which used gold as a standard of value as well as a currency metal, this
would result in an increase in the volume of currency in circulation and,
ceteris paribus, a rise in the general price level. The only point in
converting gold into coins would be to use the coins to spend, and the
increase in spending power would tend to force up prices. Similarly, an
increase in the supply of silver would tend to raise prices in those

countries which used silver as a standard of value. But for a country such as Britain, which was on a monometallic gold standard, even a large increase in the supply of silver available for minting would have no immediate effect on the price level. Silver token coins were minted by the state according to the perceived needs of the economy and not according to the state of the metals markets; the Royal Mint would not accept silver for coining except on the terms stipulated by the Treasury.

This is what is meant by saying that Britain was on a gold standard in the nineteenth century. It meant that the course of the British economy was determined in part by factors beyond the control of the British people, such as the world's supply of gold. This was an inevitable result of having what we call a commodity standard. The simplest way of operating a commodity standard is to use the commodity directly as money (in full-bodied coins) and this is what happened with the precious metals, from the earliest times until well into the twentieth century. The advantages of commodity standards will readily be appreciated. There is no possibility of the currency inflating unless the total supply of the commodity is suddenly and massively increased, and in any case people have great faith in a currency which is known to possess precisely the same scarcity value as a commodity such as the precious metals. It is not surprising, then, that serious academic economists have argued in favour of returning to commodity standards in recent years. In the 1980s the Reagan administration in the United States went as far as setting up a gold commission to look into the prospects of a return to gold. The arguments advanced are not dissimilar to those supporting the concept of an independent central bank. Governments, it is argued, simply cannot be trusted not to intervene in the supply of money; since the breakdown of Bretton Woods system (of fixed exchange rates set up by the victorious Western Allies after the Second World War), most governments in western countries have typically failed to restrict the money supply, and hence money creation should be taken out of their hands. An independent central bank, such as existed in West Germany, might be better trusted to look after the money supply, but in most countries there were misgivings about taking the control from politicians and giving it to bankers. Creating a commodity-money standard would achieve independence for the currency without bringing in another group about whom there might be as much concern as there was with politicians. This does not mean that operating a commodity standard such as a gold or silver standard is a cheap option. A well-managed fiat-money system can do just as well as a commodity standard in terms of stability of prices and exchange rates (the price of the commodity money in terms of foreign currencies) and it can do so at a lower social cost. The reason is that paper money avoids the inefficiency inherent in tying up large stocks of a valuable commodity for purely monetary use. In fact a paper money can be issued at near-zero social cost because the cost of the intrinsic substance – paper – is negligible. The problem is that of ensuring that the paper money is well managed. Arguably it was only in the late twentieth century that we finally achieved this. In Britain it has come very late in the day for, as Friedman pointed out, the successful operation of a fiat-money standard requires the exercise of considerable restraint on the part of the issuing authority. And, as Artis and Lewis (1991, p. 23) have written about commodity standards:

> The whole point of a commodity-based system is to impose such restrictions upon the monetary authority, in particular to prevent inflationary policies. A commodity-based system can be thought of as a paper money standard in which there is inbuilt monetary regulation and control. So long as the monetary structure is tied to a commodity the volume of money is limited by the supply of the commodity. [But] ... the linking of money to an external object – one or more commodities, another currency, or some index of items – should not be looked upon as giving value to money. The principal part of the linkage is instead to ensure confidence and sustain the convention [that money is worth what it says it is worth] by protecting against the over-issue of money and otherwise restricting the set of feasible policies which can be pursued by the authorities.

In the nineteenth century there was usually (with notable exceptions) little debate about the wisdom of trusting governments or other authorities with fiat moneys, since few people had yet had cause to doubt the essential wisdom of using a commodity money. In wartime it was not possible to retain commodity convertibility, that is, to keep the currency on a standard, because of the exigencies of war itself: the inevitable shortage of specie which was used to pay for essential *matériel*, the need to expand the money supply to pay for the war effort in general, and so on. So commodity standards broke down in wartime. But the intention – apart perhaps from the French creators of the *assignats* and *mandats* of the revolutionary period – was always to return to convertibility of some kind as soon after the end of the war as possible.

Commodity moneys, then, were the general rule and almost all monetary authorities based their currencies on either gold or silver, or both. Where both precious metals were used we often use the term 'bimetallism' or 'dual standard' to describe them. But therein lies a problem. The term bimetallism is to a large extent governed by the context in which it is used. It has been taken to mean, variously: an ancient system of currency long outdated and discredited; a monetary regime tirelessly promoted by the French in the nineteenth century against the good sense of England and the gold standard; a pitiful nostrum advocated by economic cranks to reverse the worst effects of the 'Great Depression' of 1873–96; or a synonym of, if not euphemism for, the American populists who advocated the restoration of silver as an easy means of raising primary-product prices in the Midwest during the late nineteenth century. We shall see also that in a formal sense there are several different kinds of bimetallism according to the geographical extent to which advocates believed the dual standard should be extended and according to what kind of metal ratio (between gold and silver) should be pursued. These varieties of bimetallism are clearly identifiable in economic history but, unfortunately, have never been adequately delineated or labelled either by contemporaries or by historians. The labels, or categories, are however required to make full sense of what was being argued and the implications of such arguments during what we might call the 'great currency debate' of the 1890s.

So bimetallism may have meant many things to many people, but it is now clearly understood that bimetallism in its broadest sense was the prevailing type of monetary regime in the history of the world economy from the late Renaissance, when Spanish gold and silver became available in large quantities, until well into the nineteenth century. The late success, or rather the late preponderance, of the international gold standard by the time of the First World War, meant that in the interwar period establishments in the western countries invariably saw a 'return to normalcy' as meaning a general commitment to the restoration of the gold standard. It was more widely believed in the 1920s than it is today that the pre-1914 international gold standard had been an unmitigated success. Its return, it was confidently thought, would secure the essential needs of both the nation state and the international economy in the postwar years – price and exchange-rate stability and a return to confidence in money. The late flowering of the gold standard, arguably, had served to confuse people into thinking that the yellow metal was the only one which should ever be considered as a monetary commodity or as a standard of value. This view has prevailed down to the present day.

If this has been true for western thinking generally, it was even more true of thinking in Britain, where the only serious competitor as monetary metal, silver, had long since been abandoned and only the gold standard was reckoned within living memory. Britain was unique in having given up silver long before it became clearly advantageous to do so, though it should be noted that even Britain had operated a *de jure* bimetallic regime until 1844.

Thus in recent times those economists who have given serious thought to monetary regimes have tended to think of gold as the only conceivable commodity standard metal. Common ancestry of modern economic thought in David Ricardo might also have served to emphasize gold monomania – though even Ricardo had been converted from silver – but whatever the reason, there has been a less than perfect understanding of the true place of bimetallism and bimetallic theory in modern economic history, especially in Britain.

Bimetallism and monometallism

Of all prominent economists and economic historians it has been the American, Milton Friedman, who has campaigned longest and hardest for a restitution of bimetallism to its proper place in economic history. In so doing, Friedman has consistently challenged the conventional wisdom about the merits and demerits of a dual standard as opposed to monometallism. The conventional view is, or was, that a dual standard was always unstable and unsatisfactory, and that it necessarily involved frequent shifts between the monetary metals. Friedman has challenged the view that monometallism was always preferable, and that gold was preferable to silver. As an influential monetary economist (and monetarist), Friedman clearly has certain axes to grind which are not of concern to this chapter, but in focusing our minds on actual historical experiences with monetary regimes – Friedman is the most empirical of economists – he has helped us to see that the drift towards the gold standard was not necessarily a progressive one. Interestingly, much of his output on the subject has been non-prescriptive, and some of it has constituted empirical economic history as much as normative economics.[2]

However, Friedman has not been alone in arguing that monetary regimes such as the international gold standard of 1873–1914 have come about as much by happenstance as by either rational deliberation or by some sort of natural progression towards a superior system. Kindleberger's (1984) conclusion was that the world 'backed onto' a gold standard in the late nineteenth century, and more recently Gallarotti (1994) has argued that there was a 'scramble for gold' after 1873. Indeed, Gallarotti believes that random political factors were just as important as purely economic ones in the creation of the 'cosmopolitan gold standard'. He writes in terms of 'monetary chain gangs' – the movement of any one or a few nations to gold during a period of nervousness or uncertainty about future specie prices – and concludes firmly that 'gold won by default' in this period.

Something of a consensus is now emerging which supports the interpretation that the movement to gold of post-1873 was pragmatic at best, probably accidental, and certainly without careful deliberation by the international economic community. If this was the case, there is no reason to argue that a gold standard was ever intrinsically superior to a bimetallic system. Recent scholars of economic theory have reached the same conclusions about the relative merits of single and double standard regimes without even having to resort to empirical data.

It should also be noted that in any case a *de jure* bimetallic regime could at various times result in *de facto* gold or silver standards. Thus the eighteenth-century gold standard in Britain developed within the context of bimetallism and the American gold standard of the late nineteenth century developed within a bimetallic constitution, notwithstanding the 'Crime of '73' (1873) which prevented the minting of silver coins for a period. In fact there are essentially three main conditions under which any bimetallic regime employing gold and silver can exist:

1. *De jure* bimetallism with *de facto* gold standard
2. *De jure* bimetallism with *de facto* silver standard
3. *De jure* bimetallism with full bimetallic system and statutory gold/silver ratio.

These are not purely hypothetical cases – the nineteenth century offers illustrations of all three. Perhaps this should not surprise us since, as we have said, formal, or *de jure*, bimetallism was the essential monetary order of the 'civilized world' until the late nineteenth century and for this reason alone requires more serious attention than it has been accorded until recently. Political élites were usually willing to accept whichever precious metal was most profitable to them as the statutory standard of value. Silver, as we have suggested, was more often than not the preferred monetary metal since its relative value was most appropriate to most kinds of common trade; the high scarcity value of gold meant that it commanded too high an exchange value as either bullion or coin and it was always a security risk even when it was not being transported. Élites therefore tended to prefer silver since it proved to be a more effective activator of trade for the simple reason that trade and currencies together provided them with the source and the means of taxation, but of course they were always willing to accept gold for its own sake.

Yet bimetallic regimes emerged remarkably early in the history of money. According to some sources the very first true coins were struck by the ancient Lydians of Asia Minor, in the land of the legendary King Croesus, who were fortunate enough to have access to copious supplies of electrum, a natural alloy of gold and silver, along the banks of the Pactolus River. The Lydians were great traders and must soon have realized their naïvety in using the precious electrum, which must have varied to some degree in its relative proportions from one find to another, if not within the same find. Indeed the sheer imprudence of offering electrum coins on to any market lends credence to the view that these were indeed the first coins ever to be struck, at least in that part of the world, and one cannot help wondering if the fabulous king gained his reputation via the bimetallic electrum rather than gold.

As in so many aspects of cultural history, the great exception to the rule of bimetallism seems to have been China, whose currency arrangements developed independently of, and parallel to, western practice. The Chinese never abandoned the barter concept of money until the twentieth century; silver was cast into ingots known as *sycee* and traded as bullion rather than coin. The *sycee* traded alongside ancient bronze coins, which were mere tokens. But the West regarded China as being on a silver standard in the late nineteenth century and ironically it may have been the East's propensity to import silver at this stage which facilitated the West's move to a gold standard – yet another chance factor in the eventual displacement of silver by gold. Generally speaking it is true that the West (Europe, that is) produced the precious metals – or procured them from the New World – and exported them to the East in return for goods which were much in demand in Europe (spices, tea, pottery, porcelain, and so on). The eastern countries represented a 'hard-currency' area, since Europe produced little else that the East wanted. Yet statesmen such as Lord Salisbury, the British prime minister at the end of the nineteenth century, could be scathing about the Indians' profligate use of the precious metals in ornaments and jewellery, but realized that without it there might have been little trade with India.[3]

India, because of its great openness to the West commercially and because of its imperial ties, was not wedded to ancient currency arrangements and possessed both gold and silver moneys over time. By the mid-nineteenth century, however, India was on a full silver standard and together with China played its part in absorbing the surplus silver of the West. As we shall see, though, Indian currency questions were the cause of much controversy throughout the western world in the nineteenth century and attention to them more than anything else resulted in the 'great currency debate' of the later decades, especially since many observers in Europe and the United States wished to see India move on to a bimetallic standard. Moreover, investigation of the Indian currency led to the creation of the system of international exchange which was introduced throughout the world in the post-First World War years (the gold exchange standard). Needless to say, examination of the subcontinent's convoluted monetary history also provided one John Maynard Keynes with a stimulating economic education.

It is therefore necessary to have some understanding of currency regimes and the relevance of bimetallism and monometallism within these regimes to be able to explain satisfactorily the development of monetary policy and monetary systems until well into the twentieth century. This is despite the fact that there was no serious movement to replace gold with a dual standard after 1900. Bimetallism may have retained its adherents, but the great monetary issue of the 1920s was how to restore convertibility of any kind. Given the rapid expansion of the international economy before 1914 under a gold regime, perhaps it was inevitable that there would be a presumption about gold after 1920. Gold became associated with expansion thanks to the so-called 'Edwardian climax' in world trade, even though the gold standard had also presided over the 'Great Depression' of 1873–96.

As if to emphasize the primacy of bimetallism in modern economic history, however, it has recently been argued that a monometallic commodity currency system such as the gold standard was not even a feasible proposition until the nineteenth century. Redish's (1990) view is that effective gold monometallism only became possible when Britain developed the steam-driven stamping press to produce a credible subsidiary token coinage. The provision of a token coinage which could not easily be forged obviated, so it is argued, the need to maintain a full-bodied circulating coinage, while at the same time allowing gold to continue as the standard of value. These factors, together with the willingness of the Bank of England and the Royal Mint to accept the role of maintaining the value of the token coins, explain, for Redish, the success of the British-inspired gold standard in the nineteenth century. Her explanation not only constitutes a heroically simple, single-cause, explanation of nineteenth-century monetary history, but also suggests that the great international gold standard was yet one more product of the classical Industrial Revolution of the late eighteenth century. However, Redish is puzzled by the evident reluctance of other countries to follow Britain's lead, or even to recognize the extensive benefits which steam technology had released. But it should be pointed out that the British themselves seem to have been largely unaware of them, and the all-importance of an incorruptible token coinage was apparently lost on the participants in the currency debates of the era. Moreover, Redish (1990) seems to be blithely unaware of the widespread support for bimetallic systems on many other grounds than the mere management of the circulating coinage.

International standardization

If Britain led the way in the development of a true monometallic regime, perhaps an essential precondition of a modern currency system, it was certainly not the case that Britain pioneered the internationalization of currencies. This is surprising when we consider Britain's role in encouraging free trade in the nineteenth century, but one might argue that liberalism ultimately prevented the state from interference even in British commerce, let alone in the internal affairs of other countries. It was left to the much more *dirigiste* French to promote developments in this direction and they and their European allies made successive attempts to introduce common currencies in the nineteenth century. But France was a much more avid proponent of general standardization than the Anglo-Saxon countries, frequently calling for the universalization of weights and measures – to say nothing of the rationalization of sporting codes – in the late nineteenth century. No doubt this was due to their republican sense of *raison d'état*. Certainly, the Revolution and the reforms of Napoleon (though surprisingly he was no advocate of metrication) had educated the French in the advantages of standardization if only because the currency and other economic matters were in such a parlous condition under the *ancien régime* that even the mad-hat ideas of John Law (variously, the 'first millionaire' or the 'first Keynesian') had been enthusiastically received (see Chapter Three).

This is not to say that Britain was not responsible for eventual standardization under the international gold standard; rather that the British did not will it in any conspicuous way, any more than they willed the expansion of the English language as *lingua franca*. The British view was always that the onus lay with each country to determine its own economic affairs, unless of course that country was within the British Empire. If this meant adopting the gold standard, or feet and inches as a standard of measurement, or English as an official language, then all well and good. But the initiative was always left to other sovereign states, even when it came to adopting Greenwich Mean Time as the prime meridian. The French perhaps felt that they had more to gain by standardization because, as was ultimately shown, it gave them a better chance that their own inventions – the franc or the metre or a prime meridian over Paris – would prevail over the British variants. Even today, a stronger emphasis on the links between sovereignty and an independent currency is perhaps more apparent in Britain than in other European countries.

Perhaps it should not surprise us, given the need for international standardization, that the late nineteenth century witnessed a very large number of international conferences looking into such matters in a wide variety of subjects (from chart-making and geodesics to time-keeping and statistics), nor that the French were more 'proactive' than the seemingly complacent British in bringing about change. The period saw the most rapid expansion of international trade hitherto experienced, and this was accompanied by mass migration and significant cultural interchange. The need for standardization was becoming apparent to all but the British, whose splendid isolation applied to more than mere foreign policy-making. Perhaps it was felt in Britain that imperialism itself was a form of standardization. At any rate, international standardization was not something which much occupied the minds of British politicians or civil servants in the age of Gladstone and Salisbury.

This meant that the British necessarily did not seek to promote currency standardization fully, even within the Empire. It is a remarkable fact that as late as the 1890s Britain and its largest imperial possession and trading partner, India, operated on completely different monetary standards: Britain was at the centre of the international gold standard and India was the world's largest trading economy still using silver. And only when this state of affairs actually threatened economic and political relationships between the two great centres did the British seek to change it. The point also needs to be made that Britain had much more to lose than other countries from any kind of exchange-rate difficulties, with India or any other great trading nation, since Britain was more dependent on foreign trade than any other country. But the British response to this was to set up its own committees and commissions of inquiry, rather than seek a concert with other states. Hence the high profile of currency matters with such bodies in the late nineteenth century, making them second only in importance, in the amount of time taken up by the Houses of Parliament, to the Irish question.

Yet to the man in the street, in Britain at any rate, currency arrangements were largely technical matters which could safely be left to 'experts' or to specialized institutions. In Britain this inevitably meant the City; in France it might mean the government or the civil service. But rarely if ever was currency reform seen as a threat to national sovereignty, not even by the most monomaniac British gold-standard die-hard. The reason for this was that commodity standards were accepted as inevitable, even as being within the natural order of things, and this in itself implied that there should always be convertibility of a kind into foreign currencies, and that the currency itself would always be reliable. Until the 1870s this even applied to currencies that were on different metal standards, for the relative value of gold and silver had altered little over a very long period. Why this might have been so, and was not so after 1873, is at the very heart of the currency debate of the 1890s, discussed in Chapter Seven.

The fact of commodity standards makes the nineteenth century very different from the twentieth century. The contributors to the 'great monetary debate' of the 1890s operated within a very different intellectual paradigm from that of their counterparts of a hundred years later for this very reason: the near-universal acceptance of the need for currencies to be exchangeable for commodities possessing intrinsic value. The nineteenth-century belief in the perfectibility of social and economic arrangements may also have come into play. Standardization offered a simple means of achieving a degree of perfection, and indeed in many instances it was a largely technical matter of no great controversy. Sometimes, however, chauvinism displayed itself in the actual choice of standard unit, with the French always pushing the metre against the much older foot (which was European rather than British) and arguing strongly against placing the prime meridian on Greenwich, even though this had become the practice on most sea-charts published by the late nineteenth century (mostly published in Britain). For similar reasons, and these are touched on by Gallarotti (1994), the French objected to the gold standard because they regarded it as British, and continued to oppose it even within the Latin Union, which by and large was pro-gold standard. As we shall see in Chapter Three, there is good reason to approach the question of nineteenth-century monetary regimes and the issues raised by the switch from bimetallism to the gold standard in the light of the general question of standardization.

In the United States attitudes towards monetary matters were very different from those in Europe. Not surprisingly, economic arrangements there were pervaded by democratic forces in a way which was still not possible in the older countries. Ordinary Americans felt that they had every right to a say in the way money was ordered; indeed that it was downright dangerous to leave such things to élites, in the form of the state, or civil servants, or bankers. At the beginning of the price disturbance which brought about the great monetary debate of the late nineteenth century, the United States was still an emergent industrial power and had only recently begun its recovery from the Civil War. The country was in the grip of a 'get-rich-quick' mentality which presaged the great railway-development era. This of course would ultimately bring it to paramount industrial status, but from the viewpoint of London or Paris in 1870, the United States was not yet a power to be reckoned with in international financial matters. On the contrary, it was still regarded as a developing country dependent largely upon primary production and benefiting extensively from injections of capital from Europe while, thanks to protective tariffs, not generating a concomitantly large volume of international trade in return. America's politics in the 'Gilded Age' (a term not etymologically connected with the gold standard) were notoriously corrupt and this prevented its leaders from being taken seriously by the European powers.

In effect the United States was on a dual monetary standard in these years, for the paper money of the Civil War – the famous, or infamous, 'greenback dollar' – continued to circulate alongside the gold specie dollar. Gresham's Law did not prevent this because the price of the greenback in terms of the official currency, and therefore in terms of gold and sterling, was determined in a free market and the greenbacks fluctuated according to local and national economic circumstances.[4] In some eastern states greenbacks predominated, while on the west coast the specie standard largely applied. Such a state of affairs would have been regarded as anathema in London but had become the normal condition in postwar America.

The enormous contrast between conditions and attitudes in the United States and Europe has not been sufficiently emphasized in considering the development of monetary practice in the nineteenth century. It will be argued here that there was never any real chance of international understanding over key issues such as the choice of standard because different countries developed different cultural stances over money and therefore over the implications of monetary change. Nor is it clear exactly where the United States stood on the essential issue of bimetallism and monometallism: the American administrations of the period followed a dear-money/gold-standard policy at home and eventually defeated powerful forces representing silver inflation/bimetallism, yet sometimes advocated a bimetallic solution to the problems of world trade, especially in relation to India, which in economic terms had become extremely important to them. They also appear to have sponsored at least two of the four international conferences of the era with a view to modifying the gold-standard *status quo*. The aim of Chapter Five is to attempt to resolve some of the problems surrounding these issues.

The subject of Chapter Seven, the 'great monetary debate', refers to the late nineteenth-century monetary controversy over the question of the continued spread of the gold standard. One of the contentions here is that, contrary to the views of the recent school which sought to reinterpret the later decades of the nineteenth century as normal years for the century as a whole, the 'Great Depression' was a distinct reality. It was perceived as such in many corners of the world economy, but also in the heart of British and European industrial regions as well as in hitherto vibrant primary-producing sectors of the world's fastest-growing economy across the Atlantic. In retrospect it is surprising that this (very real) depression did not halt the spread of the gold standard, especially since so many siren voices throughout the world had warned that gold scarcity would have a contracting effect on trade and economic activity.

A debate ensued at both international and national levels. It is argued that the gold standard spread without the international concert of nations, and this is so. Yet the important nations of the world did meet on several occasions in the late nineteenth century to discuss monetary matters and it is enlightening to look at the nature and outcome of these conferences, even though on the whole they came to nothing. There were four international monetary conferences in the years leading up to the 'great monetary debate' – in 1867, 1878, 1889 and 1892. Three of these conferences were at least in part due to the continuing depression in prices which caused British and other governments to grow increasingly concerned about the state of international trade. In the 1890s this culminated in working-class people in England taking an interest in the currency for perhaps the first time. Lancashire, the home of free trade only a few decades earlier, became associated with currency reform as a means of stimulating trade partly because revisions to free trade were still unthinkable. The Bimetallic League became centred on Manchester and a north–south rift began to appear, not simply between the 'gentlemanly capitalists' of London who continued to support an appreciating gold standard which directly benefited them, and a group of industrial capitalists who were worried about their export markets, but also between northern trade unionists and doctrinaire southern socialists, over the fate of the currency and the gold standard. It is not thought that the gold standard was ever in any real danger, even in the mid-1890s, but at least some national statesmen became interested in reform and others began to fear it as a possibility. The creation of a Gold Standard Defence Association, with backing in high places, suggests that the Lancashire interests were taken seriously in certain quarters.

The gold standard was finally internationalized during the last quarter of the nineteenth century, and Chapter Six considers a variety of reasons why this occurred. Whilst one might agree with Kindleberger (1984) that the world 'backed on' to gold in these years, this does not prevent one from concluding that there were identifiable factors which were responsible for the process, and a number of recent contributions to the economic history literature have helped outline some of these.

It will be quickly ascertained that only three of the four 'core economies' (Britain, the United States, France and Germany) in the era of the great international economy, say 1850–1914, are given a chapter in this study. Germany is omitted. The reasons for this have to do with the fact that Germany became a nation state too late to have contributed a great deal to the monetary developments of the period. The importance of a country's currency is determined in part by its sheer size. The smaller countries of Europe, and these included most of the many German states of pre-1870, were, as Clapham (1921) pointed out, unable to do without the moneys of their larger and more influential neighbours. Thus, for example, the coins of many European states circulated freely and legally in the Rhineland until well into the nineteenth century. However, the decision by the new German Empire to adopt the gold standard in 1871 is universally regarded as a seminal event, and this is investigated in Chapter Six.

Finally, it is worth pointing out at this stage that when we consider the various questions surrounding bimetallism in economic history, we need to look at an extra set of exchange statistics. These concern the rate of exchange between the two great precious metals. The figures are readily available and are non-contentious. However, they are amongst the most important of all the statistics relevant to the nineteenth-century currency debates and are probably the most illustrative of the monetary story that unfolded. A brief history of the ratio runs as follows. Until the mid-sixteenth century the annual average production of gold, by weight, seems to have been about one-tenth that of silver and therefore the market ratio between the metals was not very different from 10:1. The expansion of the Spanish Empire in South America, and especially the opening of the Potosí mines (in modern-day Bolivia) in 1545 meant that from then onwards there was a rapid increase in the supply of silver relative to gold. By the beginning of the seventeenth century, silver probably constituted about 98 per cent, by weight, of the mined totals of the two metals. The proportion of gold mined rose slightly during the eighteenth century but fell back again to 2 per cent in 1800. In the nineteenth century the relative share of gold in total output increased, at first slowly, then, after 1848, more rapidly until in the period 1850–55 it had reached 18.5 per cent. If these variations in output had been reflected directly in the market prices of the two metals, it would have been quite impossible to manage any kind of dual standard over these very long periods, but fortunately this did not happen. At the beginning of the seventeenth century the exchange rate between gold and silver had been about 11:1. But despite the large new finds of silver (which caused the output of silver to approach fifty times that of gold by weight), the ratio of exchange between the metals fell only very slowly during the sixteenth century. This must have been partly due to the fact that the monetary demand for silver was high and rising and/or that the value of silver bullion in Europe's exchanges with the East was maintained at a remarkably stable level despite the flood of new Spanish silver into the West. In the seventeenth century the ratio rose in favour of gold, reaching the 15:1 level by 1670. But generally the movement was slow and steady. After 1670 the ratio enjoyed a long period of stability at 15:1, greatly facilitating the development of bimetallic currency standards. Indeed, the ratio enjoyed an even longer stable period than in the nineteenth century and it was only the discovery of large quantities of gold in the mid-eighteenth century which upset the long period of equilibrium and caused a fall towards 14.5:1. But silver then fell again and the ratio reached the characteristic 15.5:1 of the nineteenth century soon after the Napoleonic Wars.

So we can say that throughout the modern period, and right through to 1873, the rate at which the two precious metals were exchanged was remarkably stable. It tended to drift slowly in the direction of the scarcer metal and then enjoy long periods (1670–1750 and 1815–73) of stability. As the final report of the *Royal Commission on the Recent Changes in the Relative Values of the Precious Metals* of 1888 observed, 'from the middle of the 17th century the relative value of the two metals did not vary much more than 3% in either direction until the recent divergence began to manifest itself in 1873'.[5]

This stability, a feature of both the 'drift periods' and the 'stability periods', was not principally due to human intervention in the form of any strict enforcement of a statutory ratio. Market forces and the effects of arbitrage (the process of buying a commodity in one market and selling it at more or less the same time in another market) would always work against statutory arrangements held for any length of time. It seems to be the case that bimetallic coinages ensured that the metal whose quantity was tending to increase over time was drawn into the world's mints in a correspondingly greater proportion, thereby maintaining the ratio, though custom and practice and the expectations of consumers may also have played a significant role. People, it seems, got used to a ratio of, say, 15:1 and so long as the great mass of them were prepared to accept such a rate, the rate would hold.

In the twentieth century both gold and silver reverted to being ordinary commodities, and now have little monetary role. Their prices therefore fluctuate quite widely, according to the general conditions of supply and demand.

Notes

1. Professor J. S. Nicholson: entry in *Chambers Encyclopaedia*, 1908; see head of chapter.
2. Friedman has pursued this line of argument in a large number of papers and books, between the 1960s and the present day. See for example, Friedman (1992).
3. Roberts (1999). Salisbury is quoted as saying that once the Indian peasant 'resumes that process of accumulating bangles which appears to be the final cause for which men labour with brains and hands in the Nevada mines', all would be well with the Indian exchanges.
4. Gresham's Law was named after Sir Thomas Gresham, an English financier, 1519–79, and describes the well-known fact that when two or more kinds of money of unequal exchange value are in concurrent circulation,

each being available for payments, the one of inferior value tends to drive the one of higher value out of circualtion. This is usually summarized as, 'Bad money drives out good money'. The fact that the greenback was allowed to find its own value prevented it from becoming 'bad money'.

5. *Royal Commission on the Recent Changes in the Relative Values of the Precious Metals*, Final Report, 1888.

CHAPTER TWO

Britain's golden heritage

No, Let the monarch's bags and others hold,
The flattering, mighty, nay almighty, gold.
(John Wolcott (1738–1819), To Kien Long. Ode iv)

The ancient British gold standard

The role of Britain in the drift to the gold standard seems at first sight straightforward. Apart from Portugal, effectively a client state of Britain by the eighteenth century, Britain was the only country formally on a gold standard in the mid-nineteenth century. By then, economic policy, at least in so far as it concerned the currency, was determined in large part by the prejudices of the financiers of the City of London, who dominated government thinking and ensured that successive Chancellors of the Exchequer remained faithful to gold monometallism. Gladstone may have resented this deference of Parliament but resigned himself to the fact that 'The Government itself was not to be a substantive power in matters of finance, but was to leave the money power supreme and unquestioned' (Checkland, 1957). George Goschen, Chancellor at an important time for gold, was an ex-City man, and it is thought that all Chancellors in the nineteenth century had to have the tacit consent of the City to assume office. 'A crucial qualification for the post ... was a belief that the prosperity of the country depended above all on Britain's commercial supremacy and on the banking system which supported that commerce', was the considered view of Cain and Hopkins (1993) in their recent volume. The government was, after all, like any other borrower from that private institution, the Bank of England, to some extent at the mercy of the money markets and its operators. City men by the 1870s conventionally eschewed economic theory, preoccupied as they were with the 'marshalling and assessing [of] the forces likely to impinge upon a particular price in the short run' (Checkland, 1957, p. 271). By the late nineteenth century, men of the City displayed no intellectual interest in economic supposition of any kind, even in such developments as value theory, which had an obvious relevance to their undertakings. According to Checkland, the sheer instability of the City's activities served merely to convince them of its sensitivity to events in the real world, and therefore of its essential rightness. The financiers' implicit belief in the *status quo* meant that very few of them ever questioned arrangements in any radical way, and it was therefore very unlikely that many of them would ever consider reform of the gold standard. Given their ascendancy over government in such matters, it is not surprising that they had their way.

But it is often assumed that from a much earlier date political economists in Britain had been unquestioning in their support of the gold standard, and that the monometallic convictions of the City were forged long before the late nineteenth century. Indeed it is often said that Britain had been on a gold standard throughout the eighteenth century and that this was due to the unintending efforts of that greatest of Englishmen, Sir Isaac Newton. As Master of the Mint in 1717 (even the great physicist required a remunerative day job), Newton had set the Mint's buying price for 'standard' 22-carat gold for transformation into coin at £3. 17s. 10½d. per troy ounce (equivalent to £4. 4s. 11½d fine gold). In so doing he had overvalued gold relative to silver and had thus ensured that it remained the minted metal, silver being forced out of circulation. Newton had been working at the Mint for many years before 1717 and had supervised the nation's recoinage which had been recognized as necessary since at least 1695. Seventeenth-century English coin had deteriorated to a sorry condition owing to the usual depredations of clipping and shaking and the normal erosion of wear and tear. It had been decided that the cost of the recoinage should be borne by the Exchequer rather than by the holder of coin, and a window tax had been instituted to cover the cost of the recoinage, over £2 million, a very significant sum of money at that time. This early 'hypothecated tax' accounts for the fact that it is still possible to find houses of this period with windows bricked in for tax avoidance reasons.

Gold and silver at the Mint

The minting of gold and silver in eighteenth-century England was often a result of more or less fortuitous access to the two precious metals. In 1702, for example, while Newton was early into his career at the Mint, an Anglo-Dutch naval expedition to the port of Vigo in Spain resulted in the capture of over 11 million 'pieces of eight' (coins denominated as eight Spanish *reals*) recently arrived from South America. Much of this silver was brought back to England and made up into new coins. To commemorate the expedition, the name 'Vigo' was placed below Queen Anne's bust on the 1702 edition of the shilling, crown, half-crown and sixpence. The Treaty of Utrecht of 1711 resulted in a rapid expansion of trade between England and the continent and thus, in turn, an influx of gold bullion into the country. Large new editions of gold coins were put into circulation and collectors will know that these coins are quite common even today, especially the 1714 edition (Seaby, 1985).

The Africa Company supplied much of the gold used in the eighteenth century (hence the 'guinea') and the company's elephant and castle badge appeared on some of the gold coins of the era. But until 1717 Britain had been fully bimetallic and golden guineas circulated alongside full-bodied silver coins, albeit often at a premium according to the relative prices of the two metals. By finally rating the guinea at 21 shillings, Newton and his colleagues at the Mint effectively overvalued gold relative to silver. This caused a rapid fall in the amount of silver brought to the Mint because it was now more profitable for holders of silver to export their silver bullion (or full-bodied coin) and buy gold, or have their silver minted into foreign coin which better reflected its intrinsic value. As a result, the Royal Mint issued a quarter-guinea coin but, predictably perhaps, this proved unpopular as it was too small to be convenient to handle and was very easy to lose.

However, another fortuitous event caused an expansion of the silver coinage in the early 1720s. In 1720 the South Sea Company, based on a highly speculative trade monopoly with the Americas, collapsed. Holders of government stock had been persuaded to trade them in for shares in the South Sea Company, which they were offered at par and with the approval of Parliament. The speculative boom which ensued – the 'South Sea Bubble' – resulted in the Bubble Companies Act, passed quite early in the boom, which prohibited trading in the stock of any enterprises except the chartered trading companies. But the Act came too late to prevent an inevitable collapse as stock prices reached their ceiling, and even King George I lost money in the affair. However, the activities of the company on the west coast of South America caused a large influx of silver into Britain and, notwithstanding Newton's unfavourable ratio, much of this was minted into coin. Thus many of the silver coins of 1723 have the initials SSC, for South Sea Company, placed in the angles of the shields on their reverse sides (Seaby, 1985).

Small mintages of silver coins continued until 1757–58 owing to the adventitious appearance of the white metal in Britain. But the Mint could not afford silver thereafter and 1758 coins were the last issued in any quantity for another thirty years. Some scholars reckon the gold standard to have started from about this period: 'The bimetallic system of coinage had been in crisis for some decades and, to all intents and purposes, Britain was now on a gold standard' (Seaby, 1985, p. 137).

The reign of George III (1760–1820) is notable from a numismatic point of view for the sheer scarcity of coins minted. The self-inflicted 'silver famine' continued into the late eighteenth century and even copper became so scarce that little of it was minted in this era. Then of course gold became scarce during the Napoleonic Wars, but even before the outbreak of the French wars a general shortage of coin led to another vain experiment with smaller-denomination gold coins. No large-denomination coins at all were struck during the long reign of George III, though patterns for 2-guinea and 5-guinea pieces were made. Apart from small amounts of Maundy money (specially minted silver coins produced since Charles II's reign for the monarch to hand out to the poor in Holy Week) and a limited number of shillings in 1763, no silver coins were issued in the mid-eighteenth century owing to the overvaluation of gold and the high price of silver on the world's markets. In 1787 the Bank of England commissioned the Mint to issue a quantity of silver shillings and sixpences, but these were produced at a loss to the Bank. Not surprisingly, therefore, they were hoarded or otherwise taken out of circulation and so the dearth of small coin continued. The shortage became so acute that it is surprising that the British authorities did not come off gold in these years, especially when matters came to such a pass that the Bank of England began purchasing Spanish silver *reals*, or 'dollars' as they became known. The necks of the Spanish kings Carlos III and Carlos IV were countermarked with a small oval punch of the head of George III and were issued as dollars at a valuation of 4s. 9d. The actual coins originated in Spain, Lima (Peru), Potosí (Bolivia) and (most commonly) Mexico City (Seaby, 1985).

But the Spanish coins became subject to much counterfeiting and both genuine dollars with false countermarks and false coins with genuine countermarks appeared. The dollars had to be withdrawn. As these Spanish coins were of a fineness inferior to standard British coins and were issued with a face valuation higher than their intrinsic value, they can be regarded as token, rather than full-bodied, issues. Had they been full-bodied it would not have paid the forgers to counterfeit them. This highlights the obvious need at this juncture to be able to produce token coins which could not easily be counter-feited. The solution was to mint coins that were of a high and standard technical quality, but this was difficult before the coming of the steam press. However, in 1787 the Parys Mining Company of Anglesey (which possessed the world's then biggest copper mines) began pro-ducing token copper pennies and halfpennies of exceptional quality, marked 'payable in Anglesey', or 'London' or 'Liverpool'. This issue apparently worked well because of its quality, which was difficult to replicate, though the coins in any case contained nearly their full value in copper. The shortage of coin also stimulated private entrepreneurs to issue their own moneys and John Wilkinson, the iron-master, and others, began ordering coins for the payment of their workers. Others, such as the radical Thomas Spence, began issuing coins for political and propaganda purposes (Seaby, 1985).

Britain at this time was in the throes of the classical Industrial Revolution and into the 'take-off' into modern economic growth. That it was able to achieve this in the middle of a prolonged war with France and with a severely deficient coinage is remarkable enough. Clearly, satisfactory monetization is not in itself a necessary condition for economic growth in history, not even of this example of epoch-making growth. However, the situation of money scarcity could not be allowed to continue, and efforts were made by the government to improve matters. A parliamentary committee was set up in 1787 to investigate both the coinage and the administration of the Mint. Both were found wanting, but little action was taken and thus in 1798 a new inquiry was launched in the form of a Privy Council committee. Membership of this included the Earl of Liverpool, in monetary history famous for his *Treatise on the Coin of the Realm in a letter to the King* of 1805, perhaps the most seminal of all writings on the British currency; Sir Joseph Banks, the President of the Royal Society and botanist, who possessed a large coin collection; and John Rennie, the Scottish engineer. The Earl of Liverpool recommended that in order to avoid the continuous revaluation of gold coin in relation to silver, gold should be the sole standard coin and be of full weight (or 'full-bodied'), and that silver and gold coin should be token coinages with intrinsic values below their face value. This was to be the model for the future British system of coinage and was to be fully outlined in his paper of 1805, but it was not until 1816, with the Coinage Act of that year, that it was to be fully acted upon, and it was the Earl of Liverpool's son, the second earl, who, as prime minister, would steer the measure through Parliament.

If the two Earls of Liverpool provided the intellectual and political weight behind these crucial innovations, it was Matthew Boulton who provided the *modus operandi*, not to say the necessary physical force. The Committee on Coinage were impressed by the superiority of Boulton's new steam presses at his Soho Works in Birmingham, which could provide high-quality, uniform coins which were extremely difficult to counterfeit. Boulton's enormous achievements are discussed in Chapter Six as one of the major boosts to the spread of the gold standard in the nineteenth century. But it is interesting to note that the old overlapped with the new, for in 1804 the countermarking of Spanish coins was resumed at the Mint, which was then still in the Tower of London. The head of George III in an oval frame was once again punched into the Spanish dollars but again the coins suffered from counterfeiting and in 1804 the Bank of England commissioned Boulton to overstrike completely the 'pieces of eight' with a new design. With typical efficiency, Boulton was able to do this so well that the original design was completely obliterated and replaced with a new bust of the British monarch, designed by his chief engraver, Conrad Küchler. Though these coins were reminted over a number of years they all bore the date 1804, but occasionally specimens can be found which still have the date of the original Spanish striking just visible. However, because these coins had a high silver content, a rise in the price of silver after 1812 meant that they were officially revalued at 5s. 6d. (Seaby, 1985).

The nineteenth century

Despite the continuing shortage of coin, Fetter and Gregory (1973) were able to describe British monetary history in the eighteenth century as a period of quiescence and a general lack of controversy. This is in sharp contrast to the nineteenth century, which was to be full of official inquiries and debates, which would produce a wealth of reports, articles and monographs. Eighteenth-century Britain also stood in sharp contrast to the rest of Europe, which, while being mainly on formally bimetallic standards generally, used silver far more than gold both as a unit of value and as a currency metal. However, in the late eighteenth century at least, the gold–silver market ratio, as we have seen, remained quite stable, so the existence of what was effectively two standards had little effect on the exchanges.

The early years of the Napoleonic Wars brought financial panic to many European countries, including Britain, though Fetter and Gregory argued that the wars did not initiate the crisis in Britain; rather they brought an existing crisis to a head. Nevertheless, Britain was forced off the gold standard and specie payments were suspended in early 1797 following a quickly repulsed landing by French forces in South Wales. A debate ensued immediately over how payments should eventually be resumed. Secret committees were set up in both Houses of Parliament to look into the background of the suspension and such matters as the role of the Bank of England. But for the first six years of the suspension, or 'restriction' (1797–1803), the foreign exchanges fluctuated no more than before the wars. Accordingly, the monetary situation took a back seat until 1803 when a parliamentary committee reported on the Irish exchange situation. Although little known, this report, according to Fetter and Gregory, presaged in significant ways the later and more famous Bullion Report of 1810. Some witnesses before the committee spoke up for what became known as the 'balance-of-payments' explanation of exchange-rate variations and insisted that monetary policy, as such, had little or no influence on exchange rates. The opposing 'bullionist' view emphasized that Irish monetary expansion had been the prime cause of the depreciation of the Irish exchange. This led directly to the view that the Bank of Ireland could, in principle, operate policies that would maintain a stable exchange rate. The debate was quieted when the London–Dublin exchange rate returned close to parity, along with a steadying of the continental exchanges. But in late 1809 the British pound began to depreciate against the Hamburg exchange and the 'banking versus bullionist' controversy was opened up again. The practical problems of depreciation overtook the question of the standard for the duration of the wars.

As we have seen, the gold standard was restored by the legislation of 1816, but not, according to Fetter and Gregory (1973, p. 16), 'because of any reasoned preference for gold over silver as a standard of value, but in order to make it possible to have silver coins that would remain in circulation'. The experiments with silver dollars had proved a fiasco and minds were thus turned towards the idea of a fiduciary silver coinage under a gold standard. The available evidence suggests that the initial decision after the wars to put Britain on a single gold standard was more a matter of practical expediency than any special preference for gold:

> With the hindsight of history it is amazing that a decision of such importance for England, and by England's example, the entire world, should have been made without benefit of full analysis, and largely on the basis of details of small coin convenience, and not on larger issues of economic policy. Thus was formally established the gold standard, which became effective with the resumption of cash payments in 1821 and survived for 93 years. (Ibid., p. 16)

There was, of course, no way that the British authorities could have guessed that the system they were inadvertently designing would become the blueprint for so many other countries after 1873. But the gold standard, as it was thus constituted, came under continuous attack for the next twenty-five years. Critics argued variously that resumption should have taken place with a smaller gold content (effectively a different par of exchange), and that the wartime paper currency, which had worked remarkably well, should not have been jettisoned so easily. But the most consistent attack came from supporters of silver and bimetallism, such as the bankers Alexander Baring and Isaac Lyon Goldsmith, 'men of conservative political views' (Fetter and Gregory, 1973). It has been argued that bimetallism and silver came much closer to success than history has recorded in these years, especially since there was support from such luminaries as William Huskisson, Robert Peel and the Duke of Wellington at various times. Sayers (1935) reckoned that the provision of the Bank Charter Act keeping a fifth of its reserves in silver was due to the influence of Baring.

It needs emphasizing, however, that this agitation for silver was restricted to a very few men of conservative outlook, albeit in positions of great influence, and that, as Fetter and Gregory (1973, p. 17) themselves say, 'it had none of the politically radical connotations that it came to have in the United States in the latter decades of the nineteenth century'. In any case, this early support for silver came to an abrupt end with the Californian and Australian gold rushes of the late 1840s, a process which was to be repeated some sixty years later. But there was much opposition to the revivified gold standard in the City in the postwar years and financiers were naturally prone to associate the resumption of cash payments with monetary tightness and a possible contraction of trade. David Kynaston (1994, p. 37) has recently portrayed William Huskisson as a 'key figure' in the form that the resumption took. Huskisson seems to have had a clear idea of what lay in store for Britain in the rest of the century should she adopt a gold standard of probity:

> I have no doubt that with the extent of our commercial dealings and operations of Exchange, which make this Country the Emporium not only of Europe but of America, North and South, the Bank of England would make this land the chief Bullion Market of the World ... The facility it would give to Trade in affording them the means of promptly rectifying the Exchange with any particular Country, and probably in the Coin of that Country to which it might be desirable to remit Bullion, could not fail to form one of these inducements which would make the settling house of the Money transactions of the World.

So if Huskisson had any misgivings about gold as a unit of account, he was sure that if it was done in the right way it could hold out much hope for the City of London. Proper management was what mattered, and a gold standard of wide recognition would give London a potentially pivotal role in the world economy. The hesitations and delays over resumption make one recall the current thinking (in 2000) about Britain's entry into the single European currency. Like the floating pound of the post-1992 period, the paper currency of the Napoleonic war years had worked remarkably well and had presided over rapid growth of output during the Industrial Revolution. The essential conservative principle of leaving alone a system that had ostensibly served the economy well might easily have won out at this stage and resumption might have been delayed for many more years. As with the modern question of entry to the Euro, it was felt that a return to gold, or silver, was inevitable at some future point, but that too rapid a transformation might be disastrous. However, fears about resumption were matched by fears about possible abuse by the Bank of England should it be allowed to retain the enormous discretion of a fiduciary note issue. Perhaps in the end it was the hatred of corruption by people like Huskisson which tipped the balance in favour of a return to cash payments on sound principles.

Returning to gold was seen as a cathartic process. As Kynaston (1994, p. 40) put it, 'somehow it was assumed that bringing the paper money to an end would cleanse the body politic of unpatriotic speculators and generally repair the social fabric damaged by war and its aftermath'. The second Earl Liverpool's government, ably supported by the redoubtable Huskisson, if not by his weak Chancellor, Vansittart, ultimately stood firm on the return to cash payments, despite the increase in social tension resulting from the 'Peterloo Massacre' of 1819. Legislation was enacted that Britain should return to the gold standard, with full disciplines, by 1823 at the latest.

But agitation for silver did not die out with resumption, and Fetter and Gregory (1973) reckoned that this was based firmly on the idea that silver would give a 'slightly higher price level' than gold, a position which would become familiar later in the century. If these 'silverites' had been correct, though, the flood of gold that occurred after 1848 should in turn have produced inflation. It did not. And surprisingly, the new gold, while inspiring many men to put pen to paper and forecast doom and gloom, did not spark off an explosion of parliamentary committees and government inquiries. In many ways – and this could have been alluded to much more often by the radicals of the 1890s – the new gold was a non-event for the British economy. Inflation was regarded as an anathema by the likes of Huskisson, but as long as this did not occur and as long as the exchanges remained healthy, nineteenth-century governments were not wont to intervene. And it was for this reason that Fetter and Gregory were able to conclude that 'The gold standard by the 1860s had become a cornerstone of the British economy, and virtually outside the area of debate' (ibid., p. 18).

Cottrell (1992), however, found that there was rather more support for alternatives to a gold standard, and has argued that the mild appreciation of silver in the 1840s and 1850s was enough 'to disturb European monetary arrangements and provoke thoughts even in England of introducing a silver standard' (pp. 222–3). Like the later, academic, bimetallists of the 1890s, these English protagonists for silver were concerned more with stability than any desire for higher prices or inflation. Indeed, they were fearful of an increased money supply from any cause. The main proponent for an English silver standard at this date was one James Maclaren, 'who received support mainly from the Currency School, namely Cobden, Spooner and, in France, Chevalier' (ibid., p. 223). But Cottrell arrived at more or less the same conclusion as Fetter and Gregory: the main effect of the mid-century appreciation of silver was to consolidate the British gold standard. To explain this seeming paradox, Cottrell argued that the successful gold supporters were able to deflect criticism by maintaining that the new gold was merely the result of its previous stringency (high gold prices had caused a search for new supplies) and that, in any case, an expansion of the silver supply was sure to follow on its (silver's) appreciation. In at least one of these respects – the latter – they were ultimately proven correct.

The mid-century gold discoveries

But crucially, whereas the new gold finds only served to confirm Britain's attachment to the gold standard, they did lead directly to other countries moving on to silver. Belgium and Switzerland introduced silver francs and Spain demonetized gold, along with Naples and the Netherlands (Cottrell, 1992). Gold also disappeared from the circulation of India, proving that random factors, as much as British stewardship, were at least partly responsible for that country moving towards silver in the nineteenth century. And thus it seems that certain economic forces can have very different effects in different countries: Californian gold confirmed Britain's gold standard while pushing her greatest colony, and various European countries, in the direction of a silver standard. Inevitably, this makes the disentangling of cause and effect in monetary history more difficult. And as those same European countries switched back to their favoured monetary metal, they unfortunately did so by minting coins at different levels of fineness. This would cause much disturbance at a later stage as the 'lighter' French and Italian coins drove the more full-bodied Belgian coins out of circulation. If nothing else, the British attachment to gold, while being unfashionable, no doubt insulated the country from some of the vicissitudes of the European experience, thanks to the operation of Gresham's Law on the continent. Indeed, if Cottrell is correct, it was the very fact of these intra-European arbitrage flows which led Belgium, 'a small, trade-dependent economy', to seek the establishment of a wider currency union. It is now well established that the result of this, the Latin Monetary Union of 1865, had much more to do with the management of national coins, a fairly perfunctory need, than with any broader vision of progress towards a single unit of value, such as would be the case with the spread of the gold standard after 1873, though, as we shall see, this was also multi-causal rather than visionary in origin. But what is certainly true, given the practical needs for a European union and the heterogeneous nature of continental monetary experiences in the mid-nineteenth century, is that Britain was seen to be the only player showing a consistent hand in this particular game. By the 1860s it appeared obvious to the British that staying with one suit was the only possible strategy.

The great monetary debate following resumption in Britain had had more to do with the question of convertibility than with the question of standard: the nineteenth-century British view of bimetallism was that in reality it tended towards an alternating gold/silver standard and thus was scarcely admitted to exist. In any case, the British monetary authorities retained a nominal position for silver right through to the Bank Charter Act of 1844. In other words, it is preferable to regard Britain in the eighteenth century as a country on a *de jure* bimetallic standard but with a *de facto* gold standard, and thus not formally very different from most other European countries at the time.

However, by the early decades of the nineteenth century there was a definite bias in favour of a true monometallic gold standard, and Fetter (1965, p. 142) found this to be something of a puzzle when he investigated the 'rising fraternity' of economists of the 1820s:

> In view of the philosophy of enlightenment and rationalism of most of the economists, we might have expected them to have given an understanding analysis of the possible contributions that a silver standard or bimetallism might make to greater price stability or to have considered how a conscious policy of the Bank of England could contribute more to stability in the purchasing power of the pound than did the accidents of geology and mining. Instead we find that the economists ... applied to the monetary standard a devotion to creed and dogma that they deprecated in religion and social philosophy.

Nevertheless Fetter went on to offer some basic explanations for this apparent irrationality. First, the financiers had displayed a general distrust of Bank of England policy stemming from the period of restriction of the currency during the French wars (though *ipso facto* this could have led them in the direction of a bimetallic commodity standard). Second, and in any case, they were reluctant to give discretion either to the government or to the monopoly of the Bank of England as a matter of principle because the state and the Bank could not be trusted to intervene in such matters as the setting of the bimetallic ratio. And third, there was the prevailing (Ricardian) notion in the City that exogenous changes in prices, even if they were acceptable to the financial community, would have little or no effect on the real economy of incomes and employment, arguably the most telling point. Britain therefore became a nation committed, as an article of faith for many and certainly for most of the few who worked in the Square Mile, to what was thought of as 'the ancient gold standard'. This of course was long before it became a great international system, so it should hardly surprise us that the British financial establishment remained faithful to the gold standard when it began its triumphal march across the globe in the early 1870s. Moreover, concern about monetary policy and the state of the currency was restricted to élite groups until very late in the century. In Britain, working people did not criticize the gold standard, suspicious though many of them might have been about the activities of the government or of bankers. Spokesmen such as Cobbett, for example, had no time for such matters as currency reform, believing as he did that monetary expansion was a mixed blessing and that prices would inevitably rise faster than wages (Checkland, 1957). 'Currency-mongers', thought Cobbett, would be sure to manipulate things to their own advantage, whatever was agreed in advance. As we shall see, a very different state of affairs applied in the United States in the nineteenth century, and this contrast may have had a crucial effect on the course of monetary history in the period.

The 1876 Select Committee

For most of the century, a strong consensus in Britain supported the gold standard, with the notable exception of men such as Thomas Attwood, leader of the Birmingham School, 'who had no blind faith in a metallic standard of the Ricardian kind' (Checkland, 1948, p. 7). During the 'Great Victorian Boom' of 1850–73 the monetary *status quo* was set by the Bank Charter Act of 1844 and few chose to challenge it for, as Checkland shrewdly observed, it is especially true during periods of expansion that reformers find it difficult to overcome the burden of proof which always rests with the seekers of change. From the point of view of the City, however, it must be remembered that the nineteenth century was an era of continuous expansion: the 'Great Depression' which attended the years after 1873 was felt much more in British industry and agriculture rather than in the financial sector.

Ironically the most sustained intellectual and political challenge to the gold standard in Britain came at the very threshold of its emergence as a workable international system of exchange. And to compound the irony, it was the demise of silver after about 1873 that caused the British establishment to look again at the prevailing currency arrangements. It must be appreciated that Britain had more to lose from exchange-rate fluctuations arising out of changes in the relative values of the precious metals than most other countries, for the simple reason that Britain was by far the world's leading trading nation and dominated international investment at that time. In earlier decades the fall of gold relative to silver had helped to strengthen the gold standard rather than weaken it. The fall of silver might well have resulted in a *strengthening* of silver as a monetary metal since it had normally been the depreciating metal (given Gresham's Law) which tended to become the dominant monetary metal. At any rate there was no way of second-guessing future outcomes, and therefore the 'silver problem' was taken at least as seriously in Britain as in other industrial countries. In 1876 a parliamentary select committee was set up to look into the depreciation of silver and its causes.[1] If it is true, as recent contributors are wont to tell us, that by 1870 the national economic tide was beginning to turn decisively in favour of the 'gentlemanly capitalists' of the City of London, it should be no surprise that Parliament should have ministered to their needs and responded quickly to anything that might threaten the position of the august leaders of the City.

The Select Committee found a number of reasons for the fall of silver prices. Rich discoveries of the metal had been made in Nevada, including the famous 'Comstock Lode', a fabulously rich vein of the white metal. The introduction of new gold currencies in Europe was bound, it was thought, to have affected the demand for the two precious metals: in the previous three years Germany, Holland and Scandinavia had all switched to gold. And there had also been a fall in the amount of silver shipped to India, a market which in the past had acted as a sponge to mop up surplus bullion.

A point worth noting about the findings of the 1876 Select Committee is that it concluded that demand-side factors were just as important as, if not more important than, supply-side factors. It noted that production of silver elsewhere in the world than the United States had been virtually stationary. And although the famous Comstock Lode was in full production, the State Mineralogist of Nevada had indicated that the Consolidated Virginia Mine, the largest of the enterprises, had been producing almost as much gold, in value terms, as silver – about 44 per cent of the total by value – and overall the American mines were yielding gold ores to about one-third the total value of silver. Given that in any case the annual production of specie metals represented only a very small proportion of total world stocks, it followed that the supply-side factors were relatively insignificant in determining current market prices for specie. Certainly the rapidity of the price fall of silver in the years after 1873 cannot be explained, as the bimetallists always argued, purely in terms of its increased supply.

Crucially, and this is something which has not been sufficiently emphasized, it was noted by the Select Committee that the United States was not exporting silver to Europe on any greater scale than before the price fall, partly because the American government was still substituting fractional silver coin for paper notes. This was despite the fact that the United States was at this time on a *de facto* gold standard. *The Economist* described these silver coins as an absurdity since no one actually wanted them, though it has to be said that anything which might have been seen as working against the gold standard would have invited the opprobrium of that publication at that particular time.[2] But it is worth noting that a British parliamentary report in 1876 was effectively advancing the same arguments as the later bimetallic school in seeking to explain the causes of silver's demise. It should also be noted that there is now a consensus amongst economic historians that finds of the precious metals probably do not happen entirely by accident, but are conditioned to some extent by their prevailing relative scarcity.

But the main conclusion of the 1876 Select Committee was that there was considerable uncertainty about the gold price of silver in the future and, if Gallarotti (1994) is correct, this only served to hasten the extension of the gold standard, for his view is that uncertainty and anxiety about silver caused the formation of 'chain gangs' pulling in favour of gold (see Chapter Six). Quite aside from the question of new discoveries, there were many uncertainties in the monetary world, including the vagaries of the American political scene, which meant that no one could accurately predict the form which American monetary policy might take in future years. Although the United States was not yet the industrial giant it would soon become, it was the most important producer of both gold and silver in the mid-nineteenth century, and it was already an extremely significant supplier of a wide range of other primary produce, so that European countries had come to require dollars to satisfy their trade requirements. Furthermore, the 1875 Report of the Secretary of the Treasury of the United States had refused to commit the country to a redemption rate for paper currency. The output of their mines remained uncertain and the Select Committee noted that the production of the Comstock Lode would be considerably greater if the miners were allowed to work on Sundays.

But there were greater uncertainties. The Germans held considerable quantities of silver left over from their conversion to gold after the war with France. These had apparently been sterilized, but they could be dumped on the international markets at any time. These supplies caused great anxiety in Britain and elsewhere and probably greatly enhanced the attractions of the gold standard at this juncture. Cottrell believes that the Germans stopped selling silver after the International Monetary Conference of 1878. Be that as it may, *The Economist* was still reporting in 1879 that Germany possessed between 15 and 20 million pounds sterling of silver and that the French government were unsure about

Germany's intentions regarding it.[3] There were intimations that these stocks could be used virtually as a political weapon. The anxiety experienced by the French undoubtedly augmented the effect of the indemnity payments of 1873 and helped the victors keep them in check in subsequent years, making the reparations policy of post-1873 somewhat more effective than the countervailing indemnity imposed after 1918. To what extent this helped move the Latin Union in a gold direction is uncertain, but Bagehot's journal saw the implications clearly and argued in favour of stability rather than using the crisis to force the issue in favour of gold. *The Economist* believed that Her Majesty's Government should ascertain the actual amount held by Germany and authorize the Bank of England to buy one-third to one-half of the total, on the understanding that no further sales of German silver be made for a period of five to seven years.[4] For once, as far as we know, Bagehot's advice was not taken (though Germany was prevailed upon to stop selling silver) but the position of *The Economist*, which closely reflected City opinion on most occasions, reflects the general concern of the British financial establishment for the demise of silver after 1873. Certainly the notion that British monetary authorities were nonchalant in the face of the specie price disturbance and blasé about taking any action at all can be dismissed. And if City men were sanguine about the inherent instability of their 'day-to-day operations', this did not mean that they would willingly see instability imposed upon them by quixotic foreign governments. The many government inquiries into money and finance in the late nineteenth century, given Westminster's deference to the City, echoed the deep concern of 'gentlemanly capitalism' for the condition of the pound and its exchange value in the era.

Moreover, British reprentatives attended all the international monetary conferences which took place in the period: 1867; 1878; 1889; 1892. Despite the fact that on at least three of these occasions the British delegation contained token bimetallists, the British monetary authorities could be sure that the long-standing commitment to the gold standard would be maintained. Other countries could never attain such consistency of policy. But consistency of outlook and policy does not mean that Britain was unaffected by the silver disturbance, and it must be understood that the crisis for silver in the late nineteenth century was, *ipso facto,* a crisis for gold.

Britain's commitment to gold in the nineteenth century is seen by most economic historians as largely a matter of expediency, but it has recently been argued that there were very good practical reasons for keeping a monometallic regime. The conclusions of Angela Redish (1990) are that Britain, or rather *England*, retained gold because bimetallism would not have allowed the monetary authorities the possibility of a medium of exchange with both high- and low-denomination coins circulating con-currently. New technology, in the form of Boulton and Watt's steam press, allowed the Mint to make coins that counterfeiters could not copy cheaply. High- and low-denomination coins could circulate concurrently since it no longer mattered if the market value of gold and silver varied with each other: the gold coin had intrinsic value and acted as the true numeraire, and the token coin, being difficult to copy, could be guaran-teed by the Mint. For Redish the new minting technology was crucial, for it meant that a monometallic standard was now inherently superior to bimetallism, assuming that the Mint continued to accept the responsibil-ity of guaranteeing the convertibility of the token coinage.

Indeed, Redish was puzzled by the fact that the gold standard did not spread rapidly across Europe in the first half of the nineteenth century, given that the steam-powered minting machinery was exported to the continent in the 1830s, and concluded that this must have been due to political and institutional constraints rather than purely technical ones. However, she ignores the importance of custom and tradition, which were strongly on the side of silver rather than gold in most European countries until well into the nineteenth century. It is more likely that the secure token currency allowed by the steam press would be a copper one under a silver commodity standard, rather than other variants under gold, elsewhere than in Britain. What is certain is that the advan-tages afforded by the steam press were scarcely mentioned by either side in the 'great debate' over the standard in the late nineteenth century. If the (London) Gold Standard Defence Association had reckoned this to be a material factor they would surely have advanced it as a clinching argument in the 1890s and claimed easy victory over the bimetallist school. This is not to say that Redish is incorrect about the importance of the new technology, and she reasonably claims that the failure of Britain's, and other countries', authorities to establish workable token coinages before the nineteenth century suggests that it had not been technically feasible to do so without it. The upshot of Redish's argu-ment – that the gold standard was yet one more product of the technology of the British Industrial Revolution – offers a breathtakingly heroic explanation of the spread of the gold standard in the nineteenth cen-tury, but it is not one that is easy to accept in full if only because contemporaries were largely unaware that such technical factors were conditioning their actions. Britain, it seems, was lucky to have to hand the technology to make a monometallic standard work effectively, but since other countries did not actively desire a monometallic standard they did not necessarily recognize Britain's advantage, much less wish to import it, at this stage at any rate. Further discussion of this point is offered in Chapter Six.

The Times debate of 1889

A real difficulty in assessing the role of money in the late nineteenth-century international economy is the undoubted fact that powerful economic forces in the real world were also acting on prevailing prices. In his explanation of the spread of the gold standard, Marcello de Cecco (1974) claimed to be following Keynes in arguing that the years of expansion for gold money (*c.* 1873–96) were also years of falling prices due to major cost-cutting innovations, and of course there is no question that this was so. The period encompasses both the 'Second Industrial Revolution' and the transport revolution, involving both the massive spread of the railway system and enormous improvements in oceanic transport, and there is no need to dwell further on these here. What perhaps does need emphasizing is that Britain was affected more than any other country by these improvements. By the 1870s Britain was importing over half its food requirements, and this was to rise to four-fifths by the end of the century. One need scarcely add that Britain was also the world's largest importer of almost all traded commodities at this time and, as the largest shipping country, stood to gain most by the steep fall in international, and especially intercontinental, transport costs. It is interesting to speculate what might have become of the British gold standard had this not been the case: many millions of Cobbett's countrymen might well have had a distinctly different, and far less complaisant, view of British monometallism, and cries for repeal of the gold standard would surely have been as vociferous as the clamour for the ending of the Corn Laws a generation earlier. As it was, two very different explanations for the price fall and accompanying depression were available to economic polemicists of the late nineteenth century. These versions were clearly spelt out in a debate in *The Times* in 1889, and presage the full bimetallic debate of subsequent years.

Henry Chaplin, MP, who championed the bimetallic cause on behalf of the agricultural community and who was then engaged on a tour of the country to lecture on the benefits of a dual standard, initiated a series of contributions to the newspaper which eventually drew in an eminent array of writers. Chaplin challenged *The Times*'s assertion that the Duke of Wellington had been an ardent opponent of legal tender silver coin, and claimed that, on the contrary, the Duke had often intimated to friends that he would like to see Britain 'revert to the ancient practice'.[5] The Duke of Wellington was held in such high esteem that many monometallists wrote in to deny Chaplin's claim, arguing that the Duke had merely been expressing a then common sympathy for 'bullion bimetallism', a notion which was now obsolescent, and which in any case only reflected the great man's concern for the country's military readiness and ability to pay for war should it come again. Chaplin, it would seem, failed in his quest to turn the Iron Duke into a Bimetallic Duke, but the ensuing debate represents in essence the true divide in British society over the political economy of gold and silver. Alfred Marshall wrote in to clarify his own position and to give his conditional support for a bimetallic currency, though expressing his view that the choice of ratio was crucial, and that it ought to be closer to the current market ratio of the metals than the one prevailing before 1873, which was the desired ratio of many bimetallists, especially in the United States. Marshall was essentially sympathetic to the idea of embracing the two metals, recognizing that such a regime offered real advantages of stability, but was very wary of introducing any ratio which overvalued silver and drove out gold. With the cultural prejudice of the day he wrote:

> Civilised peoples, as well as semi-civilised, would regard the hoarding of gold as a good investment. Governments would join in as they do now, in the scramble; army chests and bank cellars, private hoards and goldsmiths' safes would, I fear, take so much to render the sovereign very shortly as obsolescent as the dodo.[6]

Bimetallic enthusiasts such as H. R. Grenfell supported Chaplin, and encouragement came from overseas in the form of Henri Cernuschi, the great French proponent, who was eager to advance knowledge about the dual standard in Britain. Indeed, Cernuschi went so far as to offer a prize of 10,000 French francs to the author of the best essay on the effects of an international rehabilitation of silver. Naïvely, he asked the current Conservative Chancellor, George Goschen, to adjudicate the competition. Not surprisingly the British minister politely declined, but the debate continued to attract the attention of eminent men of the day. The (bimetallist) Duke of Marlborough countered the 'sweeping statements' of the (devoutly monometallist) Robert Giffen, who was 'too absorbed in the certitude of his own opinions' to be taken seriously. Giffen, said Marlborough, had been merely 'advocating the interests of those classes who are making hay [an unfortunate metaphor in the circumstances] out of the anomalies which have arisen under the changed conditions of trade and enterprise'.[7]

Giffen's legendary arrogance prompted Professor Foxwell, one of the two leading British academic advocates of the dual standard (the other was Nicholson), to write in from Cambridge to put the theoretical arguments for a bimetallic currency which, he concluded (after many column inches) 'would not be a perfect currency, but is a better one practicable?' This was hardly the most convincing conclusion, but Foxwell, like many academic bimetallists, did not believe that the columns of a newspaper, even those of the redoubtable Thunderer, were the right and proper place to debate the intricacies of a subject so convoluted as that of currency reform.

In February 1889, however, Sir Lyon Playfair used the opportunity of a speech at the National Liberal Club's Political Economy Series to debunk the case for bimetallism and outline the now familiar general explanation of the late nineteenth-century price fall. This too was extensively reported in *The Times*. Playfair denied that gold appreciation was the main cause of falling prices:

> Though gold had been able to buy many things cheaper since 1873, it had not been able, except in agriculture, to buy cheaper labour, for in machine-using countries wages had steadily risen even through periods of depression ... The application of machinery in the cultivation, harvesting and cleaning of cotton [for example] had been so great that, whilst in 1873 a given amount of labour produced 3.8 million bales in America, a much less amount in 1887 turned out 6.5 million bales. The economy in its manufactured products was still greater. In 1873 spindles made 4,000 revolutions in a minute; they now made 10,000. In the last fifteen years the population of the world had increased by 15%, while the production of cotton goods had increased by 86% ...[8]

Playfair also noted the much improved economy of labour in the United States and concluded that this was the main cause for the falling price of wheat, which he claimed was the 'stronghold' of the bimetallists' case. In the 1880s it was the agricultural community which made the case against the gold standard and at this stage it seemed that there was to be a rerun of the ideological battle waged fifty years earlier between protectionist agriculture and free-trade industry. Certainly it seems to be the case that bimetallism was blighted early on in Britain by being associated with tariff reform; to its opponents it was easy to make the charge that bimetallism was 'protectionism by another name', when its major proponents emanated from the farming sector. When industries such as cotton began to make out a case for reform of the gold standard, the connection had already been made and was difficult to detach.

Yet the reason why industry became involved in the monetary debate came from a different source than agriculture. India was a major supplier of wheat to the British market, and thus threatened the position of English wheat farmers, but by the later decades of the nineteenth century it was also becoming the major market for British cotton exports. It must surely be regarded as a great irony that India had been allowed to remain on a silver standard by the imperial power when the gold standard was spreading rapidly across the world economy, but in truth this had not mattered to the British when the exchange ratio between gold and silver had varied relatively little before 1873. From the 1880s onwards, however, it was the challenge posed by Indian silver which truly occasioned the great debate on currency as far as the British were concerned. The challenge was double-edged, for not only was it becoming increasingly difficult to export goods to India but the Indians by then were creating their own factory-cotton industry which could both challenge Britain within the subcontinent and threaten to intrude dangerously into the Chinese-spun cotton markets which Lancashire producers saw as their only salvation as the end of the century drew near.

Notes

1. Parliamentary Select Committee on the Depreciation of Silver, 1876.
2. *The Economist*, 12 April 1879.
3. *The Economist*, 12 April 1879.
4. Ibid.
5. *The Times*, 1 February 1889.
6. *The Times*, 25 January 1889.
7. Cernuscli letter, *The Times*, 22 September 1889; Marlborough, *The Times*, 2 January 1890.
8. *The Times*, 7 February 1889.

CHAPTER THREE

France, bimetallism and standardization

The Silver Link, the Silken Tie
Which heart to heart and mind to mind
In body and in soul can bind.
(Sir Walter Scott, *Stanza* 13)

France and the bimetallic flows

In economic history France and bimetallism are inseparable. France was prominent in the huge movements of gold and silver which occurred during the Renaissance and which are known as the 'great bimetallic flows'. Until the Crusades, France and the rest of Europe used silver as virtually the only monetary metal. The Arab world, at this time, used gold principally. Consequently there was a greater demand for silver in Christendom (because of the continuous demand for silver at the mints), and conversely a greater demand for gold in the East. It seems that the Crusaders took both gold and silver on their many expeditions, requiring both metals as they needed to pay their own troops and to buy local supplies of *matériel*. However, once the Crusaders became established in the Levant they began to mint their own silver coins and naturally these came into the hands of Muslim traders who started to use them in their own commerce. The Christians also captured, or acquired, gold coins from the Arabs and then went on to mint their own gold coins, invariably to a lower standard than the Arabs and often using captured dies. This led to a debasement of Arab currencies via Gresham's Law. However, such large quantities of silver had now reached the Arab kingdoms that it became possible for them to introduce their own silver currencies. It would seem that the result of this was to reverse the differential between the gold price of silver in Europe and the gold price of silver in the East (Ridley, 1996).

Once this had happened, a highly profitable opportunity arose for entrepreneurs who began to mint counterfeit Arab silver coins either in Christian settlements such as Acre or back in France, always the main base for Crusader trade, or Italy. These fake silver coins came to be known as *millares* and carried the legend 'There is no God but Allah'. French nobles and even bishops produced *millares* in towns such as

Arles and Marseilles, to the disgust of the pious King Louis of France, who even attempted to persuade Pope Innocent IV to ban the practice. When he did so, it of course continued underground, no doubt at even greater profit. In the thirteenth century about 3 billion *millares* were struck in Europe and sent to the East, equating to twenty-five years' peak production in the continent. The Arabs in turn paid for this silver by exporting gold to Europe, and the yellow metal became the chief commodity traded across the Sahara from the main gold mines in West Africa. It is said that so much gold was entering Egypt at one stage that its price equated with silver.

The response of European states to this new abundance of gold was to start minting it. Venice and Genoa began to use gold coins in 1252 and within a century gold coins were in circulation throughout Europe. In some ways one could argue that this was the true beginning of the gold standard, but of course it always made sense to send the cheaper metal to the mint during any disturbance of the metallic ratio.

In the fifteenth century the notorious Jacques Coeur, the chief *argentier* to Charles VII, became involved in the bimetallic flows. Coeur made his fortune by shipping galleys out of Marseilles loaded with silver coins bound for Syria. In Syria his merchants bought gold coins with them and made their return journeys. From Coeur's own financial records, which became public when he was arrested for corruption in 1453, we can establish that the great French merchant could buy 14 per cent more gold in Syria than in France with the same quantity of silver, a case of simple arbitrage. It has been argued that these bimetallic flows were in many ways the equivalent of modern currency markets (Ridley, 1996, quoting Watson, 1967).

Despite these vast movements of gold and silver, however, it remains the case that silver was by far the most important monetary metal in Europe down to the late nineteenth century. As Clapham (1921, p. 123) put it, 'the continent retained the ancient silver standard in name and to a very large extent in fact'. Indeed, the use of silver actually gained ground because the world's output of gold was typically small until the great discoveries of the mid-nineteenth century, but also, according to Clapham, because England, owing to her strong commercial and financial position, was able to draw the bulk of the world's supplies to London at this stage.

For much of the *ancien régime*, Lyon was the financial centre of France, at any rate from the transfer of the great fair from Geneva in 1461, until the failure of Bernard in 1709 (Kindleberger, 1984). From the end of the sixteenth century, however, efforts were made to shift the emphasis to Paris, principally at first by the great Florentine bankers who seem almost to have evacuated Lyon. But they appear to have succumbed to Parisian xenophobia in the early seventeenth century. The Edict of Nantes, 1598, saw the installation of Protestant bankers who had been forced out of Languedoc by Italians. In turn, the revocation of the Edict of Nantes in 1685 saw the systematic persecution of the Protestants and the beginning of the Huguenot diaspora, which worked to the great benefit of German, Swiss and, eventually, English banking.

Much like Jacques Coeur, Samuel Bernard was a banker to the French monarchy. But he made the mistake of advancing large sums of money to Louis XIV to help him fight the War of the Spanish Succession (1702–13). Bernard, however, was a Calvinist banker at a time when the majority of financiers were Catholic and thus received little help from his peers, though it seems he did recover from his rift with the state over the war finance. The temporary demise of Bernard had the effect of moving the centre of gravity of French banking decisively from Lyon to Paris.

The John Law experiment

It was to Paris in 1706 that the most famous, or infamous, of all the bankers of the early modern period came, to assert that paper money was superior to gold and silver money. John Law, the Scottish monetary adventurer, was banished at first for his fiduciary heresies, but returned in 1713 after the war, postwar periods being always times of great opportunity for those with an eye to the main chance. The death of the Sun King in 1715 provided even greater opportunities, as did the *Visa* of the same year. The *Visa* was a secret chamber of justice formed by the state after a war to cream off the excess profits of wartime munitioneers, bankers and tax farmers. Law's extraordinary and long-lasting impact on the French economy began when he convinced the Council of Finance that a new bank was needed to tidy up the financial affairs of the nation. According to Hamilton, 'no other Keynesian had ever had such a golden opportunity' (Hamilton, 1968, cited by Kindleberger, 1984, p. 97).

Law's Banque Générale opened its doors in June 1716, representing for some historians France's first real bank. Law had studied the currency systems of both Holland and England, the two most advanced of their kind at the time. He had noted that the metal holdings of these institutions were well below the value of the total of notes in circulation in their respective countries, and concluded that paper money, sensibly issued by a bank and guaranteed on land, would be more stable than even a sound commodity money, which necessarily fluctuated in value in line with the supply of the precious metals. Law took particular inspiration from the Bank of Amsterdam, of which it was said that its clients had so much confidence in it that it never needed to pay out in specie (Vilar, 1976).

In a number of ways Law flew in the face of French thinking about money. French merchants were traditionally regarded as shrewd and hard-headed and those dealing in international trade were said to accept only valid, hard-money, currencies.[1] This was certainly true of the late sixteenth century when Jean Bodin, a deputy of the Estates General, had argued that the currency should be reorganized on the basis of a single national mint producing highly standardized coin with a strict intrinsic value, something that was not fully realized until Boulton and Watt's steam presses became available over a hundred years later (see Chapter Two).

At the same time, Frenchmen were well aware of the inflationary impact of the 'abundance of gold and silver' of which Bodin had written. Vilar regards Bodin as a subtle and insightful commentator who was mindful of the need for French industry and trade to expand rapidly in order to attract specie, though he rejects the Frenchman's claim to have been the first to point out that American silver was having an inflationary effect on Europe as a whole.[2] Nevertheless, after Bodin, Frenchmen increasingly blamed their currency problems on Spanish monetary crimes. The wise Montaigne contrasted Europe with the great South and Central American civilizations which had not used money as such, but whose treasure had been torn from them by venal and money-conscious conquistadores, though even he was surprised at just how quickly the Aztec and Inca treasures had come into European monetary circulation (de Montaigne, *The Essays*, cited by Vilar, 1976). Vilar argues that from then on there was a widespread consciousness in France that gold and silver, whilst they were not in themselves wealth, were the objects, or the indication, of profitable economic activity. Consequently there was little questioning of the need for this to be recognized by the institution of a full commodity standard utilizing one or other, and preferably both, of the precious metals.

Yet John Law attacked the very concept of commodity money on the grounds that the precious metals fluctuate in value, as they clearly had done since the discovery of the American sources. He was a believer in the 'real-bills' doctrine and promised the Parisians that if the money supply were to be increased by bank note issued for productive loans, employment and output would rise proportionately and the value of money would remain stable. For several years, Law's schemes appear to have been successful and to the Banque Générale were added the Banque Royal and the Compagnie d'Occident, which merged to exploit the new Mississippi trade, setting off the famous period of intense speculation in the rue Quincampoix. Eventually John Law became French Minister of Finance and one of the richest men of his day, but inevitably the 'Mississippi Bubble' burst, alongside the South Sea Bubble (Kindleberger reckoned they infected each other), and Law was driven into exile.

Opinions vary about the extent of Law's impact on the French economy and subsequent financial history. Certainly many merchant bankers made great profits at the expense of the French people generally, by taking their yields and investing in Geneva or Amsterdam banks. It is thought that the only benefit was the evident expansion of the western seaboard ports of Nantes and Lorient as a result of the abortive attempts to settle large numbers of Frenchmen in Louisiana. Claims against Law's banks were eventually written down to one-twentieth of their original value (Kindleberger, 1984). French experience with 'the first Keynesian' was such that there was hesitation in even pronouncing the word 'bank' for one hundred and fifty years afterwards. Hence the tendency, evident to this day, for French banks to be termed 'caisse', or 'société', or 'comptoir'. There were other attempts in eighteenth-century France to provide public banking, but the Swiss-inspired Caisse d'Escompte of 1776 perhaps appeared too late in the day: its note issues were compromised by royal demands for large loans and it was then swallowed up in the Revolution.

French currency and the Revolution

French backwardness in banking development, especially compared with Britain, has been held to be partly responsible for its relatively slow economic progress in the eighteenth century, and of course may be seen to have contributed towards the disaster of the Revolution. However, French foreign trade expanded rapidly enough during the century as a whole, and for much of the time perhaps even faster than Britain's. For example, between 1725 and 1780 it grew more rapidly than Britain's and caught up, in value terms, by the latter date. Only after about 1780 did France begin to fall seriously behind her great rival, and this was due more to political than economic or monetary factors. Interestingly, Vilar (1976) argues that Britain's trade was more globalized than France's and that this accounts for its greater preference for gold in the eighteenth century, especially when one takes into account its close trading relationship with Brazil and Portugal. France developed its economic relations more with Spain and the Caribbean; hence its preference for silver. This argument is somewhat weakened by an inquiry into the powerful endogenous reasons for Britain's opting for a gold currency at an even earlier period.

Certainly France continued to be involved in the great bimetallic flows as they continued through the eighteenth century, obtaining silver from Cadiz, which incidentally was dominated by British companies, but also by directly importing silver from South America and thus circumnavigating the Spanish monopoly based upon Cadiz. This illicit trade became known as *l'interlope*. French merchants also obtained silver by trading across the Pyrenees and the Pays Basque, and as a result Bayonne grew rapidly as a banking town in the eighteenth century. But in the final years of the *ancien régime* the supply of silver began to dry up as the Spanish economy itself started to recover owing to the growth of manufacturing and closer trading links with the United States (Vilar, 1976).

To the monetary historian the French Revolution is synonymous with the remarkable phenomenon of the *assignats*. The Revolution was itself partly a result of economic change and social imbalance caused by the 'economic conjuncture' – the parallel movement in prices and population associated with the eighteenth century. But the Revolution in turn gave rise to the *assignat*. It may come as a surprise that Frenchmen were prepared to gamble on the issues of a paper money for a second time in the eighteenth century, given the fiasco of the John Law period. In fact the *assignats* were never intended to be a form of money at all but an 'assignation' on the value of confiscated Church land (Clapham, 1921). The original *assignats* were thus bonds in 1000-*livre* notes bearing 5 per cent interest and intended to liquidate the national debt, but in due course the bonds were issued at lower rates of interest and then without interest. They were then issued in smaller denominations and by April 1792, after the beginning of war, they were appearing for sums as small as 50 and even 10 *sous*. By that time they had clearly taken the form of paper money and were in wide circulation. Over-issue resulted in rapid devaluation of the *assignat*. Vilar (1976) points out that it actually rose in value after the September killings of 1792, and again after the defeat of the Russians and Austrians at Valmy, but in 1793 the currency began to fall again. Remarkably, the Constituent Assembly failed to ban free trade in precious metals until April 1793, but after that date the government tried to force the circulation of the paper money and control prices by the declaration of the 'maximum'. By this time foreign trade was only possible using gold and silver bullion and thus all metals became very scarce. Between 1792 and 1797 the Revolutionary government issued only 32 million *livres* of silver money and none of gold. *Assignats* continued in circulation through to 1796 but by that time at only a fraction of their original value. The monetary crisis over the *assignats* has been regarded as the worst in France's history but ironically the outcome was a completely new monetary system that ultimately became the envy of Europe. It is remarkable that a new monetary system should be forged in the middle of a war but even more remarkable that it should survive the epoch largely unchanged.

The outcome was a bimetallic one. The Law of 7 April 1803, or of 7 Germinal, Year XI, fixed the value of the French monetary unit. This was a silver franc weighing 5 grams, of a grade 900/1000, thus containing 4.5 grams of silver. Gold coins, also of 900/1000 grade, were also minted at a value of 20 and 40 francs and at a bimetallic ratio of 15.5:1, the same as in the reign of Louis XV (Russell, 1898). This was thus a full bimetallic system with a fixed ratio and unlimited minting of both precious metals. It heralded a period of seventy years of stable currencies in Europe at large, for the French model was widely copied outside of Britain.

However, in the following years it is reported that the French authorities became more and more annoyed by the 'diverse coinages of feudal sovereigns and ecclesiastics of high and low degree', which continued to exist in many of France's neighbouring countries (Russell, 1898). It could be that Parisian or Lyonnais financiers were blithely unaware of the great diversity that characterized their own country in some of the more backward regions until well into the nineteenth century, as we shall see later. But from 1803 there was a degree of certainty about the French official currency which possibly emanated from the career of Napoleon Bonaparte himself. The eminent American economist, Francis Walker (1898), believed that it was the very rigidity of the system that was introduced that gave it its special qualities, and that this was a matter of courage on the part of the military dictator and the 'greatness of Napoleon's mind'. This could be simply one military man (Walker had been a general in the Union army during the Civil War) expressing admiration for the greatest soldier of his century. But Walker, the soldier–economist, inevitably saw the importance of *élan* in such things. Napoleon's First Consul, Gaudin, had warned that the rating of gold to silver might have to be altered from time to time, but, says Walker, 'this was stricken out in the course of discussion, and the ratio of 151/2:1 was adopted without any suggestion of a future change'. He concluded that 'Courage is often a large part of wisdom' (p. 88). One cannot help but conclude that a similar kind of thinking underpins the French-inspired drive towards a single European currency two hundred years later: *plus ça change …*

The mid-century gold discoveries

Another reason for the success of the French currency system in the nineteenth century was that the French employed such a very large quantity of metallic money. Clearly only a small proportion of it had left the country during the Revolutionary period (most of it having been hoarded in various ways) and many people commented on the fact that France was always specie-rich, among them the British merchant banker Baring, who would one day have very good cause to celebrate the fact. Walker (1898, p. 89) was quite certain about it:

> It was this vast endowment [of specie] which enabled France for so long to carry on that great function of the exchange of the metals, one for the other, which was to save the world from more than one terrific crisis. As the modern ship [writing in 1898] is long enough to cover the interval between two or three waves, so the French reserve of metal money was large enough to outlast fluctuations in the production of the precious metals which would have completely drained away the stock of the appreciating metal from almost any other country of Europe.

Yet the prevailing view in the period was that human laws could not affect real values, nowhere more so than in Britain, and French economic history itself could be drawn upon to exhibit perfectly the folly of government interference in the form of forcing paper currencies, or, during the Revolutionary period, fixing prices and banning the export of specie – all to no avail. French *tyrannie*, it seems, was nevertheless responsible for the concept of international bimetallism in the nineteenth century. As we shall see elsewhere, the essence of formal bimetallism was the statutory fixing of the metallic ratio of exchange. It is for this reason, amongst others, that we must be able to distinguish more than one form of bimetallism, though one has to say that unfortunately the vocabulary for denoting them does not exist.

It is generally thought that the French bimetallic system overvalued silver at the mint and that hence silver found its best market in France, and consequently it flowed in from other parts of the world. There is no doubt much truth in this; Walker estimated that between 1822 and 1851 the country absorbed an aggregate of 2,630 million francs of silver. Later antagonists of bimetallism argued that this was accompanied by a large exportation of gold. But Walker refuted this, quoting Professor Émile de Lavelaye as saying that between 1803 and 1842 French mints coined 47,779,389 gold 20-franc pieces. However, Walker conceded that the mass of gold money in France had been greatly reduced in this period, but insisted that gold continued in circulation throughout. This was directly controverted by 'gold-bugs' such as Henry Dunning McLeod of the British Gold Standard Defence Association, who wrote that when he himself had been resident in France in 1839–40, 'there was no gold to be seen in common use' (Walker, 1898, p. 135). This matter proved crucial to both monometallist and bimetallist during the 'great debate', for the former argued – as we shall see in a later chapter – that bimetallism always tended towards monometallism and thus performed no obvious stabilizing function.

Nevertheless, Walker was sure that the sheer mass of metallic money in circulation in France, coupled with the bimetallic statute of 1803, was responsible for the secular stabilization of the ratio of exchange between the two metals. France was thus able to preserve her bimetallic system 'in full virtue' from at least 1819 – with full resumption - down to the middle of the century when the new discoveries of gold were made. Yet even then, France was able to carry the system on, 'through the period when gold was coming in upon her mints like the waters of a broken dam, and to maintain a stock of the *appreciating* silver until a third great change [the fall of silver] took place in the natural conditions of production; and silver, in its turn, tended to fall in comparison with gold' (ibid., p. 135).

Indeed, the discoveries of gold in California and then, only three years later, in Australia, by putting on the market such enormous amounts of the metal, posed a serious threat to all commodity monetary systems in the period. Notwithstanding the more deterministic interpretations of mineral exploration and discovery which have been advanced in recent years, it is a remarkable coincidence that two of the greatest-ever finds of gold occurred so close together. It is worth emphasizing that these gold discoveries were every bit as threatening to monometallic systems, such as Britain's gold standard, as to bimetallic currencies. Furthermore, the impact could have been expected to have been at least as great as the silver finds of the 1870s. De Cecco (1974) reckoned that the relative supplies of the two metals were never more disturbed than in the 1850s, when it was estimated that the world stock of gold literally doubled (1851–63). In the 1800s the production of silver in proportion to gold, by weight, had been 50.2:1. In the decade 1851–60 it was down to only 4.4:1. Chevalier (1857) believed that the production of gold, as compared with silver, increased five-fold between 1851 and 1857. Inevitably this meant that bimetallic France began to mint more gold coins after about 1850: in that year the value of gold coins exceeded that of every year since 1818 (Redish, 1994). A monetary commission was established in Paris to examine the causes and consequences of the fall in gold prices, but sadly none of its documents remain. In 1850 the French mints began issuing a 10-franc gold coin, and in 1855 a 5-franc piece appeared, though this latter, being tiny, was never widely used. Another French monetary commission was set up in 1861 to investigate the causes of the scarcity of coins generally, and recommended that the fineness of the silver coins be reduced to prevent them being exported for arbitrage. Clearly by this time the French 'parachute' (see page 53) was in danger of collapsing, though in fact the commission's recommendations were ignored (Redish, 1994.)

The effect of the gold discoveries on European countries generally was a massive disturbance in the international movements of both gold and silver coins. When Italy introduced a token silver coin of only 83.5 per cent fineness in 1862, the operation of Gresham's Law meant that it was inevitable that there would be an invasion of the Italian coins into France, to the intense annoyance of the French. The problems involved in using token coins led a number of countries to move to pure silver standards. For some this occurred on the very eve of their industrialization and, as de Cecco (1974) has pointed out, this would make the demonetization of silver all the more painful twenty or so years later. De Cecco went on to argue that gold was to come into its own eventually because the growth of the unit value of transactions favoured its use. The difference between the buying and selling points of the monetary metal 'would have been much greater if silver, rather than gold, had to be transported to settle transactions among nations or even between distant points within the same national boundaries' (ibid., p. 43). He is trying to explain here why the mid-century finds of gold in the event had such a slight effect on the gold–silver exchange ratio, 'when a much greater one was expected', and goes on to argue that the period 1851–66 was one of rapidly increasing prosperity and widespread industrialization. Thus there was much greater demand for the exports of Britain, the only major country on the gold standard, and so in this period sterling came to acquire its dominating status as an international currency and means of exchange. He concludes that this general prosperity allowed the silver crisis to be postponed until immediately after the 1866 crisis of London finance and especially the collapse of Overend Gurney: 'To the great chagrin of the silver standard countries, the beginning of depression coincided with a remarkable increase in silver production' (ibid., p. 43).

De Cecco's argumentation is somewhat specious – a case perhaps of shoe-horning the facts into an unsatisfactory theoretical box. The real question is why France and other countries chose to continue with silver after 1850, and de Cecco admits that this is difficult to answer. Napoleon had given the Banque de France significant discretionary powers at its 1803 foundation and de Cecco thought that the bank was therefore not eager to lose them. He does not explain how gold or silver monometallism might have reduced these powers in any way (the monometallic Bank of England was scarcely less powerful). But it seems that French *haute finance* was somehow in favour of bimetallism because 'it has been suggested [no more] that the double standard offered financiers so many lucrative arbitrage possibilities that it would be unlikely that financiers would object ...' (de Cecco, 1974, p. 44). In a stunning *non sequitur* he goes on to say that 'we cannot forget that those were the years of the Second Empire, when it was the Emperor's express desire to see all continental Europe linked in a franc-area which would exclude and isolate Germany' (ibid., p. 44).

There is cause to apply Occam's Razor at this point. The French believed in statutory bimetallism because it had worked so well in the fifty years since its inception. There is no evidence that the Banque de France itself benefited from bimetallic arbitrage; indeed the evidence suggests that French bimetallism, by stabilizing the specie exchange ratio, prevented arbitrage. And like so many people before him, de Cecco is unwilling to accept that it was the demonetization of silver which caused the price fall after 1866 (though more obviously after 1873). Furthermore, it is clear that British financiers and statesmen were at least as concerned as their French counterparts about the possible fall in the price of gold after 1851 (witness the large number of papers written on the subject and the deep concern of Parliament). Monometallic countries, for reasons that are not difficult to adduce (for example concern over future exchange-rate changes), were just as dependent on stability of the bimetallic ratio as bimetallic countries: this was readily accepted by British 'gold-bugs'. French interest in achieving greater standardization of continental currency matters in this period had little to do with France's commitment to statutory bimetallism as such, and was much more due to the practical problems of managing token coinages in a context in which national coins, in Europe at any rate, readily crossed international boundaries.

To explain the widely supported attempts to create an effective single-currency area in terms of the *folie de grandeur* of the French emperor is unacceptable. As we shall see, the French were keen on including the United States in a standardized currency scheme, and we have to concede that even Napoleon III had no colonial ambitions in North America, at any rate north of Mexico. Far from seeking to isolate Prussia economically by retaining an outdated bimetallism, as de Cecco avers, there is evidence that the French actually sought to invite Bismarck to join the monetary grouping and that the Iron Chancellor declined for his own reasons. France was keen on bimetallism for the same reasons that Britain wanted to keep the gold standard: monetary ordering is always very much a matter of custom and practice, and there was (and still is) a widespread reluctance to change the *status quo* unless a crisis of some kind is involved. There is no evidence that the French state benefited greatly from bimetallic arbitrage: the great flows of precious metals that had passed through France for centuries were not instigated by the French. Rather they were a function of France's central geographical position and the changing circumstances in the supply of, and the demand for, gold and silver which were evident in the world at large and commented on by many writers at the time and since.

The Latin Monetary Union

In 1865 France was the leading country of a group of European states which met to agree on the co-ordination of their monetary regimes. This became known as the Latin Monetary Union and at first it included France, Switzerland, Italy and Belgium. Redish (1994, p. 68) has argued that the union states came together because they each found themselves on *de facto* gold standards as a result of the mid-century gold discoveries and the subsequent influx of gold into Europe. Yet each of them, for various reasons, retained *de jure* bimetallic systems. The rapid fall in the price of gold drove silver out of circulation in these countries and, as we have seen above, the smaller-denomination gold coins that were introduced in their place proved less than popular. The disappearance of the full-bodied silver coins led to a chronic shortage of circulating, small-denomination coins, and it was this that led to the minting of 'token' coinages. It will readily be appreciated that under a bimetallic system on, say, a *de facto* silver standard, in which silver coins of full intrinsic value are in circulation, there is no problem of acceptance of coins. A French full-bodied coin of a given weight is exactly equal in value to an Italian or Belgian coin of the same weight and metallic make-up. But once token coins were introduced, this was no longer the case. Individual countries could choose their own degree of fineness and their own denominations. As Redish (1994) says, efficient management of the token coinage (given the need for such coins to circulate freely between these European states) was now necessary and this in turn required international co-operation.

Redish argues that the Union emerged at a time when there was a general climate of economic integration. This was, after all, the age of free-trade expansion, of the Cobden–Chevalier Treaty (1860), and the *Zollverein-Münzverein* (customs and currency union). The fact that the French 5-franc coin was chosen as the standard unit of international account had less to do with French political hegemony (though obviously it reflected this) than with a widely perceived desire to choose the most abundant coin amongst the candidate currencies. Selecting the Belgian franc instead would have been, to say the least, sub-optimal. In the end the decision was made by a sub-committee of the 1867 International Statistics Congress, at which there was unanimity among the twenty-two attending states (which included the United States but not

Britain) that a gold standard should be the norm. It is worth pointing out that the choice of the French franc was highly convenient to the United States, whose gold dollar had been equal to 517 centimes at par. Thus a very small reduction of 17 centimes (3½ cents) would have left the dollar an exact multiple of the French unit and the equivalent of 5 francs (Russell, 1898).

Greece and Romania joined the Union in early 1867 and at the same time Napoleon III invited Bismarck to bring Prussia in (Russell, 1898). So much for France wanting to exclude and isolate Germany, as de Cecco argued. Bismarck declined, in a note sent to Paris on 2 February 1867, on the grounds that the North German Confederation was just then entering upon 'a political programme which may include its own local monetary systems', and that once this was achieved the Chancellor might then turn to international unification (ibid.). It seems clear, then, that the formation of the Latin Monetary Union had much more to do with European *raisons d'état* than French chauvinism. Recent research suggests that the making of the Union was indeed a 'natural' phenomenon and a result of market forces rather than political aggrandizement on the part of Napoleon III. Flandreau (1995, p. 84) concluded that, 'insofar as the Latin Union had emerged as a franc zone, it was despite the will of the Bank of France'.

It seems clear that the United States came preciously close to joining the Union at about this time: such a move would surely have ended French monetary hegemony. Russell reported that the American commissioner of 1867, Ruggles, was willing to go along with unification if the existing union would be prepared to coin a 25-franc gold piece. The French objected to this on the grounds that if the dollar were made equal to 5 francs, the next level of denomination would see the American gold eagle equivalent to 50 francs. It was also pointed out that a new 25-franc piece would make the 20-franc *Napoléon* virtually redundant. There is here a sense of the currency being partly a matter of French face and Napoleonic pride, but Russell (1898, p. 40) also pointed out that Parieu, the French commissioner of 1867, was at least prepared to consider modifying the terms of the Latin Union Treaty, 'if it seemed to the United States essential to that such a coin be made'. This must remain one of the great hypotheticals of nineteenth-century monetary history, but one cannot help thinking that a Franco-American monetary union would have had a major impact on subsequent monetary events, always assuming that it would have lasted the course.

In fact the Latin Union came to consist of France and a few satellite economies. Switzerland was an insignificant industrial country at midcentury and had not yet shown any real evidence of its future financial importance. Belgium was more significant industrially but possessed a population of only 5 million in the 1860s. Italy was much larger in every sense, though very backward in industrial terms, but the finances of the new state were already in a parlous condition even before the country entered into a wasteful and meaningless war with Austria-Hungary. As Russell (1989, p. 41) wrote, 'It is probable that the other members of the Latin Union could together exert but a fraction of the influence upon the monetary metals of which France alone had shown herself capable'. But this was not because France had eschewed the involvement of other great powers in order to assume leadership of the smaller group. The accession of Romania and Greece to the Union in 1867 scarcely changed the situation. It is worth noting that many small countries in Europe (Switzerland included, at this stage) possessed no mints of their own and were thus entirely dependent on the currencies of neighbouring states. When they did attempt to introduce their own coins they found that if their commodity coins were undervalued they immediately disappeared from circulation and if they were only slightly overvalued they were not accepted by foreign merchants.

The French 'parachute'

Despite the many divergences between economists of the nineteenth century, and since, over the merits of bimetallism against monometallism, and of silver against gold, there does seem to have been a large measure of agreement that France performed the useful function of stabilizing the exchange ratio between the precious metals until at least the 1860s. Francis Walker was a bimetallist of conviction but was able to show that he had the support of many leading economists of his day in pointing out the merits of the French 'parachute'. Jevons was cited as saying that,

> As to the equilibrating action of the [French] double standard, no-one who has inquired into the matter can doubt it any more than he can doubt that one scale of a balance will go up when the other goes down ... The French currency law has thus no doubt assisted to keep silver and gold at a nearly invariable price, as compared with the other.[3]

In 1876, Walter Bagehot wrote about the bimetallic system, which he certainly did not wish to see extended, in the following terms: 'Whenever the value of the two precious metals altered, these countries [France and her Latin Union allies] acted as equalising machines.'[4] Chevalier, the doyen of French economists of the nineteenth century, though not always one arguing for bimetallic reform, believed his country had prevented a 'catastrophic fall' in the price of gold after 1850:

> If down to the present time [1857], the immense production [of gold], of which Australia and California have been the theatre, has not produced a greater fall in the value of gold, it is France which is the cause. It is she that has retarded the depreciation of gold. She plays in relation to this metal, the part of a parachute.[5]

Whether or not Chevalier first uttered the phrase is not known, but the metaphor is apt. It is curious that the action of a parachute was known long before the appearance of the first aeroplanes; we can only assume here that they were used in connection with air balloons, such of those of the pioneering Montgolfiers, though other explanations are possible (see Chapter Six).

The British Herschell Commission was, despite its metallically heterogeneous personal composition in terms of the standard, nevertheless unanimous about the action of the Gallic chute:

> Looking then at the vast changes which occurred prior to 1873 in the relative production of the two metals, without any disturbance in their market value, it appears difficult to us to resist the conclusion that some influence was then at work tending to steady the price of silver, and to keep the ratio which it bore to gold approximately stable ... Undoubtedly the date which forms the dividing line between an epoch of approximate fixity in the relative value of gold and silver and one of marked instability is the year when the bimetallic system, which had previously been in force in the Latin Union, ceased to be in full operation.[6]

For Walker himself, the matter had passed beyond controversy and he was able to add Sidgwick and John E. Cairnes to the august group who supported his view of the French system. Like Chevalier, Walker believed that France had saved the world from a major economic catastrophe in the 1850–70 period, such had been the enormous potential disturbance to the relative values of the money metals. In the light of this, Redish's (1994, p. 81) conclusion that the Latin Union was 'a step toward, not away from the gold standard' seems at first paradoxical. The stabilizing function might have been expected to support the *status quo*, rather than invite change. But Redish argues that the Latin Union came together essentially to solve the practical problems of running a token coinage where coins are likely to circulate internationally. The token coinage had become inevitable, given the preponderance of gold in this era and the fact that a circulating, full-bodied coinage had proved unworkable. Yet the Union remained on a *de jure* bimetallic system and had, for Walker, continued the good work which the French economy itself had provided before 1865. Necessarily, the perspective of Walker, an ardent advocate of the double standard, will be different from that of Redish, a modern economic historian. Walker was, after all, setting out the intellectual basis for a return to a statutory bimetallism and, like many others, drew inspiration from recent French economic history. Redish seeks to show that the spread of the gold standard in the nineteenth century was an eminently rational process which depended on developing a system of managing a token coinage. Elsewhere (Redish, 1990) has argued that this had been technically possible since the late eighteenth century when Boulton and Watt first produced their steam press capable of minting a perfectly uniform coinage. She was puzzled as to why European countries had not followed Britain's lead in the first half of the nineteenth century. Nevertheless, for Redish the Latin Monetary Union was one step along the road towards a modern currency system, but there is no reason why an effective token coinage should not have appeared under statutory bimetallic regimes had the world's economies chosen to take this direction in the late nineteenth century.

France and the age of standardization

Cottrell (1992) found it puzzling that France pulled the Union in a bimetallic direction in the context of silver arbitrage flows and the drain to the East which had created a *de facto* gold-based franc, but ultimately resorts to de Cecco's argument that the *haute banque* – senior French financiers – wanted to retain the advantages of bimetallism for arbitrage reasons, a notion which, as we have said, has now been discredited.

Chown (1994) suggests that the French wanted to retain bimetallism as a bargaining counter, hoping that by giving way to gold at some future point they could obtain concessions in the form of greater overall standardization. He cites Russell as saying that the object of Parieu, 'the vice-president and guiding genius', was to suggest 'the easiest means for [co-ordinating] other systems with the French on any standard so long as France was the centre of unification' (ibid., p. 90). As we shall see, this rings true when we consider the role of France in the associated areas (at least perceived as such in the nineteenth century) of standardization of weights and measures and the setting of standards in such things as geodesics, cartography and international time-measurement.

It is worth noting that at precisely the same time as much of the world was reconsidering its currency arrangements following the gold discoveries, some of the leading nations were intent on arriving at new standards for a range of matters, not all of them directly related to economic phenomena. This can be viewed as something of a coincidence but it is true that a number of factors were operating in this period which necessitated reform. The railway age had only really begun some twenty years before the gold finds of California and Australia and this, as is well known, precipitated the need for the setting of standard time in order to facilitate railway timetables. By 1848, Bradshaw was able to report that most (British) railway companies were keeping Greenwich Mean Time (Howse, 1980). In the next twenty years or so, European countries were still arranging their own national times, and by the 1870s it was becoming apparent that these in turn should be co-ordinated by agreeing on a universal set of meridians. Clearly this was much more important for continental railway companies, whose trains increasingly crossed national boundaries, than for British companies, though of course the need for a universally accepted set of meridians also affected nautical navigation. However, since British publishers dominated the production of nautical charts and British shipping companies monopolized oceanic trade, this was proving less of a problem in practice. In any case, British *laissez-faire* principles applied and British authorities did not seek international standardization, partly because *pax britannica* was already effecting a standardization of sorts. Thus it was left to continental European countries to provide the driving force behind standardization. Germany at this time was still in process of, as it were, standardizing its own affairs through the *Zollverein-Münzverein* and later the Empire. Thus it was left to France to lead the way. We might argue that, in any case, standardization always appealed to the French philosophical turn of mind before, and especially after, the Revolution.

At the International Geographical Congress of August 1871, meeting in Antwerp, it was agreed that the Greenwich meridian should be adopted for all passage charts of all nations by 1886. The French representative at Antwerp, M. Levasseur, while insisting that, had the meeting been convened in the seventeenth or eighteenth century, Paris (that is, the observatory in Paris) would surely have been the choice, nevertheless accepted that it was sensible to accept the Greenwich meridian. 'Le livre habituel du marin' was the '*British Nautical Almanac*', and British chart publishers, he conceded, now sold 20,000 copies of their product annually, against the 3,000 copies of the *Conaissance des Temps*, the French equivalent (Howse, 1980).

However, this magnanimous sentiment was advanced in the context of Britain's accepting in return the French metric system. Nothing therefore came of the proposal because Britain was always unwilling to make any such change, preferring as always a complaisant, *laissez-faire*, approach over what might now be called a 'proactive' one. Surprisingly, however, even by the 1880s, only twelve nations were officially counting longitude from Greenwich; the French continued to prefer the Paris meridian (Howse, 1980).[7] As with matters of currency standardization, the British did little or nothing to persuade other nations to adopt Greenwich Mean Time or the Greenwich meridian. Even the British Astronomer Royal, Sir George Airy, was lukewarm about setting the prime meridian on his observatory:

> Let Greenwich do her best to maintain her high position in administering to the longitude of the world, and National Almanacs do their best, and we will do our best without special claim to the fictitious honour of Prime Meridian.
>
> (Howse, 1980, p. 135)

Howse was surprised that the British government showed no interest in interfering in a matter which concerned important 'social usages'.

The agenda of the Third International Geographical Congress of September 1881, meeting in Venice, again included the setting of a prime meridian and a universal standard time and led to the International Geodesic Conference of October 1883, which assembled in Rome. This came down strongly in favour of Greenwich and provided a thorough rationale under the headings of seven resolutions. But again, calls were made for Britain to conform by adopting the metric system and again these calls went unanswered by the British government. At the International Meridian Conference of 1884, forty-one delegates from twenty-five major countries met to decide finally the matter of a universal set of meridians.

The general view of this conference was that it was meeting to establish a specific set of meridians, but now the French demurred and insisted that the meeting was only to agree the principle of a prime meridian. Sandford Fleming, the great Scottish–Canadian proponent of international standardization, deployed a powerful set of statistics in demonstrating that Greenwich Mean Time (GMT) was already being used by 65 per cent of the world's ships' captains (72 per cent by tonnage), whereas only 10 per cent were using Paris and only 5 per cent Cadiz.[8] Fleming's demonstration seems to have carried the day (a seminal example of the efficacy of statistics) but still did not convince the French, who argued forcefully, if illogically, that the prime meridian should not cut across a major continent; in other words, if Paris were not to be used, then neither should London or any other major city. In a sense the French remained undefeated on this issue until the First World War. While most other nations accepted GMT, the French insisted on calling it Paris Mean Time 'diminished by 9 minutes 21 seconds' (Howse, 1980, p. 153). Throughout the 1884 conference the French continued to call for universal metrification and were prepared to use acceptance of GMT as a bargaining counter to achieve this. There was a lengthy debate at the conference over whether the metric system was truly neutral, as the French insisted, or whether it was in fact a French invention, as the British and Americans argued. We could say that in the end the French adopted a 'limping meridian' which in many ways complemented their 'limping gold standard'. A similar story could be told about the international standardization of weights and measures. The French maintained a keen sense of leading nation in these matters, and there is no doubt that there was a strong feeling that French paradigms should be promoted as the internationally accepted ones; to this day there is resentment in France that English became the world's leading language in these years.

France at the end of the nineteenth century

The clear impression given by these accounts of international conferences of various kinds, whether they concerned the standardization of currencies, or of time, or of weights and measures, is that the French were a disciplined people long used to running a highly rational and uniform set of systems in their own country and highly desirous that the rest of the world should see sense and adopt their prescriptions. Nothing could be further from the truth. In 1790 Talleyrand had sent a report to the Constituent Assembly proposing the idea of a uniform system of weights and measures. Surprisingly, the great man suggested collaboration with the British (through the Royal Society of London). The Assembly passed a decree requesting that the British Parliament should meet with the Assemblé Nationale 'to produce an invariable model for all weights and measures' (Connor, 1987). This came to nothing, but at the end of the year the Assembly set up a commission of five great scientists (Lagrange, Laplace, Borda, Mongé and Condorcet) to decide the issue. Their report of March 1791 initiated the metric system. Although the standards that were recommended contained a clear set of scientific principles (for example, to use, 'one ten-millionth part of the arc of the Earth's quadrant as the standard unit of measure, the unit of weight to be a declared volume of distilled water *in vacuo* at the freezing point' (ibid., p. 345), and so on), the choice was in fact an arbitrary one. But the metric system as we know it was perhaps the most enduring product of the French Revolution.

However, the expansion of the metric system even in France was painfully slow in the nineteenth century. For one thing, Napoleon himself was no admirer of metrification, contrary to popular belief, and is reported as saying, 'What are metres? Speak to me in *toises*!' (Connor, 1987, p. 346). In fact the metric system did not become obligatory in France until January 1840, and for a long time the French themselves continued to use the old units: the *toise*, the *pied* and the *ligne* (respec-

tively these were approximately 2 metres, one-third of a metre and
1/432 part of a metre). Nevertheless the French were keen to encourage
other nations to use the metric system and a commission was set up in
1870 to promote the internationalization of the metric standard. An
international conference followed in 1875 – surely the 1870s and 1880s
must be regarded as the great age of the international conference – at
which eighteen of the twenty attending countries' delegates argued in
favour of subscribing to the Convention du Mètre. A Bureau
Internationale des Poids et Mésures followed and was funded by the
participating countries. In May 1874, the London firm of Johnson,
Matthey and Co. was commissioned to manufacture the provisional
standard metre, cast in platinum and iridium. Thirty specimen bars
were eventually ordered and were dispatched to the world's leading
trading nations, Britain receiving bar no. 16. In 1889, a general conference on weights and measures was convened in Paris and new standard
bars were later distributed. These remained remarkably constant in
length, and in 1901 the International Prototype Metre, as this came to
be known, was agreed by the conference.

   Thus was Charles Gille able to opine that:

> Challenging routine and hatred,
> Taking its stand on useful things,
> The measure of the Republic,
> Has overthrown the foot of kings.[9]

In fact, however, Weber (1980) has shown that the kings proved easier
to overthrow than the measures associated with them, and that a great
deal of uncertainty ruled for many years after the metric system became
law. Indeed, ancient measures survived, even thrived, into the twentieth
century. In 1914, the people of the Landes region were still using the
journal as the standard measure of land area, even though this was
based upon labour input rather than actual physical area (that is, a
journal would represent a larger physical area of poor land than of
good land). The *rod* of northern France was consistently larger than its
southern equivalent and was used through the nineteenth century, and
in many remote parts of France the *saumade* (or 'donkey-load') was still
in use through to the 1880s. The state did attempt to police the metric
system but seems to have failed often enough. The number of trials for
the unlawful possession of 'false weights' dropped through the 1860s
and the old measures remained deep-rooted, causing a French teacher
to remark: 'All the peoples of Europe admired and envied the French
system of weights and measures [but] at least nine-tenths of the French
people still ignored it' (Weber, 1980, p. 31).

   In central, western and south-western France, the metric system was
still not in use in 1874, and in the Tarn region the decimal system was

'still in its infancy' in 1893, and 'unknown' in the Corrèze. French milestones may have displayed their distances in kilometres, but the country people themselves knew only *leagues*, and textiles continued to be sold by the *inch* and the *line*. A priest is quoted as saying in 1895, 'Our villagers have passed their military service and our children have [passed through] school but the metric system has not passed into custom yet' (Weber, 1980, p. 32).

What was true of weights and measures was equally the case with the currency. The standardization of the franc of 1803 is supposed to have created a stable currency on which the French economy, and savings in particular, thrived for the next 120 years. In some respects this is true, but the new currency had to compete with earlier forms which continued to circulate alongside it for much of this period. It is reported that *liards* circulated in poorer regions such as Brittany and Burgundy until well into the 1850s; that fourteenth-century *blancs*, obsolete *crowns* and *reaux* (atavisms of the Spanish occupation), were still in use in the 1860s. Bretons normally calculated in *reals* through the late nineteenth century and used 12-franc pieces as the equivalent of 20 *écus*. This was apparently the case in Quimper (Brittany) until 1917. An English traveller in Quercy (south-central France) in 1893 was astonished to find peasants and dealers still transacting business in *pistoles* and *écus*, the 'the currency of the Three Musketeers' (Weber, 1980, p. 33).

Ironically, one reason why these obsolete coins continued to exist through the mid-nineteenth century was the general shortage of coin brought about by the effects of the gold discoveries of 1849 and later. As we have seen, France and other nominally bimetallic countries were forced onto a 'limping' or *de facto* gold standard as a result, but gold – unlike silver – could not easily perform the function of a circulating medium because of its high relative value. Token coins were then introduced but this produced the problem that coins of inferior fineness (such as the Italian coins of the 1860s) drove out the fuller-bodied coins such as the French francs.

Thus the monetary picture of France in the late nineteenth century which presents itself to us is one of a highly civilized state unable to maintain the currency standards of its own making. Paris may have been a great world metropolis, and certainly it had become the undisputed centre of finance under the Empire, but it was not able to bring the provinces along with it. Yet at the same time it sought to extend French-invented systems to the rest of the world, and the French government was always at the forefront of attempts to bring about international standardization of various kinds. The French overseas empire also grew apace and again it is true to say that French authorities were generally more successful than the British at transplanting their way of life (by exporting their 'systems') to the new colonies. And in some areas the French succeeded in passing on their own ways to other European countries. The French Commercial Code of 1807 gradually became the basis of company law in Belgium, Holland, Switzerland, Italy and Spain, and even Germany (though this was later modified) (Clapham, 1921). Clearly there were great benefits to be had from such standardization of law across European trading nations, with perhaps none of the costs associated with currency standardization; certainly the merchant communities in each country had much to gain in the way of stabilizing trade and defining the terms of commercial contracts. Clapham argued that by the mid-nineteenth century Western Europe, including Britain, was already becoming harmonised into a single commercial and industrial society. Common characteristics were becoming evident in social needs and economic diseases. However, it seems that Britain, while becoming part of this common European economy, was generally unwilling, because of its *laissez-faire* attitudes, to assume a leadership role in promoting many of the conditions which might bring this about, though of course it was more active in the field of free trade. It was thus left to a more *dirigiste* France, which in any case had more to gain from an internal expansion of European trade, to take the helm. Ironically, this was despite the fact that the French economy was more ramshackle and far less standardized than the British economy at this stage. Moreover, the French were unwilling to import successful British paradigms, such as Greenwich Mean Time, the imperial system of weights and measures (which had more in common with traditional French measures than the metric system), and the British gold standard, even when operating a 'limping gold standard' after 1850.

It has been argued that some countries chose to remain outside this movement towards greater European integration (including the drift to the gold standard) for the simple reason that they were not yet part of what Clapham called a 'single industrial society'. Austria-Hungary and Russia remained tied to silver because both were large exporters of agricultural products and both were still ruled by ancient oligarchies deriving their power from land ownership. As such they were interested in maintaining the competitiveness of their products by means of what was effectively a depreciating exchange allowed by a silver standard. De Cecco (1974, p. 52) argued that 'Continuous exchange depreciation constituted their last stand against the rock bottom prices at which agricultural products were being sold by the United States'.

Thus we encounter the classical socio-economic cleavage between agriculture and industry engendered by currency changes and currency reform in the nineteenth century – a cleavage which in this case was complicated by, on the one hand, the industrialization of Austria while

Hungary remained an immense granary, and on the other hand, the French-inspired modernization of imperial Russia under Count Witte, later in the nineteenth century. It would be interesting to inquire into what, if any, the connections were between French monetary policies, especially their attachment to bimetallism, and their foreign policies with regard to the economic support for Russia towards the end of the century. Of course, a movement towards international bimetallism would, in large part, have removed the potential friction between industry and agriculture at both a national and international level. But at the moment this must remain a closed book.

It has to be said that France's position in the 'single industrial society' of Clapham was far less secure than either Britain's or Germany's in the critical period from 1870 onwards. So if we can see clear identities of interest between silver-and-agriculture and gold-and-industry, it is harder to compartmentalize France. On the one hand, if France is seen as being on the cusp of a transition to modern economic growth between 1850 and 1870, it is not the case, as it certainly was later with Russia and several other countries, that France was in any great need of foreign capital. The fact that France was a capital-rich country in itself removes one of the justifications for France to want to move decisively on to a gold standard in the nineteenth century. France, to use modern parlance, did not need to possess the '*Good Housekeeping Seal of Approval*', which the gold standard afforded to would-be industrial countries in the nineteenth century, to advance into industrialism (Bordo and Rockoff, 1996).

It is certain, however, that France and later the Latin Union did exert a significant influence on the relative prices of gold and silver up to the 1870s. Walker, as we have seen, was able to show that all the important authorities were agreed on this. During the 'great debate', the bimetallists remained convinced that the French 'parachute' had been one of the most influential and beneficent inventions of the nineteenth century, and could not help but draw the conclusion that if a powerful bimetallic union had been maintained after 1870 it would have had a material influence on the metallic ratio and thus have prevented the fall of silver and the consequent international depression. As a prominent monetary theorist, Leonard Darwin (1897), pointed out, the arguments of the gold-standard supporters hinged upon the impact of a different set of inventions, the cost-reducing industrial innovations of the 'age of improvement'; gold-bugs generally argued that even without the demonetization of silver these would have ensured a secular price fall in the period. Following from this, they would have said that the passing of true bimetallism, the collapse of the Latin Union, and France's adoption of a limping gold standard, all had little real consequence. Yet at the same time they argued that a restoration of bimetallism at the old ratio would cause a massive and unwanted rise in prices, causing Darwin (ibid., p. 164) to ask: 'If the abolition of bimetallism produced no fall in prices, why should its restoration cause a rise?' Gold-standard defenders might answer that the cost-reducing impact of industrialization came after 1870 rather than before, the earlier period being more disturbed, but were never able to substantiate this with figures. Bimetallists could parry with the fact that the most cost-effective invention of all – the railway – had its day long before 1873.

Darwin, among many others, was convinced that changes in monetary standards were indeed responsible for general nineteenth-century trends in prices:

> Looking at the century as a whole, there can be no doubt that prices have shown a general downward tendency, which is quite consistent with the view that an increase of production tends to produce that result. But the rise in prices which took place after 1850 had every appearance, and was at the time believed to be due, in great measure, to the Australian gold discoveries. The severity of the fall in prices since 1873 is certainly consistent with the view that the increase in demand for gold since that date has materially augmented the fall in prices which the production would have tended to have produced. All these considerations seem to me to make it clear that average gold prices have been materially affected by the conditions primarily affecting the currency, and that they would now [1897] be considerably above their present level if bimetallism had been effectively maintained.
>
> (Ibid., p. 173)

From such a line of argument, it is not difficult to see why bimetallists of all countries in the nineteenth century found inspiration in the 'France of the dual standard' of 1803–73. Bimetallic France became the champion of their cause. A problem with this was that it tended to strengthen the position of the 'low-ratio school', which wanted to return to the old French ratio of 15.5:1, for the reasons outlined by Darwin (p. 173). The idea was seductive: the French system worked well; it was bimetallic at a ratio of 15.5:1; therefore we should return to 15.5:1. This weakened somewhat the case of the 'academic bimetallists' who tended to want a more realistic high ratio, closer to the current market ratio of the two commodities. This school argued that it was the existence of a statutory ratio, rather than the precise level of the ratio, which would effect the cure by stabilizing the exchanges. Indeed, the most desirable ratio would be the one likely to maintain the largest possible proportion of the two metals in monetary circulation. But when the market ratio under the limping gold standard had fallen to 20:1 or more, a return to the French ratio was bound to result in a flood of silver to the mints and, as its detractors warned, a *de facto* silver standard. Of course there were people who wanted a silver standard, but few of these were to found this side of the Atlantic Ocean.

French experience also gave sustenance to what I have called 'unilateral bimetallism'. Most bimetallists believed that a global dual standard was only workable if the majority of important trading countries instituted it, but a minority came to the view, again following the French example, that it only required one or two such countries to go bimetallic, perhaps indeed only one major country. Sir David Barbour (1886), Financial Secretary to the Indian government, was definitely of this view:

> The United States were at one time bimetallic at 16 to 1 and France at 15½ to 1. The result was that gold was coined in America and that silver flowed to France. The stream of silver that flowed to France was not of sufficient volume to totally exclude gold from her currency; and the world still retained the benefits of the bimetallic system at the French ratio, namely 1 to 15½, the effect of the American ratio of 16 to 1 being to render the United States for the time practically monometallic.

Barbour, then, concerned about the future of the finances of India, saw possible salvation for the country whose economic stewardship he had inherited, not in the ancient gold standard of England, but in the alien monetary system of another great European power which had once coveted England's empire in southern Asia.

Notes

1. Vilar (1976) cites the published opinions of 224 French merchants who met at the Maison des Merciers in Paris in 1572.
2. Vilar argues that the Spaniards Mercado and Azpilcueta had already advanced this interpretation (p. 184).
3. S. Jevons, *Money and the Mechanism of Exchange*, 1876, cited by Walker (1898), p. 319.
4. Walter Bagehot, cited by Walker (1898), pp. 133–7.
5. M. Chevalier, 1857, cited by Walker (1898), pp. 133–7.
6. The Royal Commission on the Recent Changes in the Relative Values of the Precious Metals, Final Report, 1888.
7. Portugal used Lisbon, Spain used Cadiz, in the 1880s.
8. Sandford Fleming was the Engineer-in-Chief of the Canadian Pacific Railway and was 'fired with enthusiasm for uniform time'. He had suggested a modern system of time zones since 1876, and received the support of the British government. See Howse, (1980).
9. Quoted by Weber (1980).

CHAPTER FOUR

India and the silver rupee

MISS PRISM: Cecily, you will read your Political Economy in my
absence. The chapter on the Fall of the Rupee you may omit. It is
somewhat too sensational. Even these metallic problems have
their melodramatic side.
[*Goes down the garden with* DR. CHASUBLE.]
(Oscar Wilde, *The Importance of Being Earnest*, 1899)

The Mint and the melting pot

India entered onto the world monetary stage in the nineteenth century
in a highly significant way because of the breakdown in the economic
relationship between gold and silver. If India was, as Disraeli put it, the
'jewel in the crown of the British Empire', it was set in a clasp of silver
until near the end of the century. It may seem perverse that Britain, the
progenitor and guardian of the gold standard, should have maintained
its most ancient and most highly prized imperial possession on a silver
standard for most of the modern era. Reasons why this was the case
will be suggested later in the chapter, but it will be appreciated that this
fact would not have posed an economic problem had the ratio of
exchange between the two currency metals remained constant. Clearly
the decline in the gold price of silver which began in 1873 changed the
circumstances entirely, causing Fetter and Gregory (1973, p. 18) to
write that 'silver again came into the arena of British economic controversy by the side door of India'.

India's economic importance to Britain was obvious enough by this
stage. The failure of free trade as a global movement and the barriers
that were being placed against its exports by spreading protectionism
meant that Britain was having to rely more and more upon the markets
of the Empire as the century entered its last quarter. Between the late
1870s and the early 1880s, India's share of British exports increased
from 8 per cent to 13 per cent and the subcontinent became the most
important market in the Empire. Between 1870 and 1913, the volume
of India's exports to Britain increased six-fold, and by the 1880s India
had become the biggest market for British cotton goods. By the end of
the nineteenth century, Lancashire cotton was making up two-thirds of
the total of British exports to the territory. Cain and Hopkins (1993)
are clear about the reasons for the growth of trade with the subconti-

nent in this era: the rise of consumer demand in Europe for Indian exports (jute, cotton, tea and indigo); railway construction after 1850; the opening of the Suez Canal in 1869; the extension of British sovereignty across new states in the mid-century period, and the transfer of power from the East India Company to the British Crown after 1858.

The predominance of cotton in the sale of British goods to India explains in large part Manchester's involvement in the monetary debates of the period and in Indian affairs generally. Karl Marx believed that this was a reflection of the rise of the industrial bourgeoisie – for which Manchester cotton stood as proxy – and indicated clearly the capitulation of the oligarchy of the City to the 'millocracy' of Lancashire. But as Cain and Hopkins argue, Marx overstated the power of the new industrial classes and exaggerated their role in the direction of British government policy in India. If India was being transformed, it was more through the agency of gentlemanly capitalists than parvenu millowners, much though the Lancashire men were in favour of the development of the territory throughout the period of the Raj. Nevertheless, it was widely appreciated, both in the City and in Lancashire, that a continuous fall in the price of silver would ultimately affect India in a number of adverse ways and that the consequent drying up of the Indian market would have a more deleterious effect on the cotton county than on the City. As the fall of silver gave way to what was obviously a prolonged depression of trade, which affected Lancashire more than any other manufacturing district, the region's spokesmen directed their attention more and more towards the problems of the Indian connection (see Chapter Seven).

However, we must look first at the fiscal problems of governing India to discern the causes of British concern at its monetary condition. Paradoxically, as we have seen, it was the government of Britain, the home of the gold standard, which carried out more research into the exchange problems resulting from the fall in the price of silver after 1873 than any other country. To say, as some observers have done, that this 'led to serious consideration of the possibility of international bimetallism' (Fetter and Gregory, 1973, p. 19) may be something of an exaggeration, but it was this concern that was the mainspring for the setting up of the Parliamentary Select Committee of 1876, which continued to report right down to 1896, and for the appointment of the Herschell Committee of 1888, the Fowler Committee of 1898 and the Royal Commission of 1913. And were it not for India's perceived currency problems, it is doubtful if Britain would ever have participated at all in any of the international monetary conferences of the period.

If we add the City's concern about the fiscal probity and the creditworthiness of India to Lancashire's concern about the retention of her most important overseas market, we can understand why the British government saw fit to investigate in this way. But there were other, less tangible, reasons for British intellectuals and politicians to become interested in the Indian currency problems in the late nineteenth century. As Chandavarkar (1989, p. 3) has pointed out,

> The sheer complexity and uniqueness of Indian monetary experience have invested the problems of Indian currency with a distinctive intellectual appeal and even an indefinable element of mystique. No wonder Indian monetary experience since the advent of British rule seems to have exercised a singular fascination for some of the most acute contemporary economists.

Alfred Marshall was keenly interested in Indian economic affairs at least from the time of his appointment as a Fellow of Balliol College, Oxford, and thereby became Lecturer in Political Economy to the selected candidates of the Indian Civil Service, helping its young men to become those 'Christian gentlemen who combined refinement with licensed muscularity' (Cain and Hopkins, 1993, p. 330). As the mentor of John Maynard Keynes, Marshall naturally passed on his curiosity, and the great Cambridge man thus wrote his first book on the Indian currency (*Indian Currency and Finance*, 1911). Keynes's other great teacher, Lionel Abrahams, was even more obsessed with Indian economic issues and was referred to, rather flatteringly, as 'the moulder and manipulator of India's involved but efficient financial system' by Keynes himself (Chandavarkar, 1989). Arthur Balfour, one of the most intellectual politicians of modern British history and perhaps the best economist–prime minister before Harold Wilson, also cut his teeth on the Indian currency problems: his first speech in the House was on precisely this subject (McKay, 1985).

It is as though India was regarded as a great laboratory for social, political and economic experimentation by British intellectuals of the late nineteenth and early twentieth centuries. Whereas British practice, whether it be in relation to the gold standard or even the British constitution itself, was a result of, and was sanctioned by, ancient custom and practice, or even by the Almighty, Indian practice could be regarded as highly variable within certain constraints. And whereas the essential parameters of British policy were a priori and inviolate, the treatment of India could always be altered or reformed at the behest of the British authorities. Even without an exogenously generated crisis of the kind occasioned by the fall of silver, intellectuals and others would have continued to ponder Indian issues in so far as they constituted a wholly legitimate area of concern to the policy-makers of the mother country. But the silver crisis gave them their head.

India's silver currency

How and why did India ever develop a silver currency? In Bengal, the most important region of India to the eighteenth-century British, the foundations for continued imperial rule were laid down under the last of the Great Moguls. The Mogul's governor in Bengal, Murshid Quli Khan, ruled almost as an independent prince, built a new capital in Murshidabad, and organized a large cash revenue without which, it has been argued, Bengal would have been useless to the British. His banker, Fatehchand or Jaget Sheth ('Merchant of the World'), controlled access to the mint and was able to purchase silver at prices he himself dictated. Typically, the British chose to work with him rather than against him, and were thus able to gain a key position in the trade of Bengal by exploiting the existing power structure (Kulke and Rothermund, 1986).

A boom in trade between Britain and Bengal began in the second decade of the eighteenth century. In order to pay for the produce of Bengal, the British began to export silver, readily available to them in Europe, in large volume. In the 1710s, about £2 million were transferred in this way. Fortunately, this did not lead to local price inflation since the Moguls sent much of it to northern India. At the same time the British began to build factories in Bengal, even sending out their own artisans to train Indian workers. They then eliminated the prosperous Bengali middlemen by deploying their own agents to deal with the local weavers and other craftsmen. If the Mogul rulers of India resented the entrepreneurial activities of the British, they must have been mollified somewhat by the steady stream of silver which accompanied their often unwonted incursions.

Later incursions were of a distinctly more military kind and the middle decades of the eighteenth century saw the British and French at war in India, each determined to emerge as the heirs to Mogul rule. The ultimate defeat of the French was followed by a period of rapacious looting by the British, which in itself shook the foundations of the Mogul Empire. By the time of the Battle of Plassey (1757) and certainly by the time of the Battle of Buxar (1764), the economic exploitation had been on such a scale that the Moguls were unable to put up a respectable fight against the British army under Major Hector Munro. By 1765, Robert Clive was master of Bengal and soon became responsible for the collection and disposal of the many millions of pounds of revenue yielded by the vast region he had conquered. In a fashion which was to become typical of British rule, the emperor was bought off with an annual allowance of £260,000, which kept him in a diminished state of affluence at Allahabad. With the effective emasculation of the Mogul, the British inherited not just a territory but a whole fiscal system, which they continued to mulch for close on another two hundred years. As Cain and Hopkins (1993, p. 320) have put it, 'the managers of the Raj took readily to India partly because they were able to merge their own rent-seeking and capitalist purposes with the apparatus of "military fascism" left by the Mughals'.

But in taking on the administration of India and by extending the principles of bureaucracy, hierarchy and centralization (more often than not through the insights of political economy and, later, utilitarianism), the British inevitably hastened the monetization of the subcontinent. As well as extending taxation systems, which presupposed a degree of monetary circulation, the imperial power also hastened India's participation in the multilateral international economy, which in turn depended on further monetization. This is not to say that India was by any means fully monetized at this stage: as late as the 1950s, the share of the non-monetized sector in the Indian economy was reckoned to be around 43 per cent for rural areas and between 8 per cent and 11 per cent for urban areas. Kumar (1983) reckoned that it must have been more than 50 per cent in the nineteenth century, when wages were still typically paid in grain in most districts. But the spread of imperialism inevitably saw the growth of the money supply if only in order to pay the wages of soldiers and servants doing the bidding of 'John Company' or, later, the Raj.

Indeed the Moguls had significantly improved the supply of money to India during their stewardship for partly the same reasons. But they had been hampered by the fact that different regions used different degrees of discount and by the essential problem that India as a whole frequently suffered a scarcity of the precious metals, owing to its dependence on their import. Thus the value of commodity coins fluctuated wildly at times. The British inherited a crude and chaotic system and the East India Company was at pains to correct this. In any case they understood that the right to coin money in itself represented an important symbol of authority and that its acceptance was part and parcel of their becoming fully accepted as the valid rulers of the country. Senior members of the company stressed the need for its servants to assimilate the monetary affairs of the various territories that were added to its empire during the course of the nineteenth century. Such was the case in Bengal: 'We wish such a reform to be made in the coinage of Bengal, as may put all persons upon an equal footing, leaving no room for fraud, and as little as possible to be affected by power.'[1] Ambirijan goes on to point out, however, that the problems connected with money and credit often baffled the best minds of both 'John Company' India and the British Raj. True to type, governors-general and viceroys alike were prone to be more interested in big-game hunting and military matters than in mundane matters of finance, a reflection of the 'traditional aristocratic view' (Ambirijan, 1984). In 1842 Governor-General Lord Ellenborough felt that 'the best thing to do regarding currency was to do nothing'. This might sound like startling complacency but could be taken to reflect the normal 'mind of the City' with regard to monetary reform in the age. Alternatively, it could be taken as mirroring the conservative–empirical approach encapsulated in the maxim 'If it is not necessary to change, it is necessary not to change.' Either way, the fact is that there were many periods of crisis in Indian monetary history even before the 1870s and these necessarily caused senior administrators to turn away, at least for a while, from fishin' and shootin' and the like. This led them to seek the advice of British 'experts' in political economy, and led Ambirijan (1984, p. 8) to the following conclusion:

> In no field in the domain of public policy-making in nineteenth century India has expert knowledge played as major a role as in monetary management. With British rule and British-trained bureaucrats it was inevitable that British monetary ideas should have had a marked impact … In this context the erection of a monetary framework in India really meant the entry into India of institutions developed elsewhere.

Indian currency confusion and the bimetallic experiments

As we have seen, the British inherited a dynamic but chaotic monetary system from the Moguls, based on the circulation of silver coins. The currency was confused for two basic reasons. First, there had long been a regional scarcity of silver, and second, there was a multiplicity of circulating coins and a lack of standardization essential to an efficient system. Thus the Indian economy had already become dependent on imports of bullion from Europe and it was reported in 1750 that a trade recession would settle on Bengal as the *diwani* (the land tax) was collected and sent to Delhi (Ambirijan, 1984). At first the efforts of the East India Company failed to obviate the recession as the collected bullion was sent on to China to finance the company's 'investment' there. As company policy also discouraged the importing of replacement bullion, it is not surprising that there was a further contraction of the specie circulation.

However, given certain British prejudices even in the eighteenth century in favour of gold, it is surprising that the authorities at first hit on the idea of a bimetallic currency system, but it would seem that Robert Clive, for one, was largely ignorant of current economic thought in Britain. The idea of a bimetallic currency was that it would encourage Indians to bring gold to the mints by giving a premium to the metal (and presumably waiving the normal seigniorage charges) since it was well known that they possessed large quantities of it in the form of jewellery and ornaments. European suppositions about Indian hoarding of this kind were to colour British prejudices throughout the period of the Raj and even affected the thinking of John Maynard Keynes. In the event, gold-holders were encouraged to bring their gold forward but, since it was overvalued, it seems that this was at the expense of silver, which rapidly began to disappear from circulation. The bimetallic experiment thus made it profitable to hoard, melt and export silver rather than gold and can only have reinforced the monometallic orthodoxy of British economic experts in the era (Ambirijan, 1984).

The problem of a bimetallic system which included circulating gold for late eighteenth-century India is not difficult to apprehend. The smallest practicable gold coin was of too high an intrinsic value to be useful as a circulating medium, and it is surprising that the authorities had not understood this. But in any case, overvaluing gold in this way was a cardinal error. At this juncture the European ratio of exchange between the two metals stood at about 14.8:1. The ratio imposed by the company, thanks partly to the premium, represented 16.45:1, giving no chance for silver to rehabilitate itself. Attempts were made to reduce the ratio in 1769 but these proved unsuccessful.

So the unfortunate effect of this bimetallic experiment was to saddle the Indian territories with an unmanageable *de facto* gold currency, requiring action by the East India Company as it threatened the state of trade, at least in Bengal. The Court of Directors wanted to return to a monometallic silver currency but perversely chose a bimetallist, Sir James Steuart, to present a report on the matter. *The Principles of Money Applied to the Present State of the Coin of Bengal* was published in 1772 and in it Steuart proposed the setting up of a central bank on the model of the Bank of England which, he concluded, must be kept independent of the East India Company. Against his own instincts he further proposed a return to a silver commodity standard on the grounds that silver 'was the money of account of the land' (Ambirijan, 1984). In 1777, Governor-General Warren Hastings stopped the coining of gold *mohurs*, but this led to pressure on silver and it had to be resumed. Hastings's successor, Cornwallis, tried again to create a workable bimetallic standard at the more realistic ratio of 14.86:1 and set up the Harris Commission of 1787, which cited Adam Smith in arguing that gold and silver should be adjusted to reflect their natural market scarcities (ibid.).

In 1792 a major new influx of silver coins came into the possession of the East India Company in the form of a war indemnity from the Tipu Sultan (he of the notorious 'Black Hole of Calcutta') and later the government of Madras (another of the presidencies under the East India Company) further enhanced the value of silver at the expense of gold, reversing the effects of the earlier premium. Thus was India reinstalled on a silver standard: partly as a result of dithering by the authorities and their ignorance of current economic thinking at the metropolitan centre, partly by calling on the wisdom of the greatest economic thinker of the age, and partly as a result of random factors beyond the control of Briton or Indian.

A continuing problem was that the Indians themselves were always prone to melting down coin to use the metals for other purposes. This was partly due to their adherence to ritualistic religions and partly due to cultural factors which placed a high premium on stores of wealth which were incorruptible. This tendency would perhaps always threaten the proper working of a bimetallic system of all but the most sophisticated kind, yet the scarcity of metal was, in turn, good reason to have a bimetallic system which made use of both specie: a true monetary dilemma. A further complication was the sheer diversity of coins in circulation owing to the breakdown of the Mogul Empire and its replacement by many new, minor states and principalities under the aegis of the East India Company. Inevitably this resulted in a complete absence of a general standard of value and Ambirijan (1984, p. 16) concluded that 'after nearly forty years of tinkering with the currency system, the British had achieved at the beginning of the nineteenth century not much improvement'.

In the 1800s the Court of Directors explicitly blamed bimetallism for the massive losses to the company and the considerable inconvenience to the public of India. In coming to the conclusion that a monometallic system should be introduced as soon as possible, they derived great comfort from Lord Liverpool's *Treatise on the Coins of the* Realm, 1805, in which had been set out, for the first time, a complete scheme for the management of a monometallic currency with a subsidiary token coinage. It must be remembered that at this stage Britain was still on a *statutory* bimetallic system itself (in 1797 at a mint ratio of 15.21:1), so India's *de facto* bimetallism should not be seen as *formally* unorthodox in any sense. In any case, it was the exigencies of the Napoleonic Wars that led to the Liverpool memorandum. (Fetter and Gregory, 1973). Britain had been forced onto a paper currency during the wars but in 1798 the price of silver had begun to fall relative to the inconvertible pound and the government had felt it necessary to prevent silver coming into the mints in too great a volume. Hence the memorandum.

Where the Court of Directors did not follow Lord Liverpool was in recommending a monometallic silver rather than a gold currency. This serves to underline the fact that at this stage the choice of metal was not one which was fraught with prejudice or bound by dogma. It is worth remembering that even Ricardo 'had discussed, without much conviction one way or the other, the relative merits of the two metals as a standard, at one time showing a preference for silver, and later for gold' (Fetter and Gregory, 1973, p. 15). So it would seem that the reason why Britain and India found themselves on different commodity standards in the nineteenth century can simply be explained by the fact that at its beginning there was no British orthodoxy for gold, only a growing consensus that the currency should be monometallic. Yet Ambirijan points out that Liverpool preferred a gold currency for 'England' because it was a rich country much dependent on foreign trade. The obverse of this, of course, would apply to India, a poor country with a small foreign trade sector. We shall come across this mode of thought again, when it is argued that its prevalence may have been partly responsible for the demise of silver after 1873.

Nevertheless, there was validity in the argument of Governor-General Sir John Shore that gold was not fit for the purpose of a generally circulating coinage in nineteenth-century India, even the smallest possible gold coin being of too high a value for most perceivable transactions at that time. The Court of Directors again followed the advice of Lord Liverpool in advocating a subsidiary copper coinage under a silver commodity standard, as against the silver and copper subsidiary coinage under a gold standard, which he preferred for England.

However, it took nearly thirty years for this plan to become adopted by all the Indian states. Under the East India Company the subcontinent was divided into three presidencies: Bengal, Madras and Bombay. In the 1800s, the governor of the Madras presidency, Lord Bentinck, was reluctant, it seems, to accept what amounted to the Bengal system in his own province since he was at that time still trying to stabilize existing currency arrangements and furthermore was involved in the Mysore Wars. In any case, Bentinck was an Englishman to a fault and, thus, 'a great enemy of all Revolution' (Ambirijan, 1984).

To say that there was currency confusion in India in the early nineteenth century would be an understatement. In Madras two major coins competed directly against each other: the *Arcot* silver rupee and the gold *Star Pagoda*, but in northern India there might be many different rupees all circulating at the same time. It is not surprising that there was a general preference for bimetallism when full-bodied coins of both gold and silver were in circulation, or that the presidency governments were wont to experiment with various gold–silver exchange ratios to achieve a workable equilibrium which would keep as much money as possible in the field, especially since there was a widespread belief that there was a shortage of circulating medium.

Thus in 1806 Madras introduced a new currency on a formal bimetallic basis, against the advice of the Court of Directors of the company,
and a similar system was introduced in Bombay in 1824. There were
attempts to extend it to Bengal but these were resisted on the grounds
that it was likely to provoke rebellion, or *mutiny*, to use the preferred
term of British India. A common bimetallic currency for the whole of
India was thus narrowly avoided.

The Anglicization of India

When Lord Bentinck became governor-general in 1828 he was determined to see India move onto a common currency. Historians of the
East India Company see Bentinck's leadership as presaging an important age of social and economic planning, 'on a scale that it [the
Company] would have considered anathema a generation earlier'
(Lawson, 1993, p. 152). Bentinck's era was to be much affected by the
towering intellect of one Thomas Babington Macaulay, who was appointed to the Supreme Council of Bengal, created by the India Act of
1833. Macaulay almost single-handedly created an education policy for
India (the misnamed 'Minute on Education' of 1835) and a draft penal
code. He was also largely responsible for installing English as the language of government and education in India, and there is little doubt
that his machinations caught the 'prevailing mood of confidence in the
superiority of British institutions and culture' (ibid., p. 153).

In other respects, however, general reform failed in the Bentinck era
(1828–35). The so-called 'orientalists' in the company's employ (whose
ideas must not be confused with the modern concept of 'orientalism')
resisted centralization on the grounds that it might upset the natural
balance of constitutional forces in India. Many planned changes to the
penal system and ideas for public works schemes were put aside until
the Great Mutiny of 1858 forced reform on the British. The main
reason for procrastination was the simple fact that the East India Company lacked the resources to carry out reform: debts were accruing
from frontier wars and in 1833 the company had lost its monopoly of
the lucrative China trade. This latter included the highly profitable tea
trade, reckoned to be one of the most cost-effective and well-run enterprises the company had ever mounted.[2] Indeed, the development of the
China trade depended intimately on the expansion of Indian exports of
opium and cotton piece goods, which in turn prevented the flow of
silver specie out of India to pay for the China goods. The East India
Company, having already lost the monopoly of the India trade in 1813,
had to invent a new role for the organization. This new role was the

government of India, which in turn was lost with the Great Mutiny of 1858.

Nevertheless, the Bentinck period ushered in an age of Anglicization for India and despite many problems besetting the currency reformers, it is surprising that greater urgency was not accorded to their projects, given the British emphasis on sound currency as a prerequisite for good government. In 1829 Bentinck had written a minute urging the establishment of a single uniform currency for the whole of India, but five years passed before the Court of Directors took any notice of his demands (Ambirijan, 1984). Then in 1834 the Mint Committee of Calcutta proposed the unification of currencies and H. T. Prinsep, Secretary of the Supreme Government of India, argued that it was essential to the improvement of the financial system of the subcontinent. A uniform currency would, he argued, provide relief to the presidencies in times of emergency (ibid.). A system of rapid steamer transport had recently been set up and therefore a uniform metallic currency could be used and would not have to be recoined. This was the same kind of argument that was later used to advocate railways for famine relief purposes. Bentinck even ordered the dies for the new currency but had to give up his post before they became available. However, his successor, Metcalfe, pursued the scheme with equal enthusiasm and a monometallic currency on a silver standard was introduced in 1835.

Ambirijan (1984, p. 36) asks how far we are justified in viewing the Act of 1835 as a victory for Liverpool's monometallic ideas and concludes thus:

> We find the Court of Directors [of the East India Company] upholding the doctrine of monometallism and relying on authorities such as Locke, Liverpool, Harris and the rest. On the other hand, even confirmed Ricardians like Holt Mackenzie, and Madras civilians like Petrie and Roebuck, who were confirmed Smithians, all appeared to defend an economic heresy, namely bimetallism. As we have seen, the local administrators, in spite of being well versed in theory, were so worried about their local problems that they were ready to act against received doctrines, but the persistence of the Court of Directors in upholding the Liverpool line finally wrought a change in the attitude of the local governments. The local officials also accepted in principle the economic ideas of men like Liverpool ... but also feared the possible deflationary effects of a monometallic standard ... This made them favour actions which they fully realised were repugnant to the prevailing orthodox corpus of knowledge.

It would be wrong, therefore, if Ambirijan is correct, to imagine India responding in any simple way towards the economic/monetary needs of the imperial power. Indeed, informed economic opinion in India was just as schismatized as in Britain and the schisms were much closer to the decision-making processes. As Checkland (1957) pointed out, British monetary experts, at least in so far as they were represented by the practitioners of the City of London, remained largely unaffected by the ideas and prescriptions of the economic theorists at this stage. It could be that Ambirijan tends to exaggerate the effects of political economy in the formulation of public policy in India, but clearly Indian officials were more aware, perhaps because of their educational backgrounds at Haileybury College, of the great precepts of political economy than their counterparts in the City, who had never been required to pass examinations inspired by the great Thomas Malthus.

Yet in one other characteristic the subcontinent shared an identity with Britain, for, as Ambirijan (1984) shows, there was in India an almost complete absence of monetary interest groups within the wider society. 'As yet', he writes, 'public opinion had no sides to take' (p. 37). This would alter radically later in the century with the rise of nationalist thought, which had much to do with current economic matters since it tended to focus on the idea of the 'great drain', and before corresponding monetary interest groups began to appear in Britain.

A bank for India

In the early nineteenth century the British tended to believe that India was not yet ready to develop its own banking system, which in turn might be expected to aid the evolution of a credit system. This meant that a circulating coinage was all the more important to monetary integrity in India. In Britain, it was believed that paper credit was only feasible in advanced countries whose governments were well established and where the rule of law prevailed. Again, theory was allowed to influence Indian policy-making when the Court of Directors cited Adam Smith in arguing that paper credit should not be seen as a remedy for a shortage of specie, since the issue of a paper currency might lead to the disappearance of the circulating medium. This would be doubly unfortunate since there was, in any case, a shortage of gold and silver thanks to the depredations of nabobs such as Robert Clive, the drain of specie owing to the company's taking over of the *diwani* (tax collection) and its subsequent transmission to China and elsewhere to fund its 'investments' there. Added to this was the fact that Europe could never, it seemed, provide enough specie to feed both the monetary needs of the Indian economy and the constant demand for the metals for use by Indian handicraft workers.

Consequently there were many calls for the setting up of a major bank in India around the turn of the eighteenth century, if only because

Indian army officers were unable to send home their earnings thanks to the unsettled conditions in Europe produced by the Napoleonic Wars. The purchase of Bengal Treasury bills served this purpose for a while but the proliferation of fighting under the governor-generalship of the Marquess of Wellesley, at the beginning of the nineteenth century, led to a massive expansion of such bills and an inevitable discounting of their value. Some people wanted India to have a purely private, profit-making bank; others preferred a government-backed institution along the lines of the Bank of England. In 1805 an 'experimental' Bank of Madras was established and this was followed by a Bank of Bengal in 1807.

However, even the notes of the Bank of Bengal were not deemed to be legal tender in India and were not accepted unconditionally until 1839. This placed even greater emphasis on the coinage but of course it did mean that capital accumulation was not as rapid as it should have been. As in so many aspects of British rule in India, it was not until after 1858 that things began to improve. Clearly it was felt that the move on to a paper currency would always be more dangerous in a poor, dependent territory, or group of territories, such as India, than in a modern European country, especially in the context of the nineteenth century. And it must also be borne in mind that there was always a wide plurality of forces to be reckoned with in any proposed major change of policy in India. The Court of Directors of the East India Company was the most important one, but it was always under the purview of the British government (through the India Office) and could have privileges withdrawn at any time. Then there were the governor-general, the presidency governors, 'financial counsellors' to the Presidencies, the Indian chambers of commerce, pressure groups such as the United Planters' Association, and so on.

But although it was felt that India must depend largely upon metal money, this in itself was becoming a liability by the 1830s, when the commander-in-chief of the Indian Army reported that nearly 30,000 troops were annually being used to transport precious metals around the subcontinent. This was less of a problem than the fact that a commodity coinage simply did not allow the Indian economy to expand at a sufficiently fast rate. Mid-century gold discoveries did not help because the effect of these was to stiffen silver prices in Europe, and this made silver all the more scarce in India. Although India remained formally bimetallic, gold had ceased to be legal tender in 1835. In 1853, Governor-General Dalhousie demonetized gold altogether to prevent speculators importing it to exchange for dear silver (Ambirijan, 1984).

Another important reason for considering a paper currency was the fact that a profit could be made from it and the East India Company, especially at this time, was always on the lookout for extra forms of revenue. In any case, there were always people in England who believed that paper economized in the use of the precious metals, which were always scarce, nowhere more so than in India. The Bank Charter Act of 1844 had been a victory for the currency school (which believed in the complete separation of the functions of banking and note issue), and it was felt in England that this would be easier to achieve in India than in London, thus giving greater support for an Indian note issue. However, when a paper currency was introduced in 1862, it led to a shortage of coins and this in turn produced agitation for a gold currency, gold being relatively abundant after the mid-century gold finds. It was also felt that the Indians themselves were well used to a gold coinage and had not been prepared for a paper issue. There were even accusations by Indian merchants that the paper currency was 'a cunning device to denude the country of the precious metals'.[3]

It must also be borne in mind that this was happening at a time when British businessmen and politicians were becoming more concerned about the 'drain to the East', whereby silver, or so it was argued, was being absorbed by the Indian economy and leaving Europe in ever shorter supply. This drain was exacerbated by the Lancashire 'cotton famine' in the 1860s, which forced British merchants to import Indian raw cotton in larger volume. But there was continuing anxiety that the price–specie flow mechanism was somehow failing to operate in India and thus upsetting the market for the precious metals. The influx of silver into India should have led to a higher level of economic activity there and thus a higher price level, stemming imports and thus shutting off the inflow of silver. The ubiquitous argument that Indians were too prone to hoarding was always available, but there was also a feeling that the prevailing Indian price levels were so low that the country could continue to import specie without affecting them. An obvious answer to the problem of the drain on silver was to put India back on a gold standard – an attractive option given the relative abundance of gold and the fear that its price was falling too quickly. Furthermore, a conversion to gold would make Indian goods, imported into Europe mainly by the British, cheaper in European markets, since British merchants would not have to use relatively scarce silver to pay for them. Later in the century, the same merchant groups argued in favour of India going on to a gold standard for exactly the opposite reasons: by the 1880s India was more important as a market, and thus a depreciating silver standard made the country more difficult to export to. In the 1860s the advantages of gold were more unambiguous – gold could easily be obtained from that other British colony, Australia, whereas silver had to be obtained from the perfidious United States.

But the general consensus behind the gold standard in Britain was the main reason why there was widespread support for India's moving on to gold. In the 1860s even economists such as J. Shield Nicholson, later to become one of the leading British bimetallists and, with Foxwell, the most prominent academic supporter of the dual standard, was behind the extension of the gold standard to India for the simple reason that gold was in increasing supply at the time. Jevons and Marshall were in accord, and gold was seen as the coming monetary metal. There was little support for bimetallism in Britain at this stage, either for India or for the international economy as a whole, but the new gold finds of the 1850s were hardly conducive to this, threatening, as they did, to break the long-held ratio of exchange between the metals.

The question must then be why the silver standard was retained in India when there was so much momentum behind the spread of the gold standard at mid-century. Ambirijan's view is that ultimately the silver standard was kept in the interests of creditors, the biggest of which was the Indian government itself. Thus the current Secretary of State for India, Sir Charles Wood, was 'vehemently against' the introduction of gold on the grounds that silver was still the world's major monetary metal and Britain's conversion to gold had been for 'silly reasons'. Nevertheless, the agitation for gold continued through the 1860s and Lancashire came into play when one of its MPs, J. B. Smith, introduced a motion in the House of Commons proposing a gold standard for India. (Ambirijan, 1984). To further complicate matters, Sir Charles Trevelyan argued in favour of a transitional bimetallic standard in order to ease India on to a gold standard and to this end urged the government of India to accept the British sovereign as legal tender (ibid).

But as is always the case with currency matters, it proved easier to write or talk about currency reform than to actually bring about any change. The men ultimately responsible for administering reform had much to lose if things should go wrong and there was always the fear, heightened in this period, that if things did go wrong, it could result in rebellion.

By the 1870s other circumstances were beginning to change. The Swadeshi ('for our own country') movement, an early manifestation of Indian nationalism, first emerged in the Poona region around 1872. Swadeshism stood for the industrial development of India and the use of Indian manufactures in preference to imported goods – what we might now call import substitution. As such, it threatened the very basis of the British Raj, though its main advocates were English-educated professionals and, invariably, of the brahmin and kayastha élite castes, who were not inclined to rebellion or insurrection (Kannangara, 1968).

Nevertheless, its appearance coloured British thinking in this era and right through to the First World War.

However, by the 1880s, Indian manufacturing was beginning to expand rapidly. The government of India had actively promoted railways since 1849 and, despite the setback of the Great Mutiny, a basic railway network had developed, connecting the three great ports and Presidency towns (Bombay, Calcutta and Madras) with the Delhi plain and the Ganges valley, by 1870. This was achieved mainly by the use of private funds at a guaranteed minimum rate of interest. But then in the 1870s the state itself began to expand the network, spending over £3 million annually on construction. Occasionally there was a reversion to the private guarantee system, as in the 1878 crisis brought on by famine and war with Afghanistan, and a pronounced devaluation of the rupee caused by a severe silver depreciation. The telegraph system was also extended from the 1860s onwards and there was much expenditure on docks and harbour construction, which tended to increase after the Great Mutiny. The Raj is often criticized for failing to promote industrialization in India but it is difficult to see how industrialization could have taken off without such infrastructural investment. In any case, the state did occasionally become directly involved in industry, as when it set up pilot projects with the Kumaon Ironworks of 1855–56 and the Burwai Ironworks of 1860–61. However, even imagining that the British might have deliberately encouraged state-led industrial investment on any large scale in the nineteenth century in any part of the world always seems to me to be a misreading of economic history. Nevertheless, the state railways did run their own, large engineering shops and in 1863 the government established and operated the Central Press at Calcutta (Charlesworth, 1982). Where the Swadeshi movement could really raise its voice was in the area of tariff policies. On a number of occasions in the second half of the nineteenth century the Indian government sought to impose tariffs against British imports and were effectively prevented from doing so by the British authorities. All of these attempts were responses to short-term financial crises: it was always understood that there was no question of the British ever accepting long-term protectionism of any kind. Thus for example in the period 1859–62 the Indian government worked for a tariff to provide revenue to pay for the costs of reconstruction after the Great Mutiny and to finance Dalhousie's wars. In the 1870s tariffs were applied to finance famine relief and further wars. Each time, they were overruled by the British government after effective lobbying from British interest groups such as the Lancashire textile manufacturers.

But it is worth pointing out that there was some understanding in India, even amongst the groups who opposed free trade, that tariffs might be counterproductive in the longer term. The great Indian nationalist, Dadabhai Naoroji, was conscious of the fact that Indian manufacturers were reliant on British firms which produced the capital equipment needed to fit out Indian factories, and Kannangara (1968) has pointed out that Indian textiles were sold abroad under the umbrella of British imperial power. It was, after all, British gunboats that kept open the Chinese and Far Eastern ports, which were the main destination for Indian exporters in the late nineteenth century. And again, Indian entrepreneurs were highly conscious of the fact that they depended very intimately upon the patronage of British authorities within India to extend their enterprises: there were cotton millowners who sought mining concessions and steel mill owners who wanted to diversify into hydroelectric power, even then regarded as the key to future development of the subcontinent. In short, it is not surprising that India should ultimately enter the new century with a commercial policy 'as close to free trade as any country is likely to be' (Tomlinson, 1979).

The fact that India was kept (however willingly) in a 'straitjacket' of free trade has important implications for her currency history in the period. After all, changes in the status of a currency can have exactly the same economic effects as a protective tariff. A rapid fall in the exchange rate may be just as effective as the imposition of a tariff in stemming the flow of imports. So it is not surprising that when the Indian rupee began to fall in value after 1873, some Indian industries began to flourish as never before under the British. Not only were Lancashire imports made more expensive, but a 'miracle' of stable export prices was achieved – a phenomenon shared by (silver) Japan in the last decades of the nineteenth century. And of course Britain was an important market throughout for Indian goods such as corn (mainly wheat), jute and tea. Exports of these items were all much boosted by the fall of silver after 1873. So if the silver crisis was to have such beneficial effects on the Indian economy, why should the Indian government ever have complained about the 'exchange problems' of the rupee? The answer is that the Indian government was finding it increasingly difficult to pay the so-called 'home charges'. As we have seen, the East India Company was prepared to use the public revenue to cover the whole costs of administering the territories for which it became responsible. But as a private company it also had obligations to its shareholders, and money was expropriated for this purpose. Furthermore, large sums of money were borrowed from Britain to finance expansionary wars, and later to build the first railways and other infrastructures; the Indian taxpayer was expected to service the public debt which accrued. As Charlesworth (1982, pp. 52–3) has put it:

India was charged for her administration on a totally different basis from the white colonies. The Indian tax-payer met all administrative expenses incurred *within* India, paying, for example, the wages of the charladies who cleaned the corridors of the India Office in London. All such charges, of course, became more burdensome during the progressive devaluation of the silver rupee in the late nineteenth century.

Indian nationalists always argued that the home charges represented a 'drain' on wealth from India to Britain and the fact that there was such a movement cannot seriously be disputed. This debate does not concern us here, however, for it is about what proportion of the home charges represented a reasonable, or moral, charge on the average Indian tax-payer. Its relevance here is that the payment of the home charges *in toto* was inevitably affected by movements in the exchange rate between the pound sterling and the rupee, since the taxes were collected in depreciating silver and paid in appreciating gold. Interestingly, throughout the period after 1873, and whenever the Indian government ran into fiscal deficit (wholly or partly due to effective increases in the home charges), the Indian economy continued to have a large foreign-trade surplus, thanks in part to short-term increases in exports, but also to rapid industrialization fostered by inward capital movements and enhanced infrastructures, and the widening trade paradigm afforded by the ever-increasing imperial connections. These factors allowed India, despite the problems of the Indian government, to experience a remarkable 'treasure inflow'. It has been estimated that between 1861 and 1895 the net inflow of silver into India represented one-third of world output in the period. Thanks to hoarding, this did not result in sustained inflation, as might have been expected. This would have throttled Indian exports and reversed these trends. But it also meant that potential demand for British manufactured goods, and especially Lancashire cotton textiles, was not growing as rapidly as it might have done.

Thus we can say that the Indian economy in the late nineteenth century began to exhibit a set of very particular, if not perverse, characteristics, and it is not surprising that it should have fascinated more than a few British economists. Indian manufacturing was expanding rapidly in the middle of the worldwide depression of 1873 to 1896 – a prima-facie reason for contemporaries to blame their problems on the propagation of gold currencies at the time Yet the Indian government teetered on the brink of bankruptcy while many of its citizens continued to be visited by disease and famine, and others egregiously hoarded silver and gold, to the chagrin of westerners.

India and the currency crisis of the 1890s

By the 1890s India was of crucial economic importance to Britain. As de Cecco (1974) has pointed out, India's trade surplus with the rest of the world and her trade deficit with Britain allowed the City of London to square its international settlements on current account. Furthermore, the reserves on which the Indian monetary system was based provided a *masse de manœuvre* which gave the British monetary authorities the ability to supplement their own reserves and maintain London as the centre of the world's monetary system.

As we have seen, the issue of the Indian rupee had been of some concern in the 1870s when the price of silver had begun to fall, and in the 1880s there had been continued calls from the Indian government to be allowed to introduce a gold standard, or at the very least, to close the Indian mints to the further minting of silver. But because the silver rupee was beneficial to Indian industrialists – and therefore supported by the Indian chambers of commerce – and because rupee depreciation had a counterbalancing effect against global deflation (pronounced after 1873), these calls went unanswered by the British authorities. During the 1880s, Indian manufacturing grew apace, especially the cotton mills of Bombay. Plantation agriculture, especially tea and jute, which equally relied upon exporting its products, had also expanded rapidly and had developed important pressure groups such as the tea planters' associations. But in the 1880s the price of silver fell so rapidly that the Indian government began to face a fiscal and financial crisis of new dimensions. By 1892 the London price of silver had fallen to 39*d.* per ounce and the British government was forced to act to do something about the Indian situation. Its response was to set up another parliamentary committee to look into currency affairs and to advise urgently on the Indian situation. The committee was to be chaired by Lord Herschell, the Lord Chancellor, and its report was published in May 1893. It has been described as 'without doubt the most lucid pre-Keynesian document on Indian monetary problems' (de Cecco, 1974, p. 65).

The Indian currency crisis overlapped with the sitting of the 1892 International Monetary Conference (IMC) which was taking place in Brussels at the behest of the Americans. It would seem that one effect of the 'Anglo-Indian currency crisis' was to render the third IMC virtually redundant. From the opening of the conference, which sat spasmodically through the last three months of 1892, there were calls for its adjournment in recognition of the fact that events elsewhere might well be about to overtake it. The Italian delegate, for example, proposed a motion for its adjournment in December on these grounds and is reported to have said, 'In this struggle for the rehabilitation of silver, everybody in fact seems to say "Messieurs les Anglais, tirez les pre-miers!"' (fire the first shots!).[4] The Indian government delegates to the conference had reported that they might have to close their mints to the free coinage of silver as a crisis measure. This might in turn have induced a feeling amongst the assembly that the Indian crisis would force the British government to reconsider its intransigent gold-stand-ard stance and begin seriously to look at the alternatives. Amongst these would inevitably be international bimetallism. In truth there were other reasons for delay, including the fact that the Americans had voted in a new Democratic administration (thought certain to be a stronger advocate of an international dual standard) which would not be able to act decisively until well into the new year. The conference was wound up in December and was never to meet again (Russell, 1898).

The Indian government clearly wanted India to be put on to a gold standard as soon as possible. Failing this they wanted to be allowed to close their mints to the free coinage of silver. Obviously this latter option was as much an anathema to the Americans as the further expansion of the gold standard. The US government had been purchas-ing silver (54 million ounces annually) for some time in order to pacify the populists and silverites, who were then becoming more powerful, and of course to help maintain its flagging price. The last thing they wanted was to see India, which possessed a major world-currency sys-tem, cease minting silver coins. Alfred Rothschild (one of the British delegates to the conference of 1892) had put forward the idea that European countries should each begin purchasing silver, along the lines of the Americans, to maintain its price over, say, a five-year period. The 'Rothschild Plan' would no doubt have met with much enthusiasm from the Americans and the French had it not been for the fact that there was so much hope riding on an eventual international dual stand-ard. The optimism about this is apparent from the speeches given by various delegates at the International Monetary Conference of 1892.

But the Herschell Committee went on to recommend the closing of the Indian mints. In some quarters this was taken to mean that the British were about to introduce a bimetallic system into India: this was certainly the case in Lancashire. Many others were confused by it or saw it as a bizarre experiment with a forced currency, though in fact there had been similar episodes, notably the suspension of the Austrian coinage twenty years earlier.

As soon as the mints were closed it was no longer possible to describe the rupee as a commodity currency: the coin was not 'full-bodied' when its exchange value inevitably began to rise above its intrinsic (silver content) value. It is quite probable that many commentators failed to understand the full implications of this, and it is still not entirely clear what the real intentions of the authorities were in so restricting the Indian currency. The Herschell Committee stopped short of recommending a full, specie, gold standard for India on the grounds that for a country which did not have a well-developed banking system, a gold circulation would have represented a heavy and unnecessary economic sacrifice. In the absence of a system of banking cheques there would have to be a massive quantity of gold in circulation to maintain a given level of economic activity.

It was in this context that the 'Lindsay scheme' was put forward as a possible solution to India's problems. A. M. Lindsay, Deputy Secretary of the Bank of Bengal, had first advanced his idea for a 'managed currency' in 1876 but it had been regarded as too innovatory. By the early 1890s its time had come. Lindsay claimed to have the theoretical backing of Ricardo and argued that his 'gold-exchange standard' was in essence identical to a plan proposed by a British parliamentary commission of 1804 (whose membership included Pitt and Fox) to regulate the exchange between Britain and Ireland. The plan envisaged a gold standard reserve, based in London, and kept by a 'London Gold Standard Office'. The office would sell rupee drafts for sterling at the exchange rate of, say, 1s. 4½d. per rupee and sell sterling drafts at, say, 1s. 3½d. per ounce. Depletion of the gold reserve (£5–£10 millions raised by a long-term loan) would point to a redundancy of the rupee and the Indian government would then have to contract its currency by melting down silver coins.[5] The aim of the Lindsay scheme was to make rupees and sterling interchangeable at a fixed rate of exchange without the need to have gold in circulation in India. According to its progenitor, the scheme was not very different from the current Dutch system, in which gold was freely available for export but only sparingly granted for inland payments.[6]

Inevitably the scheme was opposed by groups such as the United Planters' Association of India, which, while accepting that it would be good for attracting capital investment, argued that the rupee should be maintained at its 'natural value' in order that the export trade, 'the backbone of the prosperity of India', should not be handicapped by an expensive currency. Planters and other exporters wanted the mints to be reopened as soon as possible. But the 'forced rupee' inevitably gained value during the period of restriction and threatened their futures. This was particularly keenly felt by such as the tea exporters who were competing directly with China in international markets. China remained on a pure silver standard throughout the period, whereas by 1898 the value of the rupee exceeded its silver content by about 25 per cent. Thus the planters and others saw the restriction as equivalent to an export tax of the same order of magnitude.

The plot thickened dramatically at this stage when new supplies of gold began to find their way into the international economy, having recently been discovered in another British Empire territory, South Africa. De Cecco (1974, p. 67) saw an obvious causal connection between this event and Anglo-Indian currency matters: 'When gold was discovered in South Africa, the mother country again stepped in to regulate Indian monetary affairs'. In 1898, yet another committee was set up by Parliament to look into the question of the rupee, under the chairmanship of Fowler, erstwhile Secretary of State for India. The Fowler Committee recommended the free coinage of gold in India and rejected most aspects of the Lindsay scheme, and in 1898 the Treasury announced that a new branch of the Royal Mint would be opened in Bombay to fulfil this purpose: Indian sovereign coins would be exchangeable with rupees at the rate of 16 rupees to the pound. However, an Indian gold-standard reserve was also to be set up, to receive the profits made by the Indian government on a new silver coinage (which naturally would remain a token stock) and to serve as a buffer stock to gold circulation.

Whether or not one agrees with de Cecco, one cannot help but conclude that the idea of an Indian gold standard had become much more popular in Britain (so much for gold being for rich countries) once the flow of the yellow metal from the Rand had increased to a flood. The threat that this carried to the City of London, long used to an appreciating currency, is obvious enough. Again, however, historical contingency intervened, this time in the form of the Boer War which, for de Cecco, represented a 'real watershed' for sterling: 'confidence in London, the *sancta sanctorum* of international finance, began to falter, which had immediate repercussions for Indian monetary affairs' (ibid., p. 68). Hostilities in South Africa caused a massive fall in the Bank of England's gold reserve and the possibility of India's being put on a gold standard at this juncture disappeared since setting it up would have caused another huge outflow of gold from London. The British again prevaricated over India's monetary future and preparations that had begun for construction of the Bombay Mint were delayed by the deputy director of the Royal Mint over trivia such as the exact size and location of the building itself. In 1902 the Indian gold standard reserve was transferred to London and management of Indian financial policy thus passed into the hands of the India Office, thereby becoming an instrument of British monetary policy. At the same time, the Indian economy began to grow faster than ever before, thanks to the international trade boom of the Edwardian years. Exports doubled between 1902–3 and 1912–13 (£85,878 million to £164,365 million).

As is well known, India's foreign trade was so structured that it realized a large deficit with Britain and a large surplus with the rest of the world, and by investing the increase in India's gold reserves, consequent upon the export boom, into British government securities, the British were able to keep interest rates somewhat lower than would otherwise have been the case. Through the Edwardian years the prices of British securities fell continually, causing a net capital loss to the Indian gold-standard reserve. The funds were lent to the City at a maximum rate of interest of 2 per cent and thus British banks were effectively able to borrow from the India Office at 2 per cent and reinvest the money at 3 per cent or more in the City. As if this were not enough, the private City firm which acted as the broker to the India Office earned a large *ad valorem* commission on the loans. In such ways the City controlled the Indian gold standard and this is what de Cecco meant by the concept of *masse de manœuvre*. Because of it we can be sure that if the Indian economy on a silver standard was important to Britain, it was even more important under a gold standard. Indeed, the conversion of India to the gold standard preserved its position in the crown of Empire. This is not to say that these developments took place without demur. The Bank of England consistently opposed the policy of the India Office and, within India, British merchants, industrialists and public opinion generally were openly hostile to the gold standard policy as it evolved. De Cecco (1974, p. 75) concluded that 'for the Indian bourgeoisie the gold standard became a nationalistic and imperialist slogan'. The scandal of the Indian gold standard forced the Liberal government in 1913 to appoint a royal commission on Indian economic affairs but this, like many another crisis, was swept aside by the outbreak of war in 1914.

Keynes and India

It would be inappropriate to close this chapter without saying something about the role of John Maynard Keynes in Indian currency affairs. Because of the time in which he lived it was inevitable that he would become interested in the subject; he wrote that, 'Apart from the practical side of the matter, India's intricate and highly artificial system presents problems of special interest to the student of currency (Chandavarkar, 1989, p. 57). As we have seen, the Indian currency crisis was the burning economic issue of the period 1890–1914, so it is not surprising that Keynes's first book was on the matter: *Indian Currency and Finance*, of 1911. By the time this was written, India had already been installed on a gold exchange standard, not dissimilar from the Lindsay scheme, which Keynes described as 'one of the two classical pronouncements on the fundamental problems of Indian finance which have stood the test of time'.[7]

Keynes's exposition is regarded as the most lucid account of the working of the Indian gold standard. He explained that under it gold did not actually circulate within the country but that the rupee had become a token coin – 'virtually a note printed on silver', which had the status of unlimited legal tender. But he also betrayed his 'orientalist' (in the modern sense) thinking when he went on to say that India (meaning the Indian people) 'already wastes too high a proportion of her resources in the needless accumulation of the precious metals', and continued to argue in favour of import taxes on specie 'to counteract an uncivilised and wasteful habit' (Chandavarkar, 1989, p. 62). Remarkably, Keynes's book was published *after* he had been offered membership of the Royal Commission of 1913, but before the Commission began collecting evidence.[8] In the debate over the 'silver scandal' of 1912, during which the bullion brokers Messrs Samuel Morgan were alleged to have secretly purchased silver on behalf of the government of India for its gold-standard reserve, Keynes had clearly taken sides. He had written to *The Times* upholding the probity of the government of India and insisting that its policies were 'more complete, more systematic and more public' than in most other countries (Chandavarkar, 1989, p. 63). It is surprising, therefore, that his membership of the Royal Commission was acceptable, but in the event his known views did not stop him from advancing his prestige by writing several key sections of the report, making most of the major recommendations, and asking one-sixth of all the questions put before the witnesses. Chandavarkar concluded that Keynes was 'truly the moving spirit of the Chamberlain Commission' (ibid., p. 72).

Although the 1913 report of the Royal Commission is outside the purview of this study, it is interesting and important to note that Keynes continued to perpetrate the orientalist notion that only rich countries were truly suited to a full specie gold standard. This essentially is why he came to the same conclusion as Lindsay that an exchange standard with a token coinage was the best solution for poor countries such as India. This is merely a one step from the nineteenth-century notion that gold was for the rich and silver was for the poor.

Given that the token coin would inevitably be a silver rupee, this left the residual question as to what would happen if silver were to rise in price against gold: clearly the rupee would then disappear from circulation. Partly for this reason Keynes recommended that the rupee be fixed at the relatively high exchange rate of 2s. 0d., to prevent the possibility of the bullion value overtaking the face value. Given his later, famous criticisms of the overvalued pound under the gold-standard restoration policy of the British in the 1920s, it is surprising to find that he could be blasé about future exchange rates for India, opining that 'I do not think it matters to Indian industrial development whether the rupee is 2s 0d or 1s 0d'.[9] Keynes felt that internal price stability for India was more important than a competitive exchange rate, partly on the grounds that the export trades were a very small fraction of the total production of the subcontinent, and partly on the basis that the demand for India's exports was highly inelastic. This might have been true of the 'jute monopoly'; it was certainly not true of the tea trade. But Keynes felt that a high value for the rupee would allow the Indian *ryot* (farmer) to clothe himself more cheaply (with English cottons) and rely on a stable price for his produce. Keynes's championing of what has been called the 'wage-goods argument' in the favour of an expensive rupee leads us to the conclusion that he would have been a doughty critic of the pre-1893 'full-bodied rupee' which had been depreciating over a long period, but it does seem to jar with his post-First World War stance on sterling. One can only conclude that, like so many of his contemporaries, Keynes saw India as part of an essentially different cultural and economic paradigm.

Notes

1. Court of Directors to India, 30 March 1774, *Bengal Dispatches*, vol. 7, cited by Ambirijan (1984, p.12).
2. H. C. Mui and L. H. Mui, *The Management of Monopoly: A Study of the East India Company's Tea Trade*,1984, cited by Lawson (1993), p. 157.
3. Mansfield Commission on Indian Currency, *Report*, vol. II, 1867–68. Cited by Ambirijan (1984).
4. The International Monetary Conference, Brussels, 1892, Report (India Office, London).
5. Report of Parliamentary Committee appointed to inquire into the Indian Currency (Fowler Committee), 1899, Cd 9390.
6. Ibid.
7. The other one was Dickson's document on the idea of a central bank. See Chandavarkar (1989, p. 102).
8. Royal Commission (Chamberlain) on Indian Currency and Finance, 1913.
9. Royal Commission, 1913, in answer to question by Mr Gubbey, cited by Chandavarkar (1984).

CHAPTER FIVE

The United States: gold and silver in the Gilded Age

Does the eagle know what is in the pit?
Or wilt thou go ask the mole:
Can wisdom be put in a silver rod?
Or love in a golden bowl?
(William Blake: *The Book of Thel*, 1789)

American money and prices

At the beginning of the specie price disturbance of the early 1870s the United States was still an emergent industrial power and had only recently begun to recover from the Civil War. The great era of railroad-building, which was to bring the nation to paramount industrial status by the end of the century, was yet to come, and from the standpoint of London or Paris the United States was not yet a power to be reckoned with in international financial matters. On the contrary, the United States was regarded as a developing country still dependent on large injections of capital from Europe while, thanks to prohibitory tariffs, not generating a volume of international trade in return. America's politics in the Gilded Age were notoriously corrupt and effectively prevented the country from being taken seriously by the Old World powers. In 1879 a youthful Woodrow Wilson described the state of his country's political system as 'No leaders, no principles; no principles, no parties.' The fact that European-style economic liberalism was re-garded with disdain in some important American political circles – Cleveland's linkage with British free-trade interests over the 'Murchison letter' lost him the presidential election as late as 1888 – could hardly serve to convince the prevailing British financial élite that American opinions on any serious issue of the day were at all worth listening to.

Neither did the plight of the currency help to persuade British or European monetary men that anything could be learned from that side of the Atlantic. In effect the United States was on a dual monetary standard in these years, but not a *bimetallic* dual standard. The paper money of the Civil War – the famous or infamous 'greenback dollar' – continued to circulate in the post-bellum period alongside the gold specie dollar. Gresham's Law did not prevent this happening because the price of the greenback in terms of the official currency, and therefore in terms of gold and the pound sterling, was determined in a free market, and the greenback fluctuated according to local and national economic conditions. In some eastern states greenbacks predominated, whilst on the west coast the specie standard largely applied. Such a state of affairs would have been regarded as anathema in London but had become the normal condition in the United States.

Yet despite the phenomenon of two, parallel, monetary forms, prices in the period fell sharply. From January 1867 to February 1879, the money stock rose at the rate of 1.3 per cent per annum, yet prices fell at the rate of 5.4 per cent per annum. It seems likely that this price fall, much faster than anything experienced in Europe, was due to a rapid rise in output rather than a decrease in the velocity of money. (Friedman and Schwartz, 1963). This should not surprise us, for in the same years there was a dramatic increase in the number of miles of railroad track, and political change consequent upon the Civil War led to a rapid extension of the area of land under cultivation. Between 1867 and 1879 there was also a doubling in the output of the manufacturing sector.

Declining prices were accompanied by a rapid rise in real incomes, since prices fell much faster, in general, than money incomes. But the price fall affected different groups unevenly and therefore introduced greater uncertainty into the national economic scene. Moreover, September 1873 saw major financial panic and widespread business failure. It has been argued that contemporary attention tended to centre on the behaviour of the stock of money rather than on the real economy (Friedman and Schwartz, 1963). Consequently, there was much more emphasis on monetary causes, at least at a popular level, than in Britain at this time. One reason must be the position with regard to the greenback, over which there was much uncertainty. The authorities continued to vacillate about the status of the paper money, despite the intention, promulgated by Secretary of State McCullough in 1865, to withdraw it as soon as possible and to substitute a 'constitutional' currency. There had been a wide consensus in support of withdrawal and this had included both labour and agricultural interests. But in the face of depression in 1873 these groups switched in favour of monetary expansion and therefore retention of the greenback.

Whether or not the greenback should have been kept need not concern us here. The point is that there was a much stronger interest at this time in the monetary causes of depression in the United States than in Britain. Further emphasis on money was gained from the fact that the currency entered prominently into the juridical domain in the 1870s. A number of cases came before the Supreme Court, which eventually decided that the greenback was a constitutional currency. Such contentions never arose in Britain, but what really brought the currency into the limelight in America was the formation of the Greenback Party in 1875. The 'Greenbackers' demanded unconditional repeal of the Resumption Act, which they regarded as a bankers' conspiracy. Opposition to British and east-coast financial interests went so far as to call for an end to 'foreign investment' – 'inward investment' as we would say – in favour of a plentiful supply of indigenous money.

The greenback agitation had come to an end by about 1880, but by then, according to Friedman and Schwartz, it had become linked to the 'free-silver' movement, which is often, though wrongly, seen as the predominant form of American bimetallism. In 1876, the same year as the report of the British Select Committee on the Depreciation of Silver was published, the United States Congress set up a monetary commission to report on the role of silver in the American economy. The American report, or reports, for there were three, proved to be somewhat more prescriptive than that of the British inquiry. The majority report favoured the adoption of a bimetallic system, whether or not this should be adopted worldwide. In other words, there was an unambiguous support within the American Congress for what we have called 'unilateral bimetallism'. One minority report favoured bimetallism only if it were to be adopted worldwide, that is, closer to the later British and European schools of bimetallism, whilst a second minority report came down forcefully against any form of bimetallism on the grounds that the market ratio would inevitably diverge from the statutory ratio over time and the result would always be that one or other precious metal would become the standard. This latter point of view was not very different from that of the enemies of bimetallism in Britain, though it is worth pointing out that such agnosticism might be found equally amongst both 'gold-bugs' and true 'silverites', each of whom desired primacy for their preferred metal.

Friedman and Schwartz reckon that the three reports accurately represented the range of American contemporary opinion. If this is so, we can conclude firmly that at this stage of the late nineteenth century there was a very wide gulf between British and American opinion. Very few people in Britain were questioning the monetary *status quo* at this stage, yet in America no *status quo* had emerged. Bimetallism, in any of its forms, was little understood or even known about in Britain because of that country's unique, gold-based monetary history, whilst in the United States, a country far less sophisticated financially, there was already a wider understanding of the currency possibilities that might prevail. In one sense, bimetallism was already an orthodoxy in the United States, for even the eastern interests which favoured the gold standard would prove to be willing to accommodate international bimetallism. Their main concern was to go along with the British financial interests on which they depended. Since it was clearly understood, in New York at any rate, that no reform of an international nature could ever be accomplished without the accord of the British, American financiers ran no risk in supporting international bimetallic reform. If support for the gold standard was an article of faith in the City of London, it was a merely pragmatic expedient in New York.

Greenbackers and money scarcity

If Britain was secure and even nonchalant about its adhesion to the gold standard in the nineteenth century, citizens of the great republic were much more divided over the currency issue. Money occupied a different and much more central position in the perceptions of Americans. British radicals may have virtually ignored the effects which currency could have on the lives of ordinary men and women, but ordinary Americans were constantly aware of the vagaries of money. Between the Civil War and the First World War, the currency matter emerged periodically as an important political issue and in the heyday of populism in the 1890s it ranked foremost amongst all the grievances expressed by Americans.

Characteristically, therefore, monetary debate was much more colourful in the United States than in Britain. As we have said, the Civil War had necessitated the introduction of the greenback paper currency and its success had inevitably created some support for paper. The 'Greenbackers' maintained that gold and silver had no intrinsic worth and that as money truly derives its value from official recognition only, it thus required no commodity, least of all a useless commodity such as a precious metal, to make it work. The United States in the late nineteenth century was a growing economy in every sense. Thus there was a prima-facie reason for opposing commodity standards of any kind: why impose a monetary standard which effectively fixed the supply of money when quite clearly the demand for money was constantly expanding owing to the rapid growth of population, mass immigration, and the ever-extending frontier, to say nothing of the appearance of new industries and new agricultural crops? If the supply of money must be fixed to the supply of a precious metal, then these circumstances dictated that that precious metal must be plentiful. When one of the precious metals evidently became plentiful, certain groups in the United States switched from support for the greenback to support for silver.

The Greenbackers had their equivalent in the British banking school of an earlier era, but whereas opinion had divided across one major boundary in post-Napoleonic Britain, there were many varied and distinct views on currency in the *post-bellum* United States. These differences all revolved around the fear that insufficient money was a great evil, and one populist, Ignatius Donnelly, devised a vivid metaphor to describe the awful condition of money scarcity:

> Take a child a few years old; let a blacksmith weld around his waist an iron band. At first it causes him little inconvenience. He plays. As he grows older it becomes tighter; it causes him pain; he scarcely knows what ails him. He still grows. All his internal organs are cramped and displaced. He grows still larger; he has the head, shoulders and limbs of a man and the waist of a child. He is a monstrosity. He dies.[1]

As we shall see, the populists were later to become very adept at producing such imagery and used it to marvellous effect in their oratory and pamphleteering. Indeed some of this imagery reached across the Atlantic in the space of a decade. This was in the years immediately preceding the great American inventions of modern mass communications, but even Hollywood would one day come to reckon itself indebted to the popular visionaries of this earlier generation, though the populists themselves had to rely on the strength of their own voices at the many mass meetings they convened. However, some of the populists were in favour of convertible currencies, since they belonged to a tradition which on the whole distrusted paper money unsecured by specie.

However, we should remember that, despite the enthusiasm for greenback retention, commodity money was the order of the day in the nineteenth century even in the Old World, and thus there was a debate in the United States as in Europe about which metal or combination of metals should fulfil the monetary function – except that even here there was more diversity of opinion on the far side of the Atlantic: some Americans felt that gold should be the sole commodity standard metal, others felt that the currency should be bimetallic, yet others were devoutly in favour of silver. A curious conjunction of circumstances led to the 'cry for silver' – the demand for the free minting of silver – in post-Civil War America. From 1792 right up to 1873 the United States was formally on a bimetallic standard with both gold and silver dollars in circulation. In the 1850s and 1860s silver, as we have seen, became relatively scarce owing to the important new discoveries of gold, notably in California. As one would expect in these circumstances, silver went out of circulation, but as this had happened without the direct agency of government, it went virtually unnoticed, and Americans quickly forgot about the silver dollar which in any case had not been in wide circulation for a long time.

In 1873 Congress passed an Act – the US Coinage Act – formally demonetizing silver and effectively sanctioning a *de facto* situation.

Little notice was taken of this Act at the time, since it scarcely affected anyone. But then in the later 1870s the United States experienced a silver boom with the discovery of the Comstock Lode (a major new find in Nevada) and silver in other western states. This led to a renewal of interest in silver as a currency metal, and many Americans quickly came to the conclusion that a dreadful mistake had been made in demonetizing it. Indeed, Americans still argue about whether or not the Act of 1873 was a mistake, or worse still a crime, as the silverites came to term it. Milton Friedman, for example, has little doubt that the Act did have seriously deleterious effects on the American economy, but confronts the orthodoxy of American academic historians who see it as fortuitously beneficial. There is little need to go into this debate here, but Friedman's view is based upon the wider hypothesis that the spread of the gold standard in the nineteenth century was a bad thing for the international economy as a whole, and there would be many economic historians who would be prepared to support him in this.[2]

As we have seen, the essence of popular American thinking on currency matters in the nineteenth century was that there could be, and often was, a scarcity of money. This scarcity was held to account for the many economic ills that a growing economy was heir to, such as low prices and depressions. Inevitably such scarcities were blamed on the gold standard, and until relatively recent times there have been American historians who were apt to embrace this view. Thus Carroll Quigley (p. 393), writing as late as 1961:

> The international gold standard became the chief mechanism by which the supply of money could be kept low and its value, accordingly, kept high. A high value of money, which implies a low supply of money, was chiefly advantageous to creditors, to whom obligations were owed in money terms. But such a high value of money clearly meant low prices of goods, and was a disadvantage to debtors and to manufacture of goods ... Thus there appeared a dichotomy between bankers and industrialists, with one eager for a high value of money and high interest rates, while the other was eager for high prices of goods ... and low interest rates ... The opposition of interests between the two appeared most clearly when there was an insufficient supply of money for the growing industrial structure ... '

Quigley here is expressing perfectly the popular and populist view of the money supply in nineteenth-century America. There is little doubt that this perception of the role of money entered deeply into the consciousness of Americans and it can be argued that it predisposed them to the expansionary notions implicit in the New Deal, to wartime monetary expansion in both 1914 and 1940, to their early espousal of Keynesianism, as well as to historical writing such as Quigley's. At any rate, the concept of money scarcity was behind the thinking of both the Greenbackers and the silverites, even though the former argued in favour of paper money and the latter supported a commodity system. The Greenbackers, it must be noted, were active long after the Civil War, since their favoured form of money had proved so durable, and in 1878, campaigning for the retention of paper, they had succeeded in winning over a million votes at the Congressional elections. That there was a wide regional divide over the issue of money is absolutely clear, for the Greenback Party polled most of its votes in the frontier regions, while the old states remained faithful to hard currency. It is claimed that American frontiersmen, whether they had occupied colonial Massachusetts or Jacksonian Tennessee, had indeed always hoped to find economic salvation in inflated paper currencies, so this is not something necessarily new to the nineteenth century.[3] Interestingly, though, this regional divide found parallels in Britain. It might seem whimsical to think of Lancashire as 'frontier' in the 1890s, but there is no doubt that Manchester bimetallists wished to distance themselves as far as possible from the 'gold-bugs' of the City of London, and there is every reason to think that both imagery and terminology were being imported directly from the United States by this time.[4] An east–west divide in the United States was paralleled by a north-south divide in Britain.

The Greenback Party fell to pieces immediately after the Hayes administration announced in January 1879 that the greenbacks would henceforth be convertible at face value into gold. This emphasizes the predictably chimerical tendency of such single-issue parties to disappear once their main grievance is addressed, but the essential concerns of the Greenbackers were carried over into other organizations and reappeared with the populists.

The United States and international monetary relations

But American monetary concerns were to be expressed at an international level as well in the late nineteenth century. Indeed, it was the United States which did most in this period to bring about international agreement on the basis of bimetallism, effectively taking up the torch which was relinquished by the French. This may seem somewhat surprising given the conventional view that late nineteenth-century American administrations were supportive of hard currency along British lines. The truth is somewhat more complicated.

In 1878 the US Congress had voted in favour of inviting a conference of the nations to 'consider the relations of gold and silver'.[5] Presumably for reasons of convenience, it was later decided that the conference should be held in Paris, but it seems clear that the initiative came from the USA, despite the fact that the great French economist Léon Say was chosen to be its president. The apparent association with France no doubt convinced observers then, and since, that the first International Monetary Conference was inspired by the French. The American delegation attended, under the chairmanship of Senator Fenton of New York, and he was accompanied by W. S. Groesbeck, and the famous bimetallist economist Francis Walker. Their secretary was S. Dana-Horton, perhaps the most avid of American bimetallists. Fortunately, Walker (1898) subsequently wrote at length about the conference and later meetings, and his reputation is such that he can be taken to have been a good witness.

Walker's contention is that the International Monetary Conference of 1878 was called at a most inopportune moment. To begin with, the Germans had stubbornly refused to send a delegation. Walker thought that Germany's demonetization of silver had been too recent for that country equably to reconsider its decision to attach to gold, though the attending delegates decided to take a recess in the hope that it would change its mind. Germany, however, remained firm. Walker felt that the situation was hopeless from the outset, though surprisingly the British delegation was highly unorthodox in the sense that its members, according to Walker, could be taken to represent a strong bias in favour of bimetallic reform. Goschen was its chairman and Walker (1898) considered him to be 'more favourably disposed toward bimetallism than the great majority of English statesmen'. This may have been an American perspective of Goschen, though it was one that was taken by some British observers. Another American witness who later wrote about the conference, Russell, saw Goschen as '*the* most conspicuous advocate of the single [gold] standard (ibid.). Such was the degree of vagueness in contemporary understanding of the issues and of the important figures in the arena of late nineteenth-century battles over the standard.

The American-inspired 1878 conference would come to nothing. 'The experience of gold monometallism had not been sufficient to bring the States of Europe to the point of action, though there were few who did not regret the tragedy of 1873' was Walker's plainly stated value judgement; for him the lurch to monometallism by Germany and other European states in the early 1870s had been tantamount to the 'crime of 1873' in the United States. The American delegates to the 1878 conference, however, were unequivocal about the reasons for the meeting. Groesbeck, in his opening speech, said, 'The object of this conference is to restore silver to its former position; to equalize gold and silver upon a ratio to be fixed by agreement.' Clearly, given the context, this meant international agreement, though not all advocates of international monetary conferences were international bimetallists in the sense of believing that it was the only way to restore silver, and there were many American advocates of what we might call unilateral bimetallism, including of course the silverites, who must have hoped that something would come out of these conferences.

The American position in 1878, however, was fatally weakened by two factors. It was widely known that the United States was the world's largest producer of silver and was even opening up new silver mines at the time of the conference. Groesbeck was evidently painfully aware of this and argued that the United States government had no interests in the production of gold or silver and that in any case the production of silver had been greatly exaggerated. This was scarcely a credible position for the American delegation to adopt. The wily and knowledgeable European representatives would have known that the silverite opposition was a growing force in American politics and the Comstock Lode, probably the world's largest find of the white metal since Potosí (Bolivia), had already achieved legendary status in Europe (Russell, 1898).

The second problem for the Americans was the unfortunate fact that they themselves had of course demonetized silver in their own country earlier in the decade with the passing of the infamous Act of 1873. Americans may still argue about the nature of the 'Crime of 1873', but there can be little wonder that it led to equivocation among monetary experts in the United States by the end of the decade.[6] Groesbeck, according to Russell, disingenuously assumed that Europeans would be largely ignorant of financial developments in his country, and thus had to explain the Act in terms of 'inadvertence'. The term was jumped upon by the erudite Goschen as soon as Groesbeck had sat down. But even Walker was keen to give a different interpretation to the Act of 1873 and candidly admitted that though he himself had occupied a chair of political economy and was lecturing on money at the time of its passing, he had been unaware of what was being done. Whether or not it is true that this most worldly of men could have missed out on such a development, the fact is that Americans were scolding Europeans for seeing out silver when it could easily be argued, and was, that they were quite as responsible for its recent demise as any country from the Old World. Russell made the point that indeed the European delegates were charitable towards the Americans, for if they had wanted to be cruel they could have pointed out, if they knew, that one of the United States delegates (Senator Fenton no less) had been a member of the finance committee which had formulated the 1873 Act.

From an early twenty-first-century perspective we might see the conference of 1878 as something of a shambles. The British had pronounced in favour of gold monometallism yet had sent along a most unorthodox delegation. The French, in President Say's words, were 'awaiting the favourable moment to re-enter the system of the double standard', implying that this was *not* the moment (Russell, 1898). Other European countries were unable to act until their neighbours had made a move; Holland for example could not go against Britain and Germany while they were both on the gold standard. The Swiss and the Belgians were both strongly advocating gold but could not go against France if France had decided to adopt the dual standard. And the Americans were plainly seen to be proselytizing for silver only a few years after they had passed an Act to demonetize it. The Dutch delegate Vrolik was honest enough to tell the Americans that Europe was simply too divided to link up with the United States in a new system, and advised the Americans to seek partners in Central and South America and the East, 'even in the English and Dutch East Indies, where the gold standard was adapted neither to the needs of commerce nor to the habits of the people' (Russell, 1898, pp. 202–47). Thus the Americans had come up against the now well-entrenched European prejudice against silver: it was the currency of backward nations.

This was despite the fact that the well-established gold-standard countries did not want to see the demise of silver, since several of the European powers possessed colonies which depended upon an ancient (or not so ancient) silver circulation. To the Americans this must have seemed duplicitous at best, and it was not to be the first time that 'innocent Americans' would be confounded by the intricacies of intra-European affairs and the manoevrings of worldly-wise Europeans. Even the straightforward Goschen was to be quoted as saying that 'though England had a gold standard she had a great interest in the maintenance of silver as money', though he did not say whether he meant silver as full-bodied money or merely as token coin, a vital distinction of course. Nevertheless, he went on to argue that England had done more than most countries to support silver, had 'borne the depreciation of silver in India without trying to shut its doors to it', and concluded that, 'England's laissez faire policy in India had done more then anything else to keep up the value of silver' (ibid.).

To be told that the country which had invented the modern gold standard was in fact a robust supporter of silver money must have confounded the American delegation. But they would also have been surprised at the extreme opposition of the Russians, who had had a very bad experience with silver in 1876 and had been forced to suspend payments and go on to a paper currency. They were determined to impose a full gold standard as early as possible, probably in the hope that it would help them attract foreign investment from elsewhere in

Europe, which of course it did in due course. The only country which gave unreserved support to the Americans in 1878 was Italy. This may not have been the most welcome source of encouragement, for the Italians were in many ways regarded as the bad boys of Europe as a result of their behaviour in the Latin Union and were still posing problems to French bankers even at the time of the conference.

The Americans might well have agreed with the sentiments of the Belgian representative who waxed lyrical, but pessimistic, about the prospects of an international bimetallic standard: 'We are thus very nearly in the position of people who see an extraordinary bird soaring over their heads but at such a height that their weapons cannot reach it' (ibid.). Should they therefore accept that it was not within range and give it up (the 'practical view'), or decide that they would like to bring it down at some time in the future (the 'declaration of a platonic desire')? By default, the 'practical view' was taken and the prospects for international bimetallism receded with the closing of the conference.

The evidence suggests therefore that there was considerable enthusiasm for monetary reform both within certain groups of American society and at a national, or federal, level. American administrations were in favour of hard currency and therefore retained the *de facto* gold-standard regime but were prepared to look at, even to advance, international bimetallism at an international level, that is, at monetary conferences. Later on, it can be argued that such promotion was to deflect the ambitions of the silver interests at home, but in 1878 these had still not come fully to the fore. The rise of populism ensured that they did.

Populism and the Wonderful Wizard of Oz

Populism as a general term is highly imprecise and applies to a great diversity of ideas from those of the nineteenth-century Russian Narodniki, to Péron of Argentina, and to Margaret Thatcher in our own era. The beginnings of populism in the United States, however, are traceable to Texas in the 1880s, the 'meeting place of West and South', when a farmers' alliance developed around a number of lecturers and preachers who, it seems, began to teach a form of primitive socialism (Canovan, 1981, p. 3). The message was that 'the non-producer has thrived while the producer has grown poor ... the farmers of this country have labored, and others have made the laws.'[7] The speakers encouraged the formation of co-operatives among the farmers and this was taken up with some alacrity, so that one historian is able to speak in terms of a co-operative crusade 'spreading like wildfire across the South and West'

THE UNITED STATES: GOLD AND SILVER IN THE GILDED AGE

(Canovan, 1981). A soaring membership was generated by sheer community spirit and by revivalist-style meetings, and the vision offered was one of solidarity among the farmers defeating the evil monopolists, such as the railway companies, who were seen to be controlling the market to the disadvantage of the 'producing classes'. Success encouraged further efforts when the farmers took on and defeated a real monopoly, or 'trust', to use the American term, in the form of the jute-bag manufacturers in 1889. Members of the Farmers' Alliance boycotted a ring of manufacturers and arranged to have cotton bagging produced in its place. Needless to say, the concept of a battle being waged between the 'producing classes' (the farmers) and the 'non-producing gold-bugs' also found its way to Lancashire in due course.

Evidence of the extent to which populist thought and imagery penetrated the minds of people of the South and Midwest is provided by a close analysis of one of the most famous of American children's storybooks, *The Wonderful Wizard of Oz* (Baum, 1900). Its author, L. Frank Baum (1856–1919), lived in Aberdeen, South Dakota, and he began his career as a newspaperman, working as editor of a trade magazine for store-window decorators. He went on to publish his own newspaper, but his first children's book was not written until his mid-forties, and the first of the *Wizard of Oz* stories only appeared in 1900. Hugh Rockoff (1900) has recently shown that the *Oz* stories, as well as being the inspiration for one of the greatest of Hollywood films, starring Judy Garland and released in 1939, is also an informed comment on the battle for free silver in the 1890s. Rockoff goes so far as to say that 'The *Wizard of Oz* [on his interpretation] becomes a powerful pedagogic device. Few students of money and banking or economic history will forget the advocates of free silver and the defenders of the gold standard when it is explained through the *Wizard of Oz*' (p. 740).

Baum was in Chicago in 1896 when that city hosted the Democratic National Convention at which William Jennings Bryan, populist turned Democratic presidential candidate, made his famous 'Cross of Gold' speech. It seems that *The Wonderful Wizard of Oz*, conceived over a number of years but written in 1899, recounts the 'first battle' of 1896 – Bryan's title for his later book about the election. The degree of allegorical fit between the children's story and the actual events and characters participating in the battles over the currency issue is so close that one can scarcely repudiate the interpretation of Rockoff. The central character, Dorothy, represents the true spirit of the United States, being honest, kind-hearted and plucky. She may be taken to represent Mary Elizabeth Lease, the 'first really effective and important [American] woman politician' (Brogan, 1985). Lease, of 'Irish birth, appearance and temperament', possessed a scorching tongue and boundless energy and told the farmers to 'raise less corn and more hell'. This pithy command became the slogan of the populists.

In the story, the cyclone, which 'came out of the west', represents the free-silver movement; the yellow brick road is the gold standard; and the Emerald City is New York. In the original story Dorothy was given silver slippers (these were changed to ruby by Hollywood, for their own reasons) and these appropriately represent the bimetallic mechanism behind which the American silverites often hid. The scarecrow is the western farmer who thinks he has no brains but who turns out to be shrewd and capable (he goes on to rule the Emerald City in the story). The scarecrow (a Forrest Gump of the 1890s?) abjures the gold standard by not wishing to traverse the yellow-brick road; the western farmer does not have to accept the gold standard just because the 'experts' of the east say it is necessary. The tin woodman, the 'tin man' of the film, is the industrial working man. He 'was once flesh and blood' in the book, but is now rusting owing to his unemployment. The populist view was that industrialism alienated the working man, or 'took away his heart', as in the story.

The lion of the story has to be William Jennings Bryan himself. The 'Great Commoner' certainly was apt to roar in his oratorical attacks on the gold standard conspiracy of the eastern bankers and their British backers, though he would have been less than flattered at being thought of as the cowardly lion of the story. However, by the late 1890s he was thought to be soft-pedalling on the silver issue and emphasizing instead anti-trust ideas and anti-imperialism, two other important planks of the populist movement. Interestingly, Baum goes on to allegorize British imperialism as an enormous black spider in one of the sequels to *The Wonderful Wizard of Oz*, *The Marvelous Land of Oz* (Baum, 1904). And the devoutly anti-imperialist Bryan resigned as deputy president to Woodrow Wilson in 1915 over the latter's anglophilia during the First World War.

The Wizard himself is thought by Rockoff and others to be Marcus Alonzo Hanna, chairman of the Republican National Committee and the brains behind McKinlay's campaigns. Hanna – the great 'spin doctor' of his day – masterminded McKinlay's 'front-porch' speeches in which he sought to convince the American people that adoption of the gold standard and 'sound money' was good for them. The metaphor of wizardry seems particularly appropriate to Hanna, as someone who preferred to manipulate matters from behind the scenes: he was very successful in raising money from the big corporations of which Bryan was so suspicious, and was hell-bent on defeating the populists. In the story, the Wizard is far from being the out-and-out villain that Hanna was to the populists, but by the time Baum was writing the first volume of his stories, the new gold discoveries were beginning to perform the same function of monetary expansion that the populists wanted silver to do in the depression of the mid-1890s.

In any case, the allegory breaks down when we consider that President McKinlay was a supporter of (international) bimetallism (and therefore looked with some favour on the silver slippers?) and as we shall see later, actually sent a commission to Europe to sound out the British and Indian governments over monetary reform, with a view to introducing international bimetallism. There is a case for interpreting McKinlay as the benign wizard, rather than Hanna, but this might be churlish. What we must realize is that bimetallism requires careful analysis and must always be considered in its immediate context. The unilateral bimetallism of the advocates of free silver was very different in nature from the international bimetallism of McKinlay. The unilateral adoption of silver by the United States at the ratios suggested by the silverites in the mid-1890s would have massively expanded the money supply and caused an unprecedented level of inflation, unthinkable to the hard-money men such as McKinlay. International bimetallism, as advocated by some Republicans, would only have been possible by negotiating with countries such as Britain, which would always insist on full convertibility, even in the unlikely event that they ever went on to accept currency reform in the direction of bimetallism.

But the political economy of late nineteenth-century America is complicated in the extreme, and there had always been the even bigger issue of the tariff by the 1890s. This in turn is complicated by the fact that special interests always got in the way of party and government. Thus the most prominent 'gold-bug' of the period had been Grover Cleveland, the Democratic president of 1892–96, who believed implicitly that all would be well with the American economy as long as he maintained the ability of the US Treasury to pay its bills in gold. And it was 'honest Grover' who went on to repeal the Sherman Silver Purchase Act of 1890, which had partially restored the status of silver, in 1892. The aim had been to stiffen business confidence, but the economy had refused to recover from the depression of the period and the way was thus opened for the populists to renew their campaign for silver and for their brand of bimetallism. It can be argued that America's future as a gold standard country had been secured by Cleveland when he called in J. P. Morgan to market government bonds on Wall Street, to be paid for in gold, between 1894 and 1896 (Brogan, 1985). But by the latter date the new gold discoveries of the Klondike and South Africa had vastly increased the supplies of the precious metal and the gold standard was therefore safe until the 1930s. Cleveland was, in any case, repudiated by the Democrats in 1896 and so the arch gold-bug was replaced by the fervent silverite, Bryan, the 'scourge of the elephant plutocrats'. In so doing, the Democrats bound their party to the poor and the weak and were thus out of power for sixteen years. Such an interpretation suggests that the silver campaigns in all the various forms in which they appeared in the 1890s were always futile. But as we shall see in later chapters, the influence of the United States was still growing internationally and thus the views of its special interest groups were transmitted across the globe. American bimetallism was still being warmly received as a potential cure for depression even though its place of invention remained firmly anchored to the gold standard.

The disturbed years of the 1890s

The 1890s, especially the years 1891–97, were amongst the most difficult in American economic history. Gold prices continued to fall, putting pressure on prices and incomes. A series of 'flights of capital' occurred, partly as a result of the silver agitation. This is something that the British economy, while possessing sectors which were just as depressed as the American economy, never suffered from, owing to an unstinting commitment to gold monometallism. The financing of these adverse capital movements in turn put further pressure on prices and incomes. According to Friedman and Schwartz (1963), this was only relieved ultimately by further gold outflows, which in turn put pressure on the money stock, or by an excess of earnings abroad made possible by lower export prices. They are at pains to point out, however, that they do not regard the fear of the lack of maintenance of the gold standard in the United States as the only factor accounting for the decline in net capital imports during the period, but 'We are inclined to believe that in the early 1890s it was the most important factor accounting for the sheer instability in capital flows, since speculative funds flowed both in and out as confidence in the maintenance of the [gold] standard waxed and waned' (ibid., p. 104).

Friedman and Schwartz liken American experience in the 1890s to British exchange crises in the post-1945 period, characterizing both examples in terms of the 'volatility of "speculative" balances under a fixed exchange rate standard where maintenance is in doubt' (ibid., p. 105).

It is also thought that the proximate cause of these disturbances was the Sherman Silver Purchase Act of 1890, wherein a Republican Congress had agreed that the federal government should buy large quantities (4.5 million ounces per month) of silver, as a concession to the western silver interests. The McKinlay Tariff of the same year reduced the demand for imports of the protected commodities and therefore of the demand for foreign currency to pay for them. But in another way, the increased protection only served to increase the impact of the silver legislation because certain items, such as sugar, were put on the free list, and thus total revenues (and customs revenues are important to a federal state) continued to fall. Meanwhile, Congress authorized higher expenditures on pensions and rivers and harbours, and the combined effect, according to Friedman and Schwartz, was to turn a Treasury surplus into a deficit. Rightly or wrongly, this was taken to mean that the government would be less able to maintain the gold standard. Naturally enough, massive outflows of gold in 1891 and 1892 had caused public misgivings about the retention of gold. Commercial depression and a run on the banks in 1893 again threatened a major gold outflow, but this was stifled somewhat by the government pressing for repeal of the Sherman silver purchases, to the horror of the silver interests. But the effect of the banking crisis was to reinforce the gold losses by demanding a higher ratio of currency to deposits. The effective total money stock declined by about 6 per cent in 1893, and for the first time since 1879, making the 'scarce-money' school's arguments the more attractive. In July 1893, the Erie Railway Company had gone into receivership and banks in New York finally restricted cash payments. These restrictions spread across the banking sector, and according to Friedman and Schwartz, the United States was left with two stark choices in the mid-1890s: a sizeable decline in US prices and a reduced rate of increase of incomes, or the abandonment of the gold standard and rapid depreciation of the dollar. It is thought that the political commitment to the gold standard was too great to contemplate abandonment and so the economy had to undergo a period of contraction and deflation.

The Venezuela crisis and American economic policy

Yet again it has to be appreciated that American and British experiences were very different in the late nineteenth century. The British economy was depressed but the overall situation was far from uncontrollable. The pound sterling was as sound as ever and, as argued elsewhere, the economy actually stood to gain from gold appreciation in various ways. But speculative pressure continued against the dollar through the mid-1890s and the American Treasury adopted one expedient after another to replenish its gold reserves, which fell to a new low in 1895.

Remarkably, in the middle of this complex and persistent depression, the American administration chose to threaten to go to war with the arch gold-standard country, Great Britain. In all probability this was in order to divert attention away from the domestic problems. In December 1894, the American ambassador in London, T. F. Bayard, had written a letter to the American secretary of state, Richard Olney, explaining that 'Britain has just now her hands very full in other quarters of the globe … and the European powers are watching like pugilists in the ring' (Roberts, 1999, p. 615). This must have given Washington an idea, and it seems that 'twisting the lion's tail' was still a strong and popular card to play in American politics. (Ensor, 1936). In any case, the incumbent president, Grover Cleveland, was by now within a year of the time when he would have to stand, if he stood at all, for re-election. As Ensor put it, 'He [Cleveland] was a gold Democrat, and the tide of bimetallism, which was to sweep his party in 1896, was already wetting his feet' (ibid., p. 230). The temptation to have a go at Britain, especially since the radical populist stance was so strongly anti-imperialist, was clearly too strong to deny. Britain at this time was facing an increasingly hostile Franco-Russian alliance, a newly unfriendly Germany and was having severe difficulties in its Mediterranean strategy. According to Roberts (1999, p. 615), Washington 'considered it an ideal time to take up the cause of Venezuela, which for half a century had claimed more than half the colony of British Guiana on which Crown subjects had worked for generations'. Venezuela and British Guiana were neighbouring states on the northern littoral of South America. In July 1895, Secretary of State Olney advised Ambassador Bayard to demand that Britain submit the Venezuela boundary dispute (which had been on the boil since about 1888) to 'impartial arbitration', and invoke the Monroe Doctrine of 1823, which formally forbade European countries from taking any new colonies in the Western Hemisphere. A letter from Olney was read by Bayard to Salisbury, the British prime minister.

Salisbury duly consulted his cabinet colleagues who, with the exception of Colonial Secretary Joseph Chamberlain, who was 'all for belligerence' (Roberts, 1999), were in favour of appeasement. Salisbury replied to Washington to the effect that Britain had long respected the Monroe Doctrine, but that it did not apply in this particular case because Britain's claims to British Guiana long pre-dated its proclamation. The United States was told in the politest possible terms that the Venezuela controversy did not therefore concern them. But on 17 December 1895, President Cleveland announced that it was 'the duty of the United States to resist by any means in its power … the appropriation by Great Britain of any lands … which after investigation we have determined of rights belong to Venezuela' (ibid., p. 616). In Ensor's words, he had 'sounded the note of war' to the British Empire.

Cleveland announced that he would appoint an American commission to define the boundary between the two South American territories and impose its award, by war if necessary, in the name of the Monroe Doctrine. Ensor (1936, p. 230) believed that this was 'one of the most unexpected, least warranted, and least excusable steps ever taken in modern times by a Great Power'.[8] Whilst the United States was swept with a wave of jingoism, British opinion was kept in check by Salisbury. To Ensor, it became obvious that 'while an Anglo-American war would be the most popular of all wars in America, in England it was regarded as fratricidal' (ibid., p. 230). Whilst the irenical Salisbury believed that a war with America at this time was even more likely than a Franco-Russian attack on the Royal Navy, he did his best to ensure that the matter blew over as peacefully as possible. For Ensor, it was Joseph Chamberlain (whom Andrews sees as 'belligerent') and his accomplice Lyon Playfair (both of whom were married to American women) who were most active behind the scenes, visiting the United States, interviewing Olney and laying the foundations for the Treaty of Washington of February 1897, which eventually confirmed British claims.

Ensor clearly makes a strong connection between the state of the American economy, the silverite agitation, and American foreign policy with regard to the Venezuela crisis. Roberts, perhaps because his subject is Salisbury and England, rather than the United States, makes no such connection. And for Ensor, it was a catastrophic fall in American stock prices resulting from the crisis which exerted a 'chastening influence' on the American leadership and which perhaps stayed Cleveland's hand as much as the diplomacy of Salisbury and his talented cabinet.

We may never know exactly what motivated the Americans in the Venezuela crisis, but the circumstances do suggest very strongly that the Democratic administration was using the dispute for its own political ends and these included the need to mollify the populists and their allies. William Jennings Bryan was often openly belligerent towards the British both because of their imperialism (populists often referred to 1776 as a war against imperialism rather than a war of independence) and in his most famous nomination speech in the 1896 Democratic campaign, Bryan (1925, p. 498) declared:

> My friends, we declare that this nation is able to legislate for its own people on every question, without awaiting for the consent of any other nation ... Therefore we care not upon what lines the battle is fought. If they say bimetallism is good, but that we cannot have it until other nations help us, we reply that, instead of having a gold standard because England has, we will restore bimetallism, and then let England have it because the United States has it. If they dare to come out into the open and defend the gold standard as a good thing, we will fight them to the uttermost.

Famously, Bryan (ibid., p. 499) went on to say:

Having behind us the producing masses of this nation and the world, supported by the commercial interests, the laboring interests, and the toilers everywhere, we will answer their demand for a gold standard by saying to them: 'You shall not press down upon the brow of labor this crown of thorns, you shall not crucify mankind upon a cross of gold'.

In later speeches, Bryan (p. 501) cited the teachings of Christ as an irrefutable condemnation of imperialism:

Imperialism has no warrant in the Bible. The command, 'Go ye into the world and preach the gospel to every creature' has no gatling gun attachment ... Compare, if you will, the swaggering, bullying, brutal doctrine of imperialism with the Golden Rule and the commandment, 'Thou shalt love thy neighbor as thyself' ... Love, not force, is the weapon of the Nazarene: sacrifice for others, not the exploitation of them, was His method of reaching the human heart. A missionary once told me that the Stars and Stripes once saved his life because his assailant recognized our flag as a flag that had no blood upon it.

The tenor of the speeches of American populists in these years, shortly before the United States began to collect its very own empire overseas, strongly suggests that they would not have discouraged an out-and-out war with the arch-imperialists should circumstances permit, despite their invocation of the Decalogue. The battle-cry for bimetallism must ultimately have been yet one more factor drawing Britain out of her 'splendid isolation' at the end of the nineteenth century. Had such a conflict broken out, it might well have been dubbed the 'war of gold and silver'. Little wonder that the American Eagle carries with it, at all times, both the laurel leaves of peace and the arrows of war.

Nearer home, the unrest which had swept out of the Midwest with the populists had spread rapidly to the towns and cities of the American states and because of the general state of the economy, labour groups had became restive as well. From 1892 onwards there were large, though unsuccessful, strikes at the Carnegie steel mills and the Buffalo rail yards. In 1894, the coal mines and the Great Northern Railroad were subject to industrial action of various kinds, and most famously, the Pullman Car Company strike developed into a general railroad strike. Federal troops were sent in to establish martial law, but this was followed by the march of 'Coxey's Army'. 'General' Jacob C. Coxey, a Greenbacker turned populist, led a march of unemployed men on Washington, demanding an issue of $500 million in legal tender, noted as one of a number of demands on the federal government. By the mid-1890s, then, the social and labour unrest had become generalized across the

American economy. The 'National Bimetallic Union' was established in 1895 and published a weekly magazine, *The Bimetallist*. This later joined forces with the 'American Bimetallic League' and the 'National Silver Committee'. The *Wonderful Wizard of Oz* was not the only fictional outpouring of the bimetallists: the monetary controversy was dramatized by William H. Harvey with *A Tale of Two Nations*, and represented in cartoons in *Coin's Financial School*.

As in Britain, the American bimetallic associations found their opponents organizing themselves in the 'National Sound Money League', funded by the bankers. But as Friedman and Schwartz (1963, p. 117) concluded, 'Many of the anti-silver group did not oppose international bimetallism ... so its arguments were not categorically in opposition to the monetization of silver'. Thus the two sides of the debate were not as clearly polarized as they were in Britain. This is vital to an understanding of the monetary history of the period, as we shall see. In the United States, gold-standard supporters were forced to admit that things were wrong with the *status quo*, as amply demonstrated by recurrent money panics and exchange crises. Even the American Bankers' Association did not turn its back against reform, as is evidenced by its daring 'Baltimore Plan' of 1894, which suggested a completely new, asset-backed, currency.

The political campaign of 1896, famous always for the oratory of Bryan and for the bitter class conflict that it engendered, as well as the 'fear and smear' techniques which would be common to later party and presidential campaigns, has gone down in history as one of the best remembered. Silverites captured many Democratic state conventions and succeeded in putting forward the populist Bryan as their candidate. But it is clear from their manifesto of 1896 that even the Republicans were not going to tie themselves to gold for ever and a day. William McKinlay accepted the Republican nomination and a platform retaining the gold standard, and he is often described as a 'champion of the gold standard', as for example in today's *Webster's Dictionary*.[9] But McKinlay favoured the gold standard, 'only until international agreement with the leading commercial nations of the earth ... can be obtained for coining gold and silver at fixed ratios' (Friedman and Schwartz, p. 118).

The Republicans won the 1896 Election and McKinlay was swept to power largely because of a short but sharp export boom which secured a recovery of prices just in time for voting day. The boom attracted the agricultural vote to McKinlay, and this factor, plus the continuing popularity of Bryan, meant that the new administration would be forced to keep its promise to promote another international conference on the restoration of bimetallism. By 1897 it is thought that the victory of

McKinlay had improved the bargaining position of the United States internationally, and the time was thus ripe for another attempt at obtaining a concert of the powers.

This, then, is the background to the Wolcott Commission of 1897. The McKinlay administration was soon to send a delegation of senators, under Senator Wolcott, to Europe to sound out the chief commercial nations about the prospects for monetary reform. In July 1897, they met a group of British and French statesmen and diplomats at the Foreign Office in London. The British included Arthur Balfour, leader of the governing Conservative Party in the House of Commons (Salisbury was in the Lords), George Curzon, soon-to-be Viceroy of India and leading proponent of imperial expansion, and Sir Michael Hicks Beach, devout upholder of the gold standard and current Chancellor of the Exchequer. The French party included the Ambassador to London, M. Geoffray, and a French finance minister.[10]

The immediate concern of the American delegation was to ascertain the likely future of the Indian rupee. As we have seen, the rupee had been suspended since 1892; that is, it was no longer linked to silver, and the Americans were keen to know whether or not the British intended to return the Indian currency to silver. But it is clear that their brief went much further than this. At the first meeting in Whitehall, Wolcott advanced a series of proposals, which included the reopening of the Indian mints to the free coinage of silver and the repeal of the order making the gold sovereign legal tender in India, to suggest that the English mints be opened to free coinage of both gold and silver, and even a new British silver dollar for use in some of the British colonies. Other suggestions included raising the silver-bullion component of the Bank of England's reserves and new agreements compelling the annual purchase of fixed quantities of new silver by the British authorities. To say that McKinlay's gold-standard administration was trying to 'do something for silver' would be rather to underestimate its intentions.

The immediate response of the British representatives is not recorded, though it is known that Balfour had been quite keen on bimetallism and was possibly denied the chancellorship in 1895 because of his apostasy on the gold standard. The British certainly took the Americans seriously in the wake of the Venezuela affair, especially since at the time of the meeting it had not yet been settled. Another meeting was held which included Lord Salisbury himself and the American ambassador to London, John Hay. Wolcott asked directly where the British and Indian governments would stand on a new international conference, and alluded to the fact that both the Prussian Parliament and the French Chamber of Deputies had spoken out for a new meeting. Indeed, the Americans claimed to have already agreed with the French on a preliminary basis, having visited Paris before coming to London. Salisbury sensibly asked the Americans what metallic ratio they were thinking of for an international bimetallic agreement, and it seems that they had already agreed with the French to go for the 'full return' of 15.5:1. At yet another meeting in London, the French ambassador confirmed that this was their intention, arguing in typical fashion that 15.5:1 was the 'normal and natural ratio for the two metals'.[11] Clearly, this would have been totally unacceptable to the British, who probably would not have attended a meeting predicated on such a high and, to them, inflationary level for silver. And it is quite remarkable that a mission which had the full sanction of the 'hard-money' McKinlay should be suggesting an inflationary return to the pre-1973 parity.

The fall-back position for the Americans was the reopening of the Indian mints in order to do something immediately for the silver interests at home. It was here that the pressure was most obviously applied. The Indian monetary crisis had been left on the back burner and would have to be sorted out sooner or later. It could be that the only obvious effect of the Wolcott Commission was to speed up the making of a decision on the Indian currency. It was unclear in Britain what the future of the rupee might be, and the restriction in 1892 had been welcomed both by gold-standard die-hards, who thought that it must presage the extension of the gold standard to the subcontinent, and the Lancashire bimetallists, who believed that India was about to go on to a dual standard. But the British would have been quite unable to reopen the Indian mints on a bimetallic basis at anything significantly above the prevailing 35:1 ratio which obtained by the time of the Whitehall meetings. The Franco-American 'full return' to silver at 15.5:1 would have so overvalued the rupee, effectively raising its exchange value from the current 16*d.* against sterling to about 23*d.*, that Indian foreign trade would have been destroyed, causing enormous damage not just to the Indian economy but also to regions such as Lancashire whose trade depended upon India. In any case, the British had no interest in merely 'doing something for silver' and were much more concerned with stabilizing exchange rates, especially between the British pound and the rupee. In this they were fully in accord with the government of India, and the result was that India was put on to a gold exchange standard in 1898. In October 1897, Salisbury wrote to the American ambassador informing him of their decision to reject the proposals advanced by the Wolcott delegation:

> In [the] circumstances, Her Majesty's Government feel it is their duty to state that the first proposal of the United States Representatives [sic] is one which they are unable to accept ... Due consideration has been given to the remaining proposals but Her

Majesty's Government do not feel it to be necessary to discuss them at the present moment. The proposals regarding the Indian mints ... are seen as the most important consideration which could be made by the British Empire towards an International Agreement, with the object of securing a 'stable monetary par of exchange' between gold and silver ... Her Majesty's Government are therefore desirous to ascertain how far the views of the American and French governments are modified by the decision now arrived at, whether they desire to proceed further ...[12]

A copy of the letter was sent to the French ambassador. The response of the Americans is not recorded, but by the time they and the French might have been in a position to convene further talks or a new conference, the whole position had been changed by the full impact of the new gold from Alaska and South Africa. From 1897 onwards prices began to rise worldwide and in the United States even more rapidly than in Europe, probably by as much as 50 per cent before 1914. The proximate cause of the inflation was the discovery of gold in several distant parts of the world, and new finds in two of these regions, Alaska and Colorado, might be expected to have had a major impact on American thinking in the late 1890s. However, it was not until March 1900 that the Gold Standard Act was finally passed in the United States, and in the autumn of 1900, Bryan's second defeat on a bimetallic programme 'sealed the doom of silver as a major issue dominating national politics' (Friedman and Schwartz, 1963, p. 119).

Notes

1. Ignatius Donnelly, *Caesar's Columns*, ed. Walter Rideout, 1960. Cited by Canovan (1981), p. 23.
2. See, for example, Friedman (1990).
3. See for example, Brogan (1985).
4. American bimetallists such as Dana-Horton visited Manchester and were well received; the Lancashire trade union bimetallist James Mawdsley visited the United States to attend a labour conference in 1894, and so on.
5. Act of 28 February 1878.
6. See for example Friedman (1990).
7. Quoted by Adam B. Ulam, *Ideologies and Illusions: Revolutionary Thought from Herzen to Solzenitsyn*, cited by Canovan (1981).
8. Ensor was writing just before the outbreak of the Second World War.
9. *The New International Webster's Dictionary of the English Language*, 1995.
10. *Proposals on Currency: Correspondence respecting the Proposals on Currency made by the Special Envoys from the United States, presented to the both Houses, Oct., 1897.* Cd Paper 8667.
11. Ibid.
12. Ibid.

CHAPTER SIX

The spread of the gold standard and the defeat of bimetallism

Silver and gold are not the only coin:
Virtue too passes current all over the world.
(Euripides, *Oedipus*, Frag. 546)

The course of monetary history must, in some part, be determined by the long-term fluctuations in the general prosperity of the international economy, or by what are referred to as 'cycles' or 'swings' in economic activity. What may seem slightly surprising is that the great monetary reordering which culminated in the relative unity of the international gold standard occurred mainly during a 'downswing' phase of the long-term trend in prices. The trend in prices was distinctly downwards between the early 1870s and the late 1890s, apart from a short upward movement of about three years in the mid-1880s. We have noted that the 'great debate' on monetary reform took place during this era and was itself as much about the causes of these price movements as about the relative merits of various monetary systems. Sadly, it is no easier today than it was one hundred years ago to be sure about the causation of these price movements. 'Playfairites', as we might call them, in the 1890s and 'Keynesians' in recent times have stressed the primacy of 'real' economic change, such as improvements in the productive capacity of the industrial economies or the cheapening effect of innovations in transport, over monetary factors such as changes in the supply of the precious metals or monetary regime changes, in explaining these phenomena. The fact that the period 1873 to 1900 was one of enormous 'real' economic change is bound to vitiate any inquiry into causes. This was, after all, the age of the 'Second Industrial Revolution' which fostered a whole host of cost-reducing innovations. Joseph Schumpeter rightly emphasized this and was as insistent as Lyon Playfair that entrepreneurs were crucial in creating an economic environment in which prices were constantly under attack from new techniques. On the other hand, it is difficult to think of any modern era which is not associated with massive underlying economic change of this kind: the postwar 'Golden Age' of 1945–73 and our own era of the 'Information Revolution' would certainly qualify, and economic historians have taught us that even the interwar period would not disappoint in these regards. It is not the aim of this study to inquire deeply into such causes, but what is certain is that the (partial) demise of Keynesianism and the (truncated) rise of monetarism in recent decades have necessarily made us reconsider our views of the nineteenth-century international economy and its underlying structures. Marcello de Cecco, writing in 1974 (p. 40), could afford to be dismissive of the nineteenth-century monetarist (bimetallist) explanation of price trends:

> To what can this famous price slump [of 1873–96] be attributed? Those monetary economists who believed in the quantity theory had no doubt: the years of falling prices had also been years of falling money supply. If the numeraire [gold] was scarce, its value in terms of goods had necessarily to rise, i.e. prices had to fall. To this *reductio ad unum* made by the monetary school the passage of time has not added conviction ...

But more recently, Foreman-Peck (1983) has had to be more circumspect, conceding that the findings for both phases of the longer period (1873–96 and 1896–1913) are indeed consistent with a monetary explanation of price movements. He concluded (p. 163) that, 'in the first phase the effects [of changes in the supply of gold] on the money supply were only partly offset by changes in the banking system and in the second phase, the link between gold expansion and monetary expansion was precise and central'.

Inevitably, as economic historians, we are governed by the current state of economic science in our judgements about past periods. Marcello de Cecco was no doubt writing in a consciously Keynesian mode in a Keynesian era, but since then we have been able to adopt a wider latitude in arriving at our interpretations, though, like Foreman-Peck, we do not have to go quite as far as Milton Friedman in the direction of a purely monetarist interpretation of economic history. At one stage, Friedman (1992, p. 112) was advancing his own *reductio ad unum* in the form of the cyanide theory: he emphasized that the new cyanide process for extracting gold from low-grade ores was invented in 1887 by three Scottish chemists, just in time to be used in the vast new goldfields that were then being prospected in South Africa:

> In the event, the ultimate result [of the great monetary debate] was decided by none of the issues offered by either side in the heated political contest. It was decided by faraway events in Scotland and South Africa that never entered the political debate.

Whether or not this should be regarded as *reductio ad adsurdum* as much as *ad unum* may be left to the reader to decide, though to be fair to Friedman he was not talking about original causes here.

Students of Keynes will appreciate that it is not at all clear how the great man himself would have interpreted the price trends of the late nineteenth century had he been writing at the time (his first publications were after 1900). That Keynes himself was influenced by the current state of thinking in his field is beyond doubt. Hutt (1979), for example (albeit a devout anti-Keynesian) has shown how Keynes shifted his position during the interwar years from a belief in the stability of prices under a 'managed gold standard' in the 1920s to an open advocacy of Roosevelt's inflationary policies, based on a dollar devaluation, in the 1930s. Even this does not help us guess which side Keynes would have taken in the great debate, had he participated. As we have suggested, some bimetallists, such as the academics Foxwell and Nicholson and the symmetallist Marshall, wanted to modify the monometallic gold standard on the grounds that it did not provide, perhaps was incapable of providing, stable prices. Vulgar bimetallists, such as the silverites in the United States, wanted broader convertibility in order to stimulate price rises. Should we thus argue that Keynes would have been more in line with the academic bimetallists in the 1920s and rather more sympathetic to the vulgar bimetallists in the 1930s? To the extent that a majority of economists have retreated from at least the later Keynes, perhaps it does not matter what he would have made of the 1890s, but I am always conscious of his potential (or counterfactual?) contribution. As Foreman-Peck has pointed out, Keynesian-style explanations of the depression in prices after 1873 and the inflation of post-1896 have followed a number of routes. Laughlin's argument that it was the total gold stock, as well as additions to it, which influenced aggregate demand was elaborated as follows:

> Banks made increased loans [after 1896] not because gold reserves were more readily available, but because of greater secure trading opportunities that warranted bank advances. The subsequent rise in American prices ... was explicable by high tariffs, agricultural readjustment, higher wages, and the increasing expenditure of the rich.
>
> (Laughlin, 1919, cited by Foreman-Peck, 1983, p. 163–4)

But this argument would not have turned the bimetallists' case had they still been around to argue their corner in the 1900s (actually they were still around but were virtually mute). The 'academic' (current-exchange ratio) school of Foxwell, Nicholson and Walker had always argued that it was indeed the total stock of the metals that counted in the end. A major thrust of their argument was that the new silver finds were not in themselves responsible for the fall of silver; that even the Comstock Lode represented only a small addition to total stock; that in any case gold and silver were invariably found together (as they had been in Nevada); and that remonetizing silver would not therefore be inflationary. They believed that a judiciously chosen statutory ratio of exchange between the precious metals could and would satisfy the needs of all parties, even the 'gold-bugs' if they could but see it.

Eichengreen (1996) takes the view that one of the major problems of explaining nineteenth-century monetary history is the need to account for the persistence of bimetallism into the middle of the century. He accepts Redish's theory that it was the advent of steam power and the powered press which made a token coinage under a gold standard a feasible, desirable choice. But he confesses to being unable to explain why bimetallic systems flourished for another fifty years after the appearance of Boulton and Watt's machinery. He rejects the 'political theory' that sectional interests were committed to silver and thus were able to insist on its monetary usage. Though this may have been true of the United States, it does not seem to have been true of continental Europe. Like other modern economic historians, Eichengreen seems to be unaware of the powerful and long-standing commitment to bimetallism based upon the long and successful French experience. In the end he settles for the partial explanation advanced by Flandreau that it was network externalities which held the European bimetallic system together; that is that there were advantages in maintaining the same arrangements that other countries had because this simplified trade. 'Hence', he concludes, 'the disadvantages of the prevailing system had to be pronounced before there was any incentive to abandon it' (ibid., p. 15). He goes on to say that the system had to come up against a series of shocks before its practitioners would abandon it. Such shocks were provided by the Industrial Revolution and the international rivalry of the powers that culminated in the Franco-Prussian War of 1870–71. This explanation is surely unfair to bimetallism. It is predicated on the notion that it was a wholly outdated system which had had its time. The fact that all sides in the great debate of the 1890s gave tribute to the efficient working of the bimetallic system right up to about 1870 tends to negate this. Eichengreen is clinging to residual explanations, probably because he has not fully considered the more substantive ones. The spread of the Industrial Revolution to Europe can hardly be regarded as a 'sudden shock', and international rivalry was clearly apparent long before the Franco-Prussian War. But the truth is that there is no satisfactory over-arching explanation of how and why bimetallism declined or – its obverse – why the gold standard triumphed in the second half of the nineteenth century. We are thus left with having to consider a wide range of contributory factors which, taken together, may or may not add up to a complete explanation.

British pre-eminence and the 'gold syllogism'

There is a powerful and seductive syllogism available for the unwary
seeker after the causes of the demise of bimetallism. As we all know,
Britain was the first country to adopt a full gold standard and for a long
time the only major country to do so (the exception being Portugal,
which was a client state of Britain's by the nineteenth century); Britain
was the home of the Industrial Revolution and for a long time was the
only industrial country in the modern sense of the term (given that we
have so far only had about two hundred and twenty years of industrialization, it is remarkable that Britain was the only industrial state for
about the first hundred of these years); therefore it must be that Britain's undoubted industrial precocity and enduring economic supremacy
had something to do with her near-unique gold-money status. It is
particularly tempting to conclude that the British Industrial Revolution
was responsible for the triumph of gold as a monetary metal. Without
entirely dispensing with the syllogism – there is, after all, something in
it (see below) – we should first look at alternative logical positions. One
is that the line of causation ran the other way: that it was the gold
standard which gave rise to Britain's industrial supremacy. Given
Flandreau's view that bimetallism conferred significant externalities on
its adherents, it would be odd if the one major European country not to
subscribe to it were to outperform all others in trade and industry. Yet
the British Industrial Revolution did in fact lead directly to a massive
expansion of trade and economic hegemony over continental Europe.
We should note here that Britain's classical Industrial Revolution pre-
cedes the appearance of the steam press which, in one view, gave the
monometallic gold standard positive advantages over other monetary
systems such as bimetallism. Yet recent general and economic accounts
of the Industrial Revolution tend to ignore monetary factors. One recent authoritative contribution (Hudson, 1992) spends more time looking
at the impact of breast-feeding on fertility rates as a factor in the
Industrial Revolution than it does on the role of money. It might be
right to do so. Of the more classical accounts, Phyllis Deane (1965, p.
181) saw advantages for Britain's being on the gold standard. Discuss-
ing the debate between the currency school and the banking school in
the early nineteenth century, she wrote:

> What both groups took for granted was that an 'automatic' mon-
> etary system in which the value of the currency was firmly linked
> to gold (and hence to the money-rates and price levels of all other
> countries on the gold standard) was the ideal to be aimed at. This
> view stands in contrast to the prevailing modern view that the
> currency values ought to be controlled by government and adapted

to domestic needs rather than to international standards. It was fully in accordance, however, with the economic liberalism of Adam Smith and his contemporaries and was to become the distinguishing feature of the Victorian age.

In a still Keynesian age, Deane appears to have no understanding of the international monetary order of the nineteenth century. The anachronisms hardly need pointing out – her financial experts were advocating an international gold standard fully thirty years before it actually appeared.

W. W. Rostow (1960) was always too concerned with model-building to be much concerned with historical facts, but even his theoretical paradigms had no place for currency factors in explaining British industrial primacy. For Rostow, 'The creation of the preconditions for take-off was largely a matter of building social overhead capital – railways, ports and roads – and of finding an economic setting in which a shift from agriculture and trade to manufacturing was profitable' (pp. 17–18). Reading Rostow forty years on from *The Stages*, it is difficult to see how we could ever have taken his work seriously, even as a heuristic device, but clearly the notion that industry somehow replaced trade after the Industrial Revolution is hardly likely to make us look at the gold standard as a potential force in industrialization.

On the other hand, we might expect that an eminent French economic historian would have had more regard for the currency when he set out to compare France with England in the eighteenth century. Yet François Crouzet (1982) saw no reason to look at the gold standard and concentrated instead on 'real' factors such as England's advantages in mining and textiles. In the end, however, he concluded that France had not been so far behind England that it could not have caught up. However, the French Revolution and then twenty years of war had certainly increased the discrepancy to a point beyond repair. So, for Crouzet, it was the little matter of the Revolution which prevented the great bimetallic state from competing with monometallic Albion: it had nothing to do with money.

Mathias (1969) made the same mistake as Deane in assuming an international gold standard before it actually developed. Like Deane, his advantages of the gold standard to Britain should be read as the advantages of commodity convertibility, which could have been secured equally well by a bimetallic standard: it was the 'automatic' nature of a specie standard that he was referring to. But the probability is that no economic historian has ever seriously advanced the gold standard, as such, as a major reason for Britain's becoming the 'workshop of the world'. Clearly, if such a notion had ever become widely entertained at the time (and much less plausible ideas have often taken hold in history), there would have been a veritable stampede for gold from the early nineteenth century as international rivalries propelled European countries to find the best means to enlarge their industrial potential and thus fill their war coffers. In the end Gladstone was probably right to aver that Britain's industrial pre-eminence was not due to a gold currency; rather it was the other way round, and he was as avidly devoted to gold monometallism as any British politician of his era. This is not to say that such a false reckoning did not have some validity later in the nineteenth century when nations sought to join the (partly irrational) 'scramble for gold' after 1873. Then the leaders of Germany might well have duped themselves into thinking that a gold standard would help project the country towards mastery of Europe, despite the warnings of Bleichröder and others (see below). Most economic historians today are probably of the view (if they ever give it much thought) that it was pure coincidence that Britain should have pioneered both the Industrial Revolution and the world's monetary system in the modern era.

The Steam Press

An exception to this generalization is Angela Redish (1990), who clearly links the two great phenomena, and whose work has already been noted. Her own synopsis of her argument runs as follows:

> In 1816 England officially abandoned bimetallism and made silver coins into token coins that were only limited legal tender. Earlier monetary authorities had lacked the ability to manage a subsidiary coinage, a necessary complement to the monometallic gold standard. A successful token coinage must be both costly to counterfeit and credibly backed to ensure that the tokens do not depreciate to their intrinsic value. These problems were solved in the nineteenth century through the introduction of steam-driven stamping presses and with the assistance of the Bank of England.
>
> (Ibid., p. 789)

Her contention is that England abandoned bimetallism in 1816 because a gold standard with a complementary and subsidiary (token) silver coinage offered the possibility of a medium of exchange with high- and low-denomination coins circulating concurrently. Thus, 'The [English] gold standard succeeded because the new technology employed by the Mint was able to make coins that counterfeiters could not copy cheaply and because the Mint accepted the responsibility of guaranteeing the convertibility of the coins (ibid., p. 805). For Redish, the English authorities seemed to have hit upon the ideal combination of gold and silver usage. Gold defined the value of the currency, and since that currency was monometallic its value would not depend upon fluctuations in the exchange ratio between the precious metals. A token coinage, that is a coinage whose intrinsic (metallic) value was somewhat less than its face value, was issued and because of the new techniques it was difficult, if not impossible, to counterfeit it. It will be appreciated that a token coin with a face value significantly higher than its intrinsic value will normally be highly prone to counterfeiting, much more so than a 'full-bodied' coin, whose face value exactly matches its intrinsic value. A full-bodied coin is much more prone to debasement by direct physical abuse such as clipping, but difficult to counterfeit at a profit: the only way to replicate a 22-carat gold coin is to make another coin in 22-carat gold, since such a coin would have the same intrinsic value as the 'authentic' coin and the 'counterfeiter' (or rather, 'replicator') would not make any profit. Subsequent holders of the replica coin would not be cheated and monetary authorities would see no reason not to accept the coins. This is why full-bodied coins of many European and Asian and Latin American countries freely circulated in Europe through to the nineteenth century. As we saw in Chapter Two, Spanish full-bodied coins were issued, with overmarkings, by the British in the eighteenth century.

Before the nineteenth century the main method of manufacturing coins was with a machine called a fly-press. This had been introduced in the seventeenth century and was capable of producing coins of reasonable uniformity, and, together with 'milling' (the engraving of the edges of the coins), it served the purposes of the mints. But while these methods partly prevented depreciation by 'clipping' (removing metal from the edges of the coins), the coins produced were not of a standard weight and therefore 'culling' (removing the heavier coins for export or melting down) was still practised. In any case, the fly-press was widely used in other industrial processes and therefore many people had the means to counterfeit the coins (Redish, 1990).

So the coins produced by the fly-press were subject to various depredations and these led to the setting up of the Privy Council's Select Committee of Council on Coin in 1795. They sought the advice of one Matthew Boulton, of Boulton and Watt, Birmingham. If ever there was a case of asking the right person at the right time, this must surely have been it, for Boulton's solution must rank alongside Kay's flying shuttle and Hutchinson's chronometer as great British solutions of the eighteenth century. Boulton had already established his works at Soho, near Birmingham, and was using steam power for his rolling mills, cutting presses (for making blanks) and coining presses (Boulton and Watt made coins to private and foreign orders). The improvements that Boulton introduced included the following: (i) a more uniform coin of

regular thickness and diameter, (ii) a large saving on manual labour –
the machine was powered and self-acting, (iii) a coin with a perfectly
smooth circular edge that was more difficult to clip than a milled coin,
and (iv) the machine could be manufactured especially for the mint and
thus could remain a 'secret', unlike the fly-press which was standard
equipment (ibid.). Boulton reckoned that his coins could resist all methods of reducing their weight by, for example, 'shaking' in bags to cause
particles of metal to fall off, filing and milling the edges, and dissolving
the surface with aqua regis (a mixture of nitric and hydrochloric acid).
It will be appreciated, however, that if Boulton could produce a secure
token coin not prone to counterfeiting, the problems of physical debasement were not nearly so acute: people would still accept a physically
debased token coin at its token value. Boulton's recommendations were
accepted by the Committee and from 1805 onwards the new Royal
Mint was built as a 'carbon copy' of Boulton's own works in Soho.

This much of Redish's case comprises what we might call the 'framework of fact' and is undeniable. What is less certain is the extent of the
true implications of the innovation. The British (or English, as Redish
would have it) had gained a lead in yet one more facet of human
achievement, and the Royal Mint of 1805 must be regarded as the first
modern mint. It has been said that the automatic coining of money was
one of the most interesting uses of steam power in the Industrial Revolution, and Mantoux (1928) reckoned that Boulton was motivated by
his hatred of forgers and copiers who had given his home city of
Birmingham such a bad name in the eighteenth century ('Birmingham'
or 'Brummagem' wares for many years indicated goods of doubtful
quality). Boulton and Watt received orders from France during the early
years of the Revolution, from Russia (where Boulton actually set up a
mint in 1799) and finally from the British government, which they
supplied with over four thousand tons of copper coins between 1797
and 1806 (ibid.). Curiously, this last point is not mentioned by Redish.
James Watt's estimation of his accomplice's achievement was: 'Had Mr
Boulton done nothing more than in the world than he has accomplished
in improving the coinage, his name would deserve to be immortalised'.[1]

There is no doubt that Boulton's contribution to the development of
coin manufacture is a very considerable one. As he himself predicted, his
methods would eventually become the standard for all the nations of the
world and his machines are still used today, albeit driven by electricity
rather than steam. It follows, then, that a modern system of coinage is yet
one more product of the British Industrial Revolution and perhaps even
makes the link we were alluding to in the 'gold syllogism'. But all this
leaves the monetary historian with a number of problems. One of these is
conceded by Redish herself: if the single gold standard plus the steam

press provided the panacea to the management of an efficient modern monetary system, why were other nations so slow to adopt the 'Boulton–Bank of England' solution after 1820? It has been suggested that some experience was needed to master the new techniques, and that the French experimented 'for years' before finally installing one of Boulton's machines in the 1840s (Eichengreen, 1996). But this does not explain why nations did not simply buy in their coins from Messrs Boulton and Watt and move straight on to a gold standard if the benefits were as great as Redish supposes. The knowledge that the French were in any case already buying 'Brummagem coins' as early as the Revolutionary period and that the Russian government had already invited Boulton to set up a mint on their behalf in Russia in 1799 makes this more difficult to comprehend. As prohibitions on the trade in machines were removed in the nineteenth century, it is surprising that the wonderful new system was not transferred more rapidly around Europe, if not the globe, especially when we consider how quickly the technology of steam in other forms, such as the steam locomotive, was spread after 1830.

There is another problem with the Redish hypothesis. As monetary experts and financiers debated the gold standard and its alternatives during the course of the nineteenth century, they seem never to have mentioned the Boulton press as a major factor explaining the success of gold monometallism. I have examined hundreds of documents which were produced before and during the great debate of the 1890s and have never come across any reference to it. Parliamentary inquiries such as the Herschell Report of 1888 give no mention of it, not even in Part II, which was signed by the gold-standard adherents. If the system was the breakthrough that Redish claims it to be, it would have been veritable grist to the mill for the monometallist campaign. The Gold Standard Defence Association could have used it as their clinching argument. They did not.

So although we can accept Redish's arguments about the advantages of the gold standard to 'England' in the early nineteenth century, we cannot say that it was a major reason for the spread of the gold standard because few people seem to have fully understood that England had these advantages at the time. Eichengreen largely rejected the theory that political support for silver, especially in the United States, was responsible for prolonging its monetary life after the steam press and the Bank of England had allegedly made it redundant as a standard of value. As we have noted, in the end he plumped for Flandreau's argument that network externalities kept silver going into its mid-century dotage. In fact there are other reasons why silver may have been kept on, but first we will consider other explanations for the rise of gold in the late nineteenth century.

The German decision of 1871

Numerous contemporary and modern accounts of the evolution of the gold standard and the demise of bimetallism assign a high degree of importance to the German decision to adopt gold in 1871. Germany – or more correctly, Prussia and her allies – had defeated France in war and the new German Empire was declared at Versailles. The political unification of Germany, the adoption of a single imperial currency, the rationalization of the banking system and the establishment of a central bank, and the move to a gold standard all came very quickly for Germany and were all, it seems, forces which helped create the powerful new Central European state from the war onwards. However, the notion that Germany was taking a new economic direction which received the support of a large majority of its population should quickly be dispelled. Economic and financial modernization was persistently held back by powerful groups such as the Prussian *Junkers*, and the many bureaucracies which served the states under the Hohenzollern Empire. The *Junkers* were 'anti-commerce, anti-cities, anti-industry and anti-banking', according to Riesser in 1911.[2] As the *Junkers* derived their wealth from the land, they were natural supporters of silver and opponents of gold. Thus 'Prussian financial history is closely associated with financing armies, on the one hand, and providing mortgage credit to the Junker nobility on the other', according to Kindleberger (1984, p. 117). Frederick the Great, with complete insouciance, debased the currency in order to fill his war coffers, and subsequent *Junker* economic history is characterized by mercantilism, monopoly, fiat money and debt defaulting. Other German states exhibited scarcely any greater economic probity, and some were more feudal than Prussia in their politico-economic arrangements despite the liberating influence of Napoleon on many of them. Monetary arrangements were often chaotic and the Rhineland in 1816 is said to have had as many as seventy different types of foreign coin in circulation at the same time. In the 1820s and 1830s the Prussian state attempted to enforce uniform standards but was only partially successful; at the same time it managed to undervalue gold at the mint and thus drive it from circulation. As Clapham (1921, p. 125) averred, silver was actually gaining ground in Europe before 1848, partly for the reason that gold was in short supply until the Californian and Australian discoveries, but overvaluation cannot have helped its cause: In the German states, silver was everywhere standard money. A certain amount of gold circulated side by side with it, as it always had, but the quantity was less than in earlier centuries'.

And so it was a silver Prussia which led the German states towards economic and then political union in the nineteenth century. The great

Prussian scientific tariff of 1818 was used, along with promises of road-building and access to trade, to induce various states into what became the Zollverein of 1834. Some German states, notably Hanover and the Hanse towns, preferred to deal with free-trading England for many a long day, but it is important to note that it was the tariff, much more than any considerations of currency, which formed the basis of national unity in the emergence of the German Empire in the mid-nineteenth century. As with another and later experiment in European unity, *Zollverein* (customs union) pre-dated *Münzverein* (currency union) and proved somewhat less controversial.

Yet by many accounts it was ultimately Germany which propelled continental Europe towards a full gold standard and destroyed European bimetallism once and for all:

> France's own bimetallic standard ended when it did because of the Franco-Prussian War of 1870–71. France suffered a devastating defeat and was forced to pay Germany a huge war indemnity in funds convertible into gold. Germany used the money to finance its own shift from a silver standard to a gold standard – a tribute to the example of Britain, which German leaders desperately wanted to surpass in economic power and which had been on gold since 1821.
>
> (Friedman, 1992, pp. 134–5)

Prussia's defeat of France, it would seem, had at least three major effects on European currency history and the status of the precious metals:

1. It established Germany, the fastest-growing and most important continental state, on a new gold standard and the indemnity drawn up against France was 'payable in gold', thus denoting Germany's clear intentions of a change of monetary regime.
2. It undermined the French bimetallic system and ultimately forced France, probably reluctantly, on to a gold standard in due course.
3. It enabled Germany to retain a large stock of silver, which could be used as a powerful bargaining weapon in future diplomacy; Germany could make veiled threats about selling the surplus silver but her mere retention of it perhaps helped prevent the reappearance of bimetallism in Europe in the late nineteenth century.

There is little doubt that Germany's belated and dramatic shift to gold helped secure her economic leadership of Europe after 1870, and certainly her hegemony over France. Yet one historian who has looked in depth at Franco-German relations in the nineteenth century gives no weight to it, preferring instead to concentrate on differential rates of growth of industrial output and population, and the decline of French politics into ultramontanism (Mitchell, 1979). This could be because money can act in an almost invisible way: it may be important but it fills far fewer newspaper columns than, for example, the German 'War Hoax' of 1875. Generally speaking, the importance of the German silver *masse de manœuvre* of the 1870s seems to have been neglected by historians, though there is evidence that the British were well aware of it and deeply concerned about it. Committed as they were to gold, the British did not wish to see the demise of silver any more than the bimetallic countries did, if only because it threatened her exchange relationships with important nations such as France and India. Indeed, paradoxically, we can say that Britain had more to lose in this way from a fall of silver in the 1870s than a still inward-looking, nascent German Empire. Yet because of its ancient commitment to gold, the Bank of England felt unable to intervene in any way in the European silver market. However, the Bank held reserves of silver which had been built up since the time of Robert Peel's ministry in the 1840s: the Bank's holdings of silver had increased from £1,700,000 in 1844 to £2,700,000 in 1846.[3] When Peel had introduced the Bank Charter Act of 1844 he had spoken at length about the policy of excluding the Bank of England from buying silver: 'We shall', he said, 'probably insure [sic] the maintenance of such a stock of silver as may give facilities for rectifying the exchanges and supplying the demands of commerce'.[4]

Incredible though it may seem, the British financial authorities had seriously considered buying up some or all of the German silver. Even more unlikely, *The Economist,* whose editor was the gold-standard die-hard Walter Bagehot, openly advocated such a move on the grounds that 'it would relieve both the trade and the finances of the Indian government, of that there is little doubt'.[5] Furthermore, it would 'sweep off the remaining influence of the sales of silver by the German government'.[6] Perhaps the analysts of the origins of Anglo-German antagonisms and the First World War should start here in the 1870s with currency diplomacy rather than in the later vicissitudes of the Kaiserreich: the first intimations of Germany's willingness to upset the European balance of power after their humbling of France in war may well be found in the monetary arena as much as in the overtly political one. The British establishment, dominated as it was by the gentlemanly capitalists of the City, cannot have been amused at Germany's vagueness about her precious metals. But by the late 1870s *The Economist* was reporting with some relief that the sales of the German silver 'were now at an end'. In June 1879, it had ascertained that the value of the thaler (silver) pieces held in German public treasuries totalled no more than £12,500,000, an order of magnitude not much larger than British reserves and no longer a threat to currency stability. By then, however, Germany was committed to the gold standard to the extent that she refused to send delegates to the international monetary conference of that year. From then on, the opprobrium of *The Economist* tended to be directed at the Americans rather than the Germans.

Ultimately it is impossible to assess the true impact of Germany's belated and sudden shift to gold in the early 1870s. Some points, however, can be made. The Germans could have sold off their reserves of silver more rapidly than they did, and this would have had an even more dramatic effect on silver prices. They chose to get rid of the silver in smaller packages and over a period of time, presumably because they did not want to disturb the ratio overmuch. On the other hand, the existence of the German hoard of silver was well known, and the fact that Germany kept these stocks through most of the 1870s can only have acted as a destabilizing factor on specie prices in the decade. However, we should remember that Germany was not nearly so important in the 1870s as in the 1890s.

The German switch to gold was accompanied at first by a boom of unprecedented proportions. In the words of Fritz Stern (1977, p. 181), 'it seemed as of an era of unlimited riches had begun ... and in three years as many ironworks, blast furnaces and machine-production factories were founded as had been created in the previous seventy years'. This boom, however, is not usually attributed to the gold conversion, but rather to the reparations of approximately 5 billion francs which the French seem to have paid with remarkable willingness and which allowed the retirement of German public debt. This in turn unleashed a vast supply of liquid funds and thus a period of 'easy money', which was quickly dubbed 'Grunderzeit': a time for empire-building, both political and economic. Opposition to gold continued and was led by the great banker and bimetallist, Gerson von Bleichröder. Pitted against him was the gold enthusiast Ludwig Bamberger, 'the virtual founder of the Reichsbank and of a single imperial currency' (ibid., p. 181 note). It is interesting to note that in 1879, according to Stern, a letter from Lord Odo Russell predicting that Germany would soon adopt a bimetallic standard was leaked to the press. Bamberger spoke in the Reichstag about the matter and pointed the finger at Bleichröder as the source of the rumour. But Bleichröder was still the personal banker to Bismarck, who in turn attacked Bamberger. The matter became something of a *cause célèbre* in Germany and an acrimonious row between principals of such high standing must have left its mark. It is tempting to suppose that it was this row which caused Germany to put its monetary house in order and dispose of the troublesome silver later in the year. British bankers, especially the great international houses such as Rothschilds and Barings, must have been fully apprised of such German financial goings-on and must have proffered advice at various stages.

One might conclude here that numerous accounts of the demise of silver in the late nineteenth century give great credibility to the view that the decision of Germany to adopt the gold standard after the war with France was a momentous one for monetary history. However, it is impossible to say how far this is due to the possibility that there is a common ancestry to many of these accounts.

The failure of the French parachute

It is almost universally appreciated that the French monetary system was instrumental in helping to stabilize the world's currencies for much of the nineteenth century. We have seen in Chapter Three that France had been the clearing-house for specie entering Europe since the heyday of the Spanish Empire, when the 'bimetallic flows' replenished the monetary reservoirs of both Europe and the East. It was important, therefore, that France continued to recognize both gold and silver as commodities for monetary standards through to the nineteenth century. Kindleberger (1984) has concluded that while Britain was 'backing into the gold standard', France was 'backing into' official bimetallism in the modern era. In early nineteenth-century France, he argues, 'no thought was given to adoption of the gold standard'. In 1803, we have seen that the French Law of 7 Germinal had, as a matter of history, established bimetallism as the essential monetary system of the nation. Nevertheless, silver was still the major monetary metal and was treated as the primary standard of value. Gaudin, the admirable finance minister responsible for 7 Germinal, had inserted a clause in the statute which provided for a recoining of the *gold* coins if and when the market ratio of the precious metals came to differ too widely from the legal (statutory) ratio, which was fixed by the French at 15.5:1. A gold coin, the *napoléon*, came to be the 'symbol of imperial prosperity' (Clapham, 1921). But no one was ever obliged to pay in gold, and gold coins came to command a premium. This is dangerously close to silver monometallism, but for ordinary exchanges the two metals circulated side by side and an effective bimetallic system emerged. Indeed, the need to recoin the *napoléon* never arose since the market ratio remained steady over a remarkable long period. As Clapham (p. 124) pointed out, 'probably, as bimetallists have always argued, the fact that the French mints were open to both metals, and so tended to absorb whichever was momentarily the more abundant, was in itself one of the causes of the steadiness of the market ratio'. Clapham went on to write in terms of France's 'monetary comfort' between 1815 and 1870, and, as we have seen, he is joined in this by almost all subsequent economic historians, to the extent that the proposition 'that French experience over a pronounced secular period proves that statutory bimetallism is a workable monetary system' is almost to be regarded as part of the 'framework of fact' in any general account of events. And it must also be appreciated that this long period of French-induced equilibrium was not sustained without many outside shocks, in the form of the rebellions of the 1830s, the Europe-wide revolutions of the late 1840s and huge new finds of both gold and silver between 1848 and 1870. France absorbed more than half of the world's total output of gold between 1850 and 1870, while retaining its stocks of silver, such that the ratio of French holdings of silver against gold increased dramatically, from 41:1 to 8:1, over the same period.[7]

It cannot be denied, then, that the French economy acted as a 'parachute', allowing gold and silver a 'soft landing' through the middle decades of the century. Even the monometallists who signed Part I of the report of the (British) Gold and Silver Commission accepted that, 'while the relative value of the production of the two metals was subject to considerable changes in the first seventy years of this century, the extreme variation in their market value scarcely exceeded 3% in either direction; while if the average values over a series of years is taken, the variation is hardly perceptible'.[8] Of course, they concluded that other factors than bimetallism were also responsible for this, namely that the relative values of the money metals could only have been maintained because there was, within the bimetallic region, a sufficient stock of both metals. In other words, 'had silver been produced in increasing quantities in the earlier part of the century, the ratio [meaning the statutory ratio] would have been powerless to prevent its falling in value, as there was no gold in the country [France] which could have given place to the increased supply of silver'.[9] In similar fashion they argued that at the time of the great gold discoveries of 1848–49, the French currency had all but ceased to be bimetallic and was composed, 'practically of silver only'. So the result – that the market ratio was not rapidly affected – was due more to the fact that France had a large stock of the undervalued metal (silver) than that it was properly bimetallic. Even so, and despite all the reservations of their school, the gold standard enthusiasts who wrote Part I of the Final Report conceded that, 'the French bimetallic system prevented a serious fall in the value of gold which could not otherwise have been avoided'.[10]

But monometallists were not wont to use the metaphor of a 'parachute' to describe the dampening effect of French bimetallism (or 'oscillating gold–silver standard', as they might have called it). The play on words would have added credibility to the alien, Gallic, system. And Francis Walker (1898, p. 85), the American bimetallist, preferred the metaphor of a long ship to describe the stabilizing effect:

> [France] was able to carry that system [bimetallism] on, through the period when gold was coming in upon her mints like the waters of a broken dam, and to maintain a stock of the appreciating silver until ... silver in its turn tended to fall in comparison with gold. For myself I entertain not the slightest doubt that, but for the hostile action of Germany between 1871 and 1873, France, with her then monetary allies of the Latin Union, would have been able to continue this beneficial function on to our own day, when the South African gold-fields were so unexpectedly opened up to human enterprise. For this reason, it seems to me that the image of a ship long enough to ride over two or three waves at once in not inappropriate.

Of course, Walker was writing at a time when marine architects could be smug about the inherent stability of the vast ocean-going liners they were then pioneering: he might not have been so willing to advance this particular metaphor a few years later. On the other hand, 'parachute' seems an odd word to use in an era which pre-dated the appearance of the aeroplane. However, it must be appreciated that a parachute as we understand the term could be used to bail out from lighter-than-air machines such as hot-air balloons, and that the word derives from the French, meaning 'in place of a fall'. Thus a safety catch which prevented a too-rapid descent in a colliery shaft, or a device which prevented a boring tool from penetrating too quickly, might also be termed 'parachutes' in the nineteenth century.

Perhaps the biggest shock which was obviated by the French parachute was the 'Gold Panic' of the early 1850s. The Californian and Australian gold finds were two of the greatest of all time and, for Walker (1898, pp. 121–2), 'one of the most marvellous coincidences of human history'. Chevalier (1857) in France noted that the production of gold, as compared with silver, increased five-fold between 1851 and 1857. Experts around the world wrote lengthy papers on the 'probable fall in the price of gold', which never came. Gloom-and-doom merchants talked of the ratio falling to 12:1, 10:1, or even 8:1. Holland demonetized gold because of the panic, and that most pessimistic of peoples, the Portuguese, went entirely over to the English sovereign for the duration. Universal bankruptcy was confidently forecast and even the British, as we have noted elsewhere, seriously considered switching to silver (though, it has to be said, not many of them). Walker quoted one English financier as declaring that gold would one day be fit only for the dustpan and Chevalier declared himself in favour of silver monometallism as the only hope of preserving industry, trade and the social structure.

'But', as Walker (1898, pp. 121–2) went on to say, 'the hearts of the men who controlled the destinies of France did not fail. Freely, that country took gold from all without fear of its becoming worthless in her hands'. France continued to influence the relative values of the two metals by buying gold on a falling market and selling silver on a rising one. It would be interesting to calculate the likely welfare effects of this action on the French economy. The decade of the 1850s was, for Walker, 'the greatest financial storm of two centuries', yet its destructive effect was limited by the French parachute. In an earlier chapter we have seen how Walker's sometimes Panglossian view of the French system was supported in varying degrees by a wide array of leading lights such as Stanley Jevons, Henry Sidgwick, John E. Cairnes and even Walter Bagehot, as well as the leading bimetallist thinkers of the day. And ironically, it was an apostate Chevalier who probably first used the term 'parachute' during the gold crisis and in his essay, first published in English in Manchester in 1857, entitled, 'On the probable fall in the value of gold, the commercial and social consequences which may ensue':

> If down to the present time [1857], the immense production, of which Australia and California have been the theatre, has not produced a greater fall in the value of gold, it is France which is the cause. It is she that has retarded the depreciation of gold. She plays in relation to this the part of a parachute.
>
> (p. 50)

The question we need to address here is why the French parachute failed to open after 1870. In truth, the system had been seriously weakened long before the Franco-Prussian War. The very fact that there was so much more gold in circulation by the 1860s than in, say, 1840 is in itself relevant and over the longer period a number of countries began, after the initial shock of its new abundance, to see gold as the inevitable metal of standard. The rapid expansion of gold forced silver out of circulation in much of France itself, as well as Switzerland, Italy and Belgium. Redish (1994) has shown convincingly that the creation of the Latin Monetary Union of 1865 'should be viewed as a step on the path to the gold standard and not as a dead-end attachment to bimetallism'. By 1865, the four 'core' countries of continental Europe were on 'limping gold standards' and were unwilling to contemplate a return to a silver standard. Nevertheless, a French commission set up by the government in 1867 still went on to argue for a retention of a bimetallic capacity, though it was reconvened and prevailed upon to change its mind (Walker, 1898). Walker conceded that the 1867 International Monetary Conference was a clear victory for gold monometallism, but only because in his view the delegates to the Paris meeting were 'out of their minds' to reach a unanimous verdict which helped kill off silver as a monetary metal:

> This all important step [of fixing gold as the only monetary metal] having been decided upon, with an ease and lightness which are today [1896] matters of amazement, the Conference had no difficulty in preparing a scheme of international coinage which reads very prettily in the report and would have been nice in Utopia.
>
> (Ibid., p. 157–8)

To underline the view that the 1867 IMC had been a charade, Walker cited the fact that the United States had not bothered to send a proper delegation to Paris. Indeed, they did not really send anyone at all, for the American representative was the resident United States commissioner to the 1867 Paris exhibition, which happened to be on at the same time. As far as we can tell, Mr. Samuel B. Ruggles knew nothing about economics or finance but was nevertheless empowered to act in that position. Walker believed that this was done merely to save the expense of sending a proper delegate. Chance factors as this have their place in history and it did not, according to many authorities, prevent the findings of the IMC from being extremely influential. Ruggles himself was quoted as saying that 'with a single stroke of the pen', the conference had simplified the world's currency systems, and perhaps it had.

The Bank of France is pictured by Walker as fighting a stolid rearguard action against the IMC and the onward march of the gold standard, and at the end of 1869 the Conseil Supérieure de l'État was summoned to report upon the advantages and disadvantages of monometallism. M. Rouland, the governor of the Bank of France, 'offered a strenuous opposition, defending the [bimetallic] law against the aspersions that had been brought against it' (Walker, 1898, p. 166).

Of course, we must remember that Walker was far from being an unbiased commentator, and Russell (1898) later defended Ruggles from Walker's comments, pointing out that he (Ruggles) had represented the United States at the Statistical Conference in Berlin a year earlier. He argued that Ruggles's 'prejudice for gold was no stronger than the government's [i.e., the United States' government] or that of any one in the country at that time' (p. 21). This is a rather ambiguous, and tenuous, defence and only confirms that Ruggles was a monometallist and a standardizer, if not an ignoramus. The 1867 conference was, after all, about how to standardize, and events perfectly illustrate the ambivalence of the French at the time: they were generally keen to see world standardization on the basis of the French franc, as was virtually agreed by the IMC, but were not certain about standardization on gold. The monometallic British were happy to see the spread of the gold standard but were none too keen on standardization on the French franc. It is perhaps because gold-standard Britain was against the recommendations of the 1867 conference that the latter has wrongly been seen, as Redish has pointed out, as pro-bimetallic.

The 'Crime of 1873'

The 'Crime of 1873' was the United States Coinage Act of that year. Until 1873 there had been in the United States, as we saw in Chapter Five, free coinage of both gold and silver, in other words, *de jure* bimetallism, at a ratio of 16:1. But during the Civil War (1861–64) and for several years afterwards, the amount of silver coin actually minted was very small. The average value of the US coinage in the ten years ending 30 June 1874 did not amount to more than $2,000,000 a year.[11] The Coinage Act of 1873 effectively suspended the free coinage of silver, and gold was made the sole legal tender for sums exceeding 5 dollars. From 1873, although the government did not trumpet the fact, the United States was on a gold standard almost as much as Great Britain. It would seem that this shift went almost unnoticed, not merely in Europe, but also in the United States itself.

The demonetization of silver, however, did affect Americans. The United States was a large producer of silver and, as we have seen, these mines were to be found in the west of the country, far away from the centres of power and finance, where economic policy generally was made. This, together with the fact that the midwestern states also contained the great new agricultural regions, whose farmers depended on high prices for their produce, partly explains why money and monetary policy became such important issues in the great federal republic towards the end of the nineteenth century. The Royal Commission of 1888 was quick to point out those characteristics of the United States which helped make American economic and monetary history so different from that in Europe. In the United States, apart from brief periods (1791–1811; 1816–36) when the so-called 'First' and 'Second' Banks of the United States were operating, no institution was in a position to accept the responsibility for controlling the credit policies of the commercial banks. In Britain and in the leading continental countries there were relatively strong central banks which had become lenders of last resort. In the United States, therefore, the government – state or federal – was the institution charged with the responsibility for correcting the abuses and shortcomings of the financial system. It is possible that this meant that money was always bound to be at the centre of political discussion and explains why the silver controversy raged louder and longer there than in Britain or Europe. In any case, currency and its creation were always at the heart of the American Constitution, as Friedman is always keen to point out. The US Congress in its earliest years, following the advice of Alexander Hamilton, passed its first Coinage Act in April 1792, and this defined the basic monetary unit as the dollar, which in turn was defined as equal to 371.25 grains of pure silver, or 24.75 grains of pure gold. Thus it authorized the free coinage of both silver and gold at a specified ratio of 15:1 (371.25 divided by 24.75 = 15.0).

This is perhaps why the silverites and their allies later referred to the Act of 1873 which demonetized silver as a 'crime'. Simply put, it was contrary to the American Constitution, which in their minds came close to being natural law: the United States was constitutionally a bimetallic state. However, we have said that the United States was on a silver standard from 1792 to 1834. But we must see that this was purely a *de facto* silver standard and not a constitutional, or statutory, one. The reasons are fairly clear: gold increased in its market value towards the end of the eighteenth century and was used for money, but only at a premium and never at its par value until 1834. Gresham's Law ensured that silver, the 'cheap money', drove out gold, the 'dear one'. The legislation of 1834 had the opposite effect, by raising the exchange ratio to 16:1, well above its actual market ratio of 15.65:1. This shifted the United States on to a *de facto* gold standard and it remained on this until the Civil War; in this period silver coins were part of a subsidiary coinage. The California Gold Rush merely confirmed gold's status in the United States by helping to move the market ratio downwards from 15.5 or thereabouts. If the French system of 7 Germinal can be seen as a near-perfect example of statutory bimetallism, the American one can only be defined as an oscillating gold/silver standard between independence and the 1870s. No wonder that even devout American bimetallists such as Francis Walker were prone to use French economic history, rather than their own, to provide ammunition for their bimetallic propaganda. Conversely, gold monometallists were more prone to refer to the more unfortunate American experiences with bimetallism.

But the American bimetallic system differed greatly from the French one. If the American dual standard was a parachute in any sense, it was one that was full of holes and had no effect whatsoever, even according to the silverites, in dampening price fluctuations of the precious metals. There may be good reasons why the American parachute was so threadbare. Friedman argues that the lurch from silver to gold in 1834 had much less to do with the tenets of any bimetallic theory than with financial politics. The Select Committee on Coins of the House of Representatives was set up to 'do something for gold', the metal having been found in a few southern states (Virginia, North Carolina, South Carolina and Georgia) long before the 1848 rush to California. The committee considered a ratio near to the market ratio but then went too far and overshot at 16:1. It must have been quite obvious what the effect of this would be. But it seems that the decision was made in the middle of the notorious 'Bank War' then raging between President Jackson and the banker Nicholas Biddle. Biddle's note issue had become very popular because of the parlous state of the official currency at the time – 'a mixture of US and foreign silver coins, plus paper money issued by the state banks' (Friedman, 1992, p. 56). Jackson was therefore part of a 'golden club' used to belabour the hated enemy, the Biddle Bank.

Unfortunately for the cause of bimetallism, the United States contained far more enthusiasts for the silver cause than France at the crucial time. American bimetallism could always be interpreted as special pleading for silver when that country produced such vast amounts of the white metal. Furthermore, this silver, as we have seen, was produced in western states that were already committed to inflationary policies because of the dominance of their primary producers. Western farmers faced near-perfect, global competition for their output and thus had no influence whatsoever on the prices they received. When these prices fell rapidly, as they did in the 1870s, they could only turn to the currency for an answer to their declining affluence, and the American Constitution held out hope that currency reform was always possible. But this meant that Europeans could never take the American position on currency very seriously. S. Dana Horton and Francis Walker might come to London to preach the dual standard, but British bimetallists could only hope that they did not talk too much about their own country's unhappy experience with a bimetallic currency for much of its recent history.

After 1873, American governments passed successive pieces of legislation to help silver in an increasingly gold-using world. The Bland–Allison Act of 1878 and the Sherman Act of 1890 were the major sops to the silver interests. They required the Treasury to purchase silver and mint it into coins exchangeable for gold at fixed ratios. Bland–Allison came in the aftermath of the admission of more of the western states to the Union, so again we can safely assume that it was a result of special pleading, rather than any wider concern for long-run currency stability. Thus we could argue that a true definition of the United States' currency position in the period 1878–1914 was 'gold standard plus silver purchases'. Because of the actual political outcome, as we have seen in Chapter Five, there was no overturning of the gold standard, no 'putting to right' the 'Crime of '73'.

As I have emphasized before, the United States in the late nineteenth century was much more concerned with economic developments within its own boundaries than with the expansion of the world economy. This means that its power élites were in a very different position from those in Europe, notably in Britain. There seems to have been very little regard for European interests in the United States when it deliberated over its own currency complexion: witness for example the 1834 decision to adopt gold, or the silver purchases of a later period. The Sherman Act of 1890 was 'a *quid pro quo* for conceding the eastern industrialists' desire for the McKinlay tariff, one of the most protective tariffs in US history, adopted the same year' (Eichengreen, 1996, p. 22). American currency history is dominated by American economics, American politics and American vital interests. There is no reason to think that anything changed during the great debate on currency in the 1890s. The men of the City of London who appreciated this can be forgiven in their gold obduracy if they saw the United States as the very last place from which they should be taking their currency cues.

Whether the Coinage Act of 1873 should be seen as a 'crime' in any sense of the word is a matter for American historians. It has been shown that no bribery took place, as was once alleged. But the effect of the Act is important: it ended the legal monetary status of bimetallism in the United States and effectively prevented a restoration of silver there, despite the clear constitutional status of the metal in the strongest of all constitutions democratically arrived at. The effects were long-lasting. Friedman (1992, p. 61) is convinced that, 'had that fateful line not been omitted [the omission of any mention of the "standard silver dollar" of the constitution] from the 1873 Act, resumption in 1879 would almost surely have been on silver not gold'. And we must always remember that the United States was of much less consequence as an international player at the time of the 'crime' than twenty years later when its consequences came fully to the fore. Had there been a greater and more long-standing commitment to silver at an earlier stage, the United States might have been able to lead the world (or at any rate a large part of it – which might have been sufficient) away from the gold standard in the 1890s. Purely adventitious factors had been at work in 1873. The Senate Finance Committee which forced through the bill had been packed with ideologues who had long wanted to demonetize silver for their own special reasons. Thus only a small counterfactual shift would have been required to change the course of American, and possibly world, economic history: as was so often the case with American developments, the Senate Committee was acting politically rather then pragmatically.

It has been argued that the failure to include provision for the standard silver dollar in the Coinage Act of 1873 was based not upon any kind of recognition of the existing economic facts but upon a calculated hostility to silver as a monetary metal. It has often been seen as a purposive and deliberate course of action by Senator John Sherman, who was largely responsible for framing the legislation and seeing it through Congress. Silverites certainly interpreted it as a result of 'malice aforethought': they saw the 'striking down' of silver as having a vast impact on the general economic prospects of the United States as the nineteenth century drew to a close.

It is perhaps difficult for us now to see how anyone could ever so despise a metal or a type of money, though an appreciation of the way in which many British people have harboured an almost visceral hatred of the Euro in recent years may persuade us that it is conceivable.

The 'Crime of '73' did not itself cause the fall of silver, though many Americans, on both sides of the debate, continued to think that it did. In fact it came too late for that. From a ratio with gold of 15.4:1 in 1870, the world market price of silver had already started to fall some time before 1873, reaching a new low of 16.4:1 by 1873. But, as Friedman (1992, p. 67) suggested, the 'crime' 'added to the upward pressure on the gold–silver price ratio, both by absorbing gold that would otherwise have been available for monetary use in the rest of the world, and by failing to absorb silver'. The American legislation of 1878 and 1890 which required the silver purchases (the Bland–Allison Act of 1878 stipulated that the Treasury buy 2–4 million dollars of purchases each month, and this was stepped up dramatically by the Sherman Act of 1890) obviously had some impact in retarding silver prices. However, it is also possible that the legislation, by defining silver as a commodity which required government support, helped ensure that governments in Europe would be more rather than less wary about remonetizing it: to have done so in the late nineteenth century meant relying on a distant country to continue that support, when in truth it could have been withdrawn at any time and as a consequence of American, not European, developments. Friedman (ibid.) calculated that the US government purchased altogether sixteen times more fine silver than gold under the purchase schemes, but he concluded that free coinage of silver would have led to much larger purchases because the stock of money would have expanded much more rapidly under bimetallism. One has constantly to remind oneself at all times that Friedman is an avowed bimetallist who blames the depression of 1873–96 unequivocally on the gold standard.

The repeal of the silver purchase requirements in 1893 would have had much the same effect as the 1873 legislation and of course came at

THE GOLD STANDARD AND THE DEFEAT OF BIMETALLISM

a crucial time for silver. Indeed, it was right in the middle of the 'great debate', though it certainly did not provoke the concern that it should have done in Europe.

It is worth pointing out, too, that discrimination against silver in the United States extended well beyond the government. Ritter (1997, pp. 185–6) has investigated this issue and has summarized the points as follows:

(i)   discrimination made at the United States mints, in receiving gold bullion for free coinage and not so receiving silver.
(ii)   discrimination by bank clearing houses which refused to offer silver certificates in payment of balances.
(iii) discrimination by the United States treasury which preferred to pay out in gold, even in circumstances where it could have paid in either metal.

Ritter concluded that free coinage alone would not have restored 'parity', that is, 16:1 or thereabouts, and therefore would not have rescued silver, contrary to Friedman. If she is correct, then the 'Crime of '73' was merely one of several such crimes committed against the metal by American authorities at many levels in the late nineteenth century.

The conclusion one is forced to draw from American experience in the late nineteenth century is that there was an ineluctable underlying shift from silver to gold and that this shift was multi-causal. It will probably prove impossible to disentangle all the factors responsible for the demise of silver in the New World. American decisions were often unrelated to events in Europe or the world at large, thus confirming the view that American monetary history is utterly different from Europe's, especially from Britain's. Factors such as the enlargement of the Union, bank wars, farm prices and political prejudices about the currency all had their part to play, and American bimetallists on European tours had no right to lecture Europeans on their lack of monetary good sense.

The gold standard as kitemark

Throughout this book so far there has been an emphasis on the so-called 'core economies' of the nineteenth-century world economy: Britain, France, Germany and the United States. India has been examined because of its special place in the currency history of the period and because of its importance in international trade. This is because, by and large, the debates and the major decisions about monetary and currency policies largely took place within these states. Of course, the United States could be regarded as 'peripheral' at the beginning of the period, but was definitely central by 1890 and already a leader in the formation of opinion, as well as much else. We have seen that the core elements of the international economy, for a wide variety of reasons and in very different circumstances, accepted the international gold standard from the early 1870s onwards.

Bordo and Rockoff (1996) have recently looked at the possible reasons why countries outside the central core moved in the direction of gold monometallism in the late nineteenth century. Although the debate as we understand it was restricted to the core in terms of contributions, it might well be that the reasons adduced by Bordo and Rockoff contributed towards the decision-making processes within the economic élite and/or resulted directly from those decisions in various ways. The main argument advanced by Bordo and Rockoff is that peripheral countries benefited by shifting to the gold standard because it improved their access to capital. This, they argue, may explain 'why countries were so determined to adhere to gold even when doing so involved substantial costs: faithful adherence [to the gold standard] lowered the costs of loans from Europe' (p. 390). Membership of the gold-standard group was seen as evidence of financial rectitude on their part and thus comparable to the 'Good Housekeeping Seal of Approval'. This particular metaphor may make more sense to American than to British scholars – it refers to the practice of a certain American magazine to present particular manufactured products or services with a seal indicating that they merited a certain standard of quality. British readers might prefer to use the term kitemark, as has recently been done to describe the proposed concept of rewarding good behaviour by allocating kitemark status to less developed countries, as for example within the Commonwealth group. Countries which can show that they live up to certain criteria on, for example, human rights, or fair and free competitive elections, may qualify for the kitemark and thus, presumably, find it easier to attract foreign capital, amongst other things. Thus membership of the gold standard 'signalled that a country followed prudent fiscal and monetary policies and would only temporarily run large fiscal deficits in well-understood emergencies' (Bordo and Rockoff, p. 390). The country in question could be depended upon to avoid defaulting on externally held debt. A by-product of this was that the gold standard served as a 'creditable commitment mechanism' which might effectively prevent the government of the country from pursuing monetary expansion for their own purposes – for example, to obtain seigniorage revenues (the charge made for minting bullion) – and thus helped prevent inflation and subsequent stagnation that has troubled developing countries in the twentieth century. It may be obvious that joining a gold standard, or any commodity standard, would prevent inflation, but the gold standard moved from being a 'domestic British practice' in 1870 to a true international standard by about 1880: the practice of fixing national currencies to gold resulted in fixed exchange rates and thus became, for Bordo and Rockoff, a 'nominal anchor to the international monetary system'.

Clearly, the main motive for 'less-developed countries' in the late nineteenth century was access to capital, which was only obtainable in the core European countries, especially Britain and France. By joining the gold standard, it is argued that such countries cold expect to pay lower interest rates on loans raised in, say, London, than other countries which could not or would not make the necessary commitment to gold. Bordo and Rockoff looked at nine countries which chose to display the 'Good Housekeeping Seal of Approval' and observed the behaviour of long-term bond yields in those countries. The data they assembled consisted of annual interest rates, real incomes, fiscal deficits and money supply during the gold standard era. Their principal findings were that 'interest rates charged on long-term bonds in core capital markets during the era of the classical gold standard differed substantially from country to country and that these differences could be correlated with a country's long-term commitment to the gold standard (ibid., p. 416). Countries which adhered faithfully to the gold standard were charged rates of interest which were only slightly above the British consol rate, whereas those countries which made only sporadic attempts to maintain convertibility and which altered their parities frequently were charged much higher rates of interest. Bordo and Rockoff concluded by saying, 'we interpret these findings to mean that adhering to gold was like the Good Housekeeping Seal of Approval' (p. 46). They are quick to point out that membership of the standard did not come cheap, and that those countries on the gold standard had to forego, for example, the flexibility which might enable them to react to factors such as supply-side shocks by following expansionary financial policies and altering their exchange rate. In the end, though, 'those countries that did not adhere to the rule [of the gold standard] faced greater supply shocks than those that did', and this might well have reduced their long-term growth prospects. Thus we have the not unexpected result that the decision to join the gold standard group hinged upon the perceived advantages of flexibility against those of stability. As Bordo and Rockoff point out, these same considerations are important today when emerging countries have to, as it were, recreate the 'Good Housekeeping Seal of Approval' by pegging their currencies to a stronger one such as the American dollar, or by establishing currency boards. The implications of this for the single European currency are obvious enough, especially as regards the Mediterranean states which have not maintained the growth rates, or the price stability and financial rectitude, of their more northerly partners in recent years. At the time of writing it is not clear whether the costs of joining the EMU in terms of flexibility are as yet matched by advantages of greater stability.

It is interesting to note here that the question of stability was one which often exercised the minds of bimetallists during the great debate of the 1890s. They tended to see the gold standard as highly inflexible, inelastic and unresponsive to the demands of their economies. Certainly the representatives of bimetallism in the midwestern and southern states of the United States saw the gold standard in such a light. A 'subtreasury' plan presented to the St Louis Convention of 1889, for example, sought to reduce 'the power of money to oppress'. It advocated a flexible currency standard that expanded and contracted according to the needs of the agricultural cycle, and a regional redistribution of the currency. Ritter (1997) sees this as a 'antimonopolist monetary system', aimed at maintaining an equal economy between farmers and industrialists, between the west and the east, and between producers and non-producers: a true democratization of the monetary system. One can only imagine the reception such a scheme would have enjoyed in the City of London, but the idea shows that the stability versus flexibility dichotomy was well appreciated in the era and that clearly western farmers were not experiencing the economic advantages that the stable gold standard bestowed upon the federation as a whole.

To what extent did the 'Good Housekeeping Seal of Approval' accelerate the spread of the gold standard in the nineteenth century? Since, thanks to Bordo and Rockoff, we now know more about differential interest rates in the late nineteenth century than contemporaries did, we can say that there were indeed clear-cut advantages to joining the gold standard, but we cannot say how widely these were understood at the time. To what extent British financiers furnished their would-be clients, such as Argentine dictators, with this kind of knowledge is not known. Latin American oligarchies were just as keen as the western farmers to retain maximum flexibility at all times, if for very different reasons. Dictators tend to live in the short term and are more concerned with the power, always determined by access to funds, to put down rebellion and retain their position, than with the long-term growth prospects of the economy. This may have changed somewhat towards the end of the nineteenth century when the South American oligarchies began to appreciate the distinct advantages that could be gained by railway-building, both to force up the price of their own land and to police the provinces against insurrection, and increasingly this became the responsibility of the state as much as of the British or French railway-builders. Even so, they tended to prefer the flexibility of a national currency against the inherent advantages of fixed exchange rates under the gold standard until very late in the century.

A case study which tends to support Bordo and Rockoff's findings is Martín-Aceña's inquiry (1994) into the Spanish economy and its external face between 1880 and 1914. Spain was on a bimetallic standard until 1883 and then suspended convertibility; thereafter it was never resumed. Spain thus never joined the gold standard and may be regarded, as it were, as a control component of the general experiment with gold monometallism in most of Europe at the end of the century. Martín-Aceña argues that this isolated Spain from the great international economy of the era. After 1883, according to Martín-Aceña (p. 155),

> the Spanish currency was detached from the international monetary system and capital mobility was seriously hampered ... until the turn of the century foreign investment ceased and therefore the economy lost the ability to earn the required surplus on capital account. Spain could have joined the gold bloc at any time and the Spanish authorities did not like a floating exchange rate for the peseta. After 1900 they intended to join the gold standard but the formal decision to resume convertibility was never made.

Autarky and isolation, concludes Martín-Aceña, exacted a high cost. Procrastination – or 'mañana' – clearly cost the Spanish the possession of the 'Good Housekeeping Seal of Approval' and deflected potential inward investment.

Bordo and Rockoff and Martín-Aceña are strong at explaining why successive peripheral economies might have moved into the gold bloc in the late nineteenth century, though it has to be said that the chronic international depression of the period cannot have encouraged countries such as Spain to accept a rigid system with an appreciating currency, and there were many other problems with the Spanish economy at this time. Spain moved out of bimetallism and into a financial wilderness, but would a bimetallic commodity coinage have served the same purpose, or is it the case that the British gold standard was essentially more rigid than any previous regime? Would a unilaterally bimetallic currency have attracted the 'Good Housekeeping Seal of Approval' and brought Spain into the centre ground of the European growth in the late nineteenth century? Was the British gold standard more 'respectable' than any other possible regime, and was this because of the unwritten 'rules of the game' which have been so much written about?

Not many of these questions are answerable at the present – not even Friedman has broached them – but Bordo and Rockoff's position is given further support by Miller (1993), who, in looking at the economic relationship between Britain and the Latin American republics in the period, has written that, '[in Brazil] as in Argentina, the adhesion to the Gold Standard was not just an acceptance of the orthodox liberalism espoused by foreign financiers. In both cases it occurred when the national government's desire for "respectability" [my inverted commas] and exchange rate stability coincided with exporters' fears of a rising currency due to the success of exports and foreign investment' (p. 176).

None of these considerations entered much into the great debate on currency of the 1890s because they simply did not concern the experts who contributed to it. The most comprehensive document of the period – the Report of the British Gold and Silver Commission of 1888 – is not concerned with it. Matters were simply not seen from the viewpoint of the peripheral countries, at least not in Europe: the United States, for the purposes of this analysis, can be regarded as part core and part periphery and hence, perhaps, the high degree of monetary schism there. One could argue that the western financial interests *should* have been interested in the circumstances of those peripheral countries which were accepting European capital, if only to understand the nature of the states they were dealing with. But the fact is that proponents of the gold standard seem never to have promulgated it on the basis that joining it would enable emerging countries to enjoy lower interest rates, or any other kind of special treatment. The metaphorical construct of a '*Good Housekeeping Seal of Approval*' has much validity as an explanatory device for modern economic historians but in some ways it is hopelessly ahistorical, in the sense that it is derived from the twentieth-century age of advertising and applied to a period largely innocent of such blandishments. If the offer of special treatment was ever made to, say, a South American dictator, in return for his country's currency joining the gold bloc, it was in an informal setting and was not known about, or credited with importance, by the theorists of the age. Perhaps this is because the great monetary debate was so explicitly, and ubiquitously, regarded as a debate between bimetallism (and sometimes silverism) and gold monometallism, and very few contributors were able to stray very far from this context. In other words, they were always thinking in terms of the respective merits of two different kinds of commodity standard, rather than looking at the merits of a common standard against a multiplicity of standards (that is, no common standard). And in so doing they failed to look at the ways in which one type of commodity standard might be preferable to others in terms of the advantages it enjoyed in helping to bring more countries in to the standard. There might, for example, have been a case for arguing that a statutory bimetallic standard would have been more successful in encouraging countries in Latin America and Asia to join a common (incidentally bimetallic) standard, for the simple reason that they would not have to make the dramatic shift from silver to gold. If there was such a case, it was never made. An explanation of these failings would also have to take full account of the highly imperfect state of knowledge in the nineteenth century compared with our own day, when for an example we have only to think of the wealth of data and political insight provided by a specialist press and available to foreign investors about the countries they are interested in funding, in an age enjoying the benefits of the Information Revolution, compared with a hundred years ago, when would-be investors might have only the scantest of knowledge about the regions of recent European settlement they were helping to develop. Ultimately (but not here) we might have to consider also the massive differences between the cultural contexts of the 1890s and the 1990s which explain the totally different attitude sets towards 'other countries' which prevailed in each period.

Scrambles, drifts and lock-ins

Other economic historians have been concerned with the spread of the gold standard *through* the core and *from* the core countries and *to* the peripheral countries in the late nineteenth century. For Gallarotti (1993), the extension through the core countries was in its nature a 'scramble' for gold. This scramble, paralleling the 'scramble for Africa' which was happening at the same time, was 'essentially a phenomenon that characterised the developed world' (he presumably regards the United States as 'developed' in the 1870s). Monetary status – the seal of approval of membership of the gold standard – was a necessity for the developed world but a mere luxury for the less-developed nations. If Bordo and Rockoff are correct, this seems a perverse starting-point: the emerging nations' hunger for capital can scarcely be said to be a 'luxury'. But Gallarotti's background principle for explaining the spread of the gold standard was the general redistribution of power from high-inflation groups (agricultural interests) to low-inflation groups (urban capitalists) that was then under way. Hence, according to Gallarotti, those countries where the former groups still predominated tended to be hesitant about joining the gold standard, whereas those where the latter held sway – the advanced industrial countries – 'scrambled' towards the gold standard and the monetary probity which accompanied it. The notion of a 'scramble' derives from the fact that there was considerable nervousness about silver, which before had been the main monetary metal:

> The compelling structural changes in the developed world in the nineteenth century created an environment ripe for monetary regime transformation after 1850. It was not until the late 1860s and 1870s, however, that a structurally predisposed developed world encoun-

tered the proximate catalysts that consummated the transformation of monetary standards. These catalysts represented various critical events (which were principally coterminous with developments in the market for the precious metals) that created and compounded nervousness over the future trends in the value of silver.

(Gallarotti, 1994, p. 31)

For Gallarotti, then, the demonetization of silver was part of a 'common trend' in the monetary history of the nineteenth century. This trend was about 'nations protecting their monetary systems against disturbances in the market for metals'. Simply put, they switched to gold after 1870 because of the fear that silver would continue to fall in value in the future and no longer offered a secure basis to a standard. They were fearful of having to maintain a depreciating silver standard because of 'multiple undesirable consequences', namely: a depreciating exchange rate against gold-standard nations; a depletion of international reserves (silver-standard nations tended to deplete their reserves when adjusting with gold-standard nations); and inflation. Exactly how internal inflation might occur when nations were on full commodity standards of any kind is not explained.

According to Gallarotti (1994, p. 38), after about 1860 there was a growing 'structural predisposition' towards gold: 'The worst-case scenarios portrayed the maintenance of silver and bimetallism when the decline in the value of silver was large, rapid and secular'. It was such misgivings which explain the transition to gold and why it was so rapid after 1870, and Gallarotti used the term, 'monetary chaingang' to describe the fact that 'movement of any one or a few nations to gold in this period of nervousness would assure that the others would follow suit'. Monetary experts expressed 'alarm and apprehensions, and even panic' about developments in the metals market that could have worrying consequences for national monetary systems. Relying on the words of one William Sumner (an Ivy League intellectual who supported the urban–industrial, east-coast, conservative Democrats), Gallarotti (ibid., p. 38) characterizes the shift to gold in the American's terms: 'they seemed to be running over one another's heels as fast as they could to get rid of silver, because the one who sold first would get the best price'. In fact, William Sumner was far from being a disinterested observer since he was a gold monometallist who wanted to discredit silver, and we have already seen above how men in the late nineteenth century could display a highly emotional antipathy towards an innocent metal. His description is not one that would fit the European metal markets for the whole of the period concerned. Most experts in Europe tended to see the fall of silver, as I have argued, in terms rather of its increasing supply, and on much of the continent silver represented the conservative position characterized more by (well-grounded) fears about joining an appreciating gold standard. One has only to think of Bleichröder and his supporters in imperial Germany at this juncture. And we cannot say that the German authorities were quite so keen to offload silver when in fact they retained copious reserves of the metal long after conversion to gold. Clearly, Germany's decision to shift to gold was not a panic measure, but rather a considered one in the context of the war with France which put monetary reform on to the political agenda. However, we can agree with Gallarotti that once Britain and Germany were installed on the gold standard there was no choice for 'little Holland' to follow suit and join the 'monetary chaingang' to gold.

Milivoje Panić (1992), an economist, saw the situation in a similar light to Gallarotti but more in terms of the need of the international economy to sacrifice what he calls 'monetary diversity'. He suggests that the gold standard triumphed because it was the most stable system, and suggests a modern inversion of Gresham's Law: 'good money' drives 'bad money' out of circulation in the long run:

> It is for this reason that the system adopted by the strongest economy (or economies), with its relatively low rate of inflation and 'strong' currency, will tend to be widely imitated in a world in which levels of international economic integration and interdependence are both high and continuously rising ... it is the monetary standard and practices employed by the dominant economy that will in the end come to dictate national and international monetary arrangements.
>
> (p. 23)

For Panić, a contributor who has been taken very seriously in the context of the modern debate over the single European currency, the drift to gold was a movement towards a rational system based upon the British model. Nations sought stability and Britain exemplified stability. In some ways this is not very far removed from what I have called the seductive syllogism: that because Britain was the first successful industrial state and at the same time employed a gold currency, there must be a causal connection between the two. If Panić is right, other nations were indeed seduced by the syllogism. On the other hand, it could just be a formal acceptance by Panić of *post hoc ergo propter hoc*, and there is a highly deterministic underpinning to his reasoning:

> One of the most obvious lessons from the gold standard experience is that it is increases in international specialisation and trade – in other words in economic links between countries – that *sooner or later* [my italics] create the need for a single unit of account, either a commodity standard or a common currency ... Monetary diversity, with the risk that independently determined policies will amplify exchange rate volatility, thus becomes increasingly incompatible in a dynamic international economy with an efficient use of resources

within the continuously rising levels of integration and interdependence.

(Ibid., p. 121)

Like so many other commentators, Panić fails to point out that the French bimetallic standard of pre-1870 would have fulfilled all the requirements he outlines, but then his brief was not to look at alternatives to the gold standard, rather it was to compare the nineteenth-century gold standard with its modern equivalents. Nevertheless, the fact that the exchange ratio between the precious metals was invariant between 1815 and 1870 means that any country on any commodity standard could benefit from exchange-rate stability. The French parachute enabled all currencies which were convertible into specie to enjoy a fixed exchange rate. Panić assumes that it was necessary for the gold standard to become generalized for this (general fixed exchange rates) to be true, but this clearly was not necessary. If we were to agree with Friedman, or Schumpeter long before him, that bimetallism would have performed a superior stabilizing role to gold, then bimetallism engendered 'good currencies' which in Panić's grand inversion of Gresham's Law should have driven out bad (inferior) currencies such as those based purely on gold.

In order to explain how an (arguably) superior system such as bimetallism should have driven out an (arguably) inferior one such as gold monometallism, it has been suggested that gold benefited from a kind of 'lock-in' process in the late nineteenth century (Kemp and Wilson, 1999). In this explanation, the switch to gold took place as a result of a series of self-reinforcing accidents of history. The spread of the gold standard is seen as a sequential movement by individual nations and as having come about not as a co-ordinated international movement (as is widely agreed), nor by being driven by widely perceived rational ends. By analogy with technological change (such as the spread of the QWERTY keyboard or the VHS videotape, both of which represented inferior but successful technology), it is argued that gold took the lead at a propitious time and was able to benefit from such a 'lock-in' after about 1870. Countries which joined the gold standard began to benefit from network externalities, and these externalities grew as the system itself grew, thus effectively preventing them from ever turning back to silver or bimetallism, irrespective of the possibility, or probability, that these alternatives may have performed better. It is difficult not to agree that the gold standard was implicated in some way in the 'Great Depression' of 1873–96, about which incidentally, Panić is silent.

Orientalism and 'bullion prejudice'

By the end of the 1870s, by all reckonings, the western world, as we understand the term, was committed to the monometallic gold standard. This commitment would survive secular economic depression, a sustained intellectual and theoretical attack from many quarters during the 'great debate' of the 1890s, and the 'threat' of massive new gold discoveries at the end of the century in South Africa and the Klondike. Commitment to the gold standard, if not the gold standard itself, even survived the First World War. As we have seen, the spread of the gold standard to the so-called periphery was a more uncertain and hesitant process. The gold standard may have acted as a '*Good Housekeeping Seal of Approval*', but many nations could not afford to buy in to this imprimatur. Thus India remained on silver, despite the tutelage of the great imperial gold-standard state until well into the 1890s, and the world's most populous country, China, stayed on silver until the 1930s. Whereas most of Western Europe (with the exception of paper Spain) was on gold by the end of the 1870s, the East largely remained on silver until 1900 and later. The same can be said for South America, where powerful silver-mining interests helped prevent the spread of gold even to Argentina, by the 1890s one of the world's richest countries. So the gold-standard club of 1870–1900 definitely represented a 'premier league' of rich European states and their satellites, the British 'white-settler' dominions, and the United States. It is not really surprising that the notion developed that the gold standard was for rich, developed countries, and silver was for backward, primary-producing, underdeveloped, countries. Although the gold–silver split was not an entirely East–West dichotomy, it may be appropriate to use the term 'orientalism' to describe the prejudices that grew up around 'gold supremacism' in the late nineteenth century. For the modern Arabist writer, Edward Said, orientalism describes the mind-set of European imperialists towards the 'exotic' non-European world, especially in the nineteenth century (though most certainly also today), and encapsulates the idea of East and West as two wholly different and separate cultures incapable of assimilation except on the terms of a dominant West, and of the 'civilized' white man. Indeed, Said's orientalism is found in its most virulent form in such writings as the Englishman Rudyard Kipling's conception of the 'white man'; he writes:

> Being a White Man was therefore an idea and a reality. It involved a reasoned position towards both the white and non-white worlds. It meant, in the colonies, speaking in a certain way, behaving according to a code of regularities, and even feeling certain things

and not others ... it was an agency for the expression, diffusion
and implementation of policy towards the world.
(Said, 1978, p. 227; italics added)

It is not surprising, then, if the 'white man' or the 'orientalist' might
seek to keep the non-white in his place by preventing him from joining
certain exclusive clubs and organizations. This has always been, after
all, a major feature of imperialism and apartheid. The British imperialist might want to categorize the gold standard as yet one more of
Britain's gifts to the world (along with the steam engine and cricket),
but it was one which should be disseminated to the non-whites, or
orientals, only when the whites deemed them to be ready to make
good use of it. The spread of the gold standard from 1870 created a
two-tier system and to some extent this was aligned along an East–
West axis (or North–South axis in the Americas). At the 1878
International Monetary Conference in Paris, the Swiss financier, Charles
Feer-Herzog, was described by Russell (1898, p. 218) in the following
terms:

> He believed in the future of gold as sole legal tender money of
> unlimited coinage, and in the future of silver as mere fractional
> coin, because silver was an inferior metal, ill adapted to the needs
> of higher civilisation, inconvenient for private persons, only fit as a
> standard for backward nations, a metal the value of which had
> constantly been depreciating for four centuries and which, when
> maintained in the rank of legal money by civilised peoples, caused
> in a certain way the emission of paper money.

We have seen in Chapter Five how the United States delegates were
deeply embarrassed by the mere suggestion that they should seek a
silver alliance with the 'backward' countries of Latin America and
India. But perhaps an even more telling point is the fact that none of the
'backward' or 'peripheral' countries had been invited to the conference
in the first place. The only countries represented were European (France,
Britain, Austria-Hungary, Belgium, Greece, Italy, Holland, Russia, Swe-
den and Norway, and Switzerland) and the United States. This alone
makes the nineteenth-century gold standard an exclusive club.

It should be noted that the admirable Francis Walker took urgent
issue with Feer-Herzog in his vision of a two-tier monetary world,
arguing that only two or three 'territorially extensive countries' in the
world were strong enough to maintain a full gold standard 'upon true
economic principles' (and incidentally he did not consider Germany to
be one of them), and he added: 'If those nations only are to be called
civilised which are prepared to receive gold as their principal money,
their sole money of full value, we must, perforce, take a somewhat

lower view than we have been wont to do of the progress of mankind' (Russell, 1898, p. 236).

However, we can be quite sure that Feer-Herzog's position was far from extraordinary in any sense, and that his orientalist prejudices were not limited to the Alpine state. Indeed, it is evident in many of the thousands of pamphlets and articles that were published during the great debate, and it was prejudice perpetrated by contributors of all kinds. When various 'backward' countries such as Chile (between 1895 and 1898) attempted and failed to maintain a gold currency, these prejudices must have been further strengthened, despite the fact that it was ostensibly in the interest of British financiers to see the South American republics adopt the '*Good Housekeeping Seal of Approval*' (see Miller, 1993).

It should also be noted that Lombard Street's enthusiasm for gold monometallism did not extend to India. It seems that London financiers were fearful of the prospect of a drain of gold from Britain in the event of the subcontinent being allowed to change metals. While the Indian silver rupee was suspended in the mid-1890s, the question of what do with the rupee was much discussed in the City, Whitehall and the Houses of Parliament. Kynaston has reported that 'the official mind still wanted India on the gold standard, but Lombard Street, it seemed, was cooling by the hour' (Kynaston, 1995). True, the situation in 1898 was much complicated by an imminent war between Spain and the United States, which might lead to 'dear bread' and the possibility of a drain on gold at such a time was unthinkable. Such are the vicissitudes which shaped monetary history as much as every other sphere of human activity. India was instead placed on a gold exchange standard as a compromise, to save on the use of gold, but only after several years of a 'forced currency', with a rupee detached from its silver base. So the City's opposition to a gold standard for India was pragmatic as much as ideological: the financial establishment possibly saw an Indian gold exchange standard as seeing off bimetallism as well as placating the Indian government. This may not have represented 'gold supremacism' or 'bullion prejudice', but the notion that Lombard Street wanted to see the whole world subscribe to a '*Good Housekeeping Seal of Approval*' should be severely modified.

In the not-so-distant past, European adventurers had been able to exploit oriental naïvety about bullion in the 'peripheral' world. For example, in Tokugawa Japan in the 1850s the government (of Japan) had exercised a monopoly over the minting of precious metals and had fixed their own silver–gold ratio at an astonishing 5:1, presumably because more gold was mined in the Japanese islands than silver, relative to the rest of the world. This was at a time, as we have seen, that the two metals were still exchanging at about 15.5:1 in Europe. Once westerners heard of this, they realized the profitable arbitrage possibilities and it is even argued that these were a greater incentive to dealing with Japan than trade itself, at least for a period:

> The possibilities of so wide a discrepancy were not overlooked by foreign merchants. They imported Mexican dollars and exchanged them weight for weight with Japanese token silver coinage; they then exchanged the latter for gold coins at a ratio of 5:1, shipping the gold to Shanghai and there bought silver at 16:1. It may well be true that the initial attraction of foreign merchants to Japan was stimulated as much by the prospect of profit from exchange transactions as by that gain of trade in commodities.
>
> (Hyde, 1973, p. 154)

This is to say nothing of the fact that an overvalued Japanese silver coinage meant that tea, silk and copperware could be purchased by Europeans at artificially low prices because of the Japanese metal ratio. By the Meiji period these conditions had changed, but Lombard Street must have retained a memory of the easy pickings which its merchants had financed, and such memories would have strengthened existing orientalist prejudices.

Ultimately, however, we can probably agree with Kynaston that the City opposed a gold standard for India because of its sheer conservatism: it opposed almost all change. In any case, by the 1900s most of the so-called 'backward countries' had been moved on to the gold standard and only China remained outside the fold. Even in South and Central America, where silver-mining interests were still powerful, gold convertibility was introduced. This does not negate the importance of the 'orientalist' bullion prejudice. The idea that gold was for developed and silver for underdeveloped countries was an important one at the critical period, from the 1870s to the 1890s, and helped reinforce the commitment of the powerful western economies to gold monometallism. In a perverse way it might also have been important in the minds of those dictators and oligarchs who took their countries into the gold bloc once the battle was won by the yellow metal. It is, after all, as an American Marx once observed, the exclusivity of a club which makes one want to join it, but we can only guess at the precise contents of many a conversation which must have taken place between a British businessman and an Argentine statesman wherein the latter was warned that if he expected a continuing stream of foreign investment in the future, he really ought to switch to gold convertibility.

Mineral discoveries and cycles

It is well understood, even if we do not subscribe to the Kondratieff Cycle, that there are in economic history observable waves of activity, from the short-term trade or business cycle to the much longer investment, or Kuznets Cycles of perhaps a 20–25-year periodicity. However, the nineteenth century was a time of relative price stability, recently described as the 'Victorian equilibrium' since the period of price stasis almost exactly covers the reign of the great queen. For one historian it was the sheer 'underlying stability' of the era which 'increased the visibility of many cyclical rhythms' (Hackett Fischer, 1996, p. 158). If, as bimetallists and others believed, it was the spread of the gold standard and the tendency of gold to appreciate that explain the sustained and general fall in prices which accompanied the success of gold as a monetary metal, then, as we have argued, we do not need any other explanation of the 'Great Depression' of 1873–96 and we can confidently apply Occam's Razor.

Yet modern economic historians tend to discount purely monetary, or monetarist, explanations of price movements in history. Even Hackett Fischer concluded that though 'monetary factors did indeed have an impact on prices throughout the [Victorian] period, they did not create the equilibrium itself' (ibid., p. 169). It is difficult to see how some purely adventitious factors, such as the supply of the precious metals themselves, or dramatic changes in currency policy, such as Germany's in 1871, *could* have worked in the direction of equilibrium. Supranational forces, such as international agreements on standardizing monetary policies, or the sequential (but perhaps chaotic) scramble for gold, might have done so, but these are not investigated by Hackett Fischer.[12]

To what extent, then, should modern economic historians concern themselves with factors such as the supply of the precious metals – a major desideratum for nearly all contributors to the great debate of the 1890s, including gold monometallists, silverites and bimetallists? Each thought that their policies would definitively influence prices, one way or another, in the future. Yet economic historians often seem to tell us that they could not have done. Most economic historians seem to be 'Playfairite' in their assumption that 'real' economic forces, such as the spread of cheap transport systems, or modern mass-production methods, were the true causes of long-term trends in prices and costs, and just about everything else. Of course, changes in the supplies of the precious metals can be offset, or more than offset, by, for example, changes in monetary policies, as we have seen. The 'price equilibrium' of the Victorian era occurred during an unprecedented increase in the supply of both gold and silver, and sometimes there were massive spurts in the production of each (gold in the 1850s and 1890s; silver in the 1870s). So, despite the nervousness about silver prices which Gallarotti (1984) has outlined, it would seem that the long historical period (1850–1900) which saw the greatest increases in specie production also witnessed the greatest price stability. Perhaps we should not be surprised by this when we consider that (even accepting a vulgar monetarist view of history) one of the two great specie metals (the greater of the two specie metals) was effectively demonetized after 1870 and sterilized as a form of money throughout most of the world.

Despite all this, we can say with some certainty that if the bimetallists or silverites had had their way in the 1870s, nineteenth-century price trends would have been very different. One is inclined to leave counterfactual history well alone, but a brave Milton Friedman did attempt to estimate the likely effects of the United States continuing a bimetallic standard after 1873. But whilst he suggested that a consistent application of a legal ratio could have kept the gold–silver exchange standard at roughly equal to the legal ratio in France in the period 1815–73 (15.5:1), he decided that the exercise was subject to such wide margins of error that the estimates could not be deemed worthwhile (Friedman, 1992). However, Friedman does believe that the United States could have successfully taken over the role of the French parachute, a highly significant conclusion and one which has not been discredited so far. It means that silver need not have been driven out as a monetary metal. And one is bound to doubt if the price level would have fallen as it did after 1873 if this had been the case. Schumpeter (who was generally sympathetic to bimetallism in his historical writings) and most mainstream economists who have followed him have believed that money was in the end a passive factor and that output was ultimately independent of monetary expansion, and Foreman-Peck (1983) has pointed out that the period of fastest growth in the British monetary stock (from the late 1840s to the late 1850s) did not correspond to the fastest growth of GNP at current or constant prices or with the price index, which was in the decade from the late 1850s.

Friedman was unable to obtain a meaningful conclusion because he could not produce estimates of some of the key variables. Among these were the determinants of the fractions of gold and silver production which go into monetary- and non-monetary use. It is difficult to see why he bothered to publish his paper, given the lack of these essential determinants. Other missing determinants were those which governed gold and silver production. More can be said about these without re-entering Friedman's counterfactual exercise.

Some years ago Blainey (1969) suggested that mineral production was not as accidental as economists such as Schumpeter, Keynes,

Tinbergen and others had assumed. Kondratieff had been brave enough to infer that gold discoveries were partly dependent upon the price cycle. He had thought that gold-mining was least profitable when the price of other commodities was high (as in 1873) and most profitable when the price of other commodities was low. Under the gold standard the latter meant that the price of gold was high, as in, say, 1896. Kondratieff's assumptions about the behaviour of gold and silver prospectors, however, turned out to be faulty, but Blainey was able to show that in Australia mineral (gold in this case) discoveries tended to be made most often during slumps in the trade cycle. The reasons he suggested can be interpolated as follows:

1. Low interest rates aided discoveries by providing cheap capital to prospecting organizations.
2. As the price of gold was fixed under the gold standard, active gold mines were amongst the few enterprises whose profits did not fall away during a slump.
3. Labour tended to be cheaper and more plentiful during a slump; local industries tended to make more men unemployed.
4. Landowners and farmers were more likely to take an interest in any evidence of mineral deposits on their land when there was a slump, as their usual economic activities were less profitable.
5. The prospect of unemployment made prospecting more attractive to would-be adventurers.

Blainey was certain that most finds made in Australia between 1840 and 1930 were made by people 'actively searching' for minerals, rather than, as the folk-lore would have it, by young boys throwing stones at crows and unearthing a precious deposit. In any case, accidental finds were often ignored if the local economy was thriving: a farmer might, for example, notice evidence of copper on his land but ignore it if his men were profitably employed looking after the sheep. Blainey saw gold prospecting as the most important type of mineral exploration and most likely to be related to the economy generally because of gold's tendency (under the gold standard) to appreciate in price during a recession. So in a way the bimetallists of the 1890s were correct when they judged that in the future new gold would be found and silver would thus become relatively scarce.

But despite this, Blainey (1969, p. 311) came to the conclusion that the history of gold discovery does not correlate in any clear way with the long-term trend in prices, or, as he put it, 'the key does not fit the lock'. He wrote:

It is true that a burst of Australian gold discovery came in the early 1890s, when the world price of gold was extremely favourable, but it is also true that a burst of copper discoveries came in the 1840s when the world price of copper was extremely unfavourable. It is true that major tin discoveries came early in the 1870s when the price of tin was abnormally high but the same period witnessed an even more important series of gold discoveries at the very time when the purchasing power of gold was as weak as that of tin was strong.

The price of metals *should* have affected the likelihood of finding a new mining field, all things being equal. But it was case of *ceteris non paribus*. Deterministic theories of mineral discovery are in the end exploded by the fact that the discovery of rich ores is always an economic blessing and 'could amply compensate for poor metal prices' (ibid., p. 312). In the end Blainey surmised that the rhythm of discovery he had outlined tells us more about the way that mineral finds could rescue a colonial economy from depression than about anything that was happening in the international economy. Another factor not mentioned by Blainey is the obvious point that gold prospectors were quite likely to find silver in their searches, and silver prospectors were quite likely to find gold: often, as in Nevada in the 1870s, the two precious metals were found side by side in large quantities. Since, however, it was often the case that prospectors were nearly always looking for gold *in the first instance*, as it makes sense to look for the most valuable metal, there is a sense in which gold prospecting and gold discovery is a special case, and not therefore subject to any generalizations about metal discovery. Furthermore, the existence of the gold standard itself gave a special quality to gold: it was the only commodity whose value would always appreciate during a depression, and one wonders therefore if Kondratieff was not after all correct to draw attention to the gold discoveries of the 1890s. We may need a different theory of discovery under a gold standard than, say, under a period of fiat money, but Blainey did not broach this question. Of course, one could go further and argue that if all prospectors are gold prospectors and if the gold standard regime gave an incentive to gold prospecting, at least during a general price depression, then *all* metals are most likely to be found during a depression if it was in the era of a gold standard. In such a case we should not be surprised that the 1890s was indeed a period of rich metal finds in several parts of the world.

None of this, however, helps us to explain the fall of silver and the consolidation of gold in the last quarter of the nineteenth century. All we can say is that, historically, a new supply of one of the precious metals would normally push a generally bimetallic world (as before 1870) in the direction of that metal, as a high fraction of the new supply would be minted into coins. Thus the new gold discoveries of the 1850s *eventually* pushed the world in the direction of gold currencies. For a variety of reasons, outlined above, this did not happen with the new silver of the 1870s. Instead, the world was weaned off the monetary metal with the greatest historical claim to being the commodity of the standard. The French parachute, which had facilitated the drawing of both precious metals to the world's mints, broke down and the Americans (despite 'helping out' silver from time to time) were as yet unable to provide a replacement. Gold took on a special lustre as it was increasingly identified with modern industrial countries, and silver was seen as the metal of backward, 'uncivilized' nations. The gold standard was refined as the centrepiece of the rapidly expanding, multilateral, international economy, which is admired to this day, and even some 'peripheral' countries in Asia and South America were drawn into the ambit of gold when it became profitable for the core countries to allow them into this exclusive group. This was especially true when many of the new territories of recent settlement required larger and larger volumes of European capital to open up and develop them. These large sums in turn required that the new countries provide evidence of their financial probity; for Bordo and Rockoff joining the gold standard provided irrefutable proof of this. As the gold standard expanded, it is possible that a degree of lock-in occurred, as the external network economies of possessing a gold currency proved irresistible. As Gallarotti argues, there was a 'scramble for gold', which paralleled the scramble for empire in the last quarter of the nineteenth century.

Notes

1. J. Watt, 'Memoir of Matthew Boulton', in Smiles (1847).
2. J. Riesser, *The German Banks and their Concentration, in Connection with the Economic Development of Germany*, 1911. Cited by Kindleberger (1984), p. 123.
3. *The Economist*, 12 April 1879.
4. Ibid.
5. Ibid.
6. Ibid
7. Royal Commission on the Relative Prices of Gold and Silver, Final Report, 1888.
8. Ibid.
9. Ibid., Part I, p. 85.
10. Ibid., p. 105.
11. Ibid.
12. Hackett Fischer does not mention the gold standard in 536 pages of monetary history.

CHAPTER SEVEN

The great monetary debate and the decline of bimetallism

MABEL CHILTERN: At lunchtime I saw by the glare in his eye that he
was going to propose again, and I just managed to check him by
assuring him that I was a bimetallist. Fortunately I don't know
what bimetallism means and I don't believe anybody else does
either.

(Oscar Wilde, *An Ideal Husband*, 1895)

We have seen that bimetallism, in at least one of the term's meanings, was
the order of the day through most – perhaps three-quarters – of the
nineteenth century; that between the end of the Napoleonic Wars and the
early 1870s this was a satisfactory state of affairs for most countries of
the world. We can even argue that it was the existence of bimetallic
arbitrage, in countries such as France, which allowed other nations such
as Britain to operate a gold standard. French bimetallism – the 'French
parachute' – steadied the rate at which the two precious metals exchanged and eased the monetary world through the potential disasters of
the mid-century gold finds of California and Australia and the silver finds
such as the Comstock Lode of Nevada of 1859. Had it not been for the
many soft landings afforded by the French system, monometallic Britain
would have faced enormous difficulties trading with non-gold-standard
countries or regions such as India or South America, or indeed many
parts of Europe. At any rate, this historical view was one of the most
powerful and cogent arguments of the bimetallic school of the late nineteenth century, and naturally such an interpretation was always contested
by the adherents of the gold standard. Today it would be difficult to
sympathize with the British orthodox school's view of their recent economic history (though this in itself does not invalidate their stance on
monometallism: there were other reasons than historical interpretation
that might be adduced in their favour). Kindleberger (1984), for one,
fully accepts what we might call the bimetallic view of monetary history
before 1873. Writing of the French bimetallic standard and the British
gold standard, he says: 'the two systems meshed smoothly and automati-
cally in response to the large increase in gold production that followed
the discoveries in California and Australia. Some estimates suggest that
world gold production rose ten-fold [as a result of them]'(p. 64).

Clearly, the supply of the two precious metals had little impact on the ratio at which they exchanged before 1873, and de Cecco (1974, p. 42) has also recognized this:

> Between 1814 and 1870, the price of silver had not been much of a problem: from 60 11/16d in 1814 it had dropped to only 60 9/16d in 1870. Nor had it ever gone below a minimum price of 59 1/2d .... The annual supply of silver between 1811 and 1880 increased almost fivefold. But gold supply in the same period increased by much more. In 1801–1810, silver production was 50 times that of gold, in 1841–45 only 15 times, and in 1851–1860, only 5 times. This drastic [relative] increase in gold production was not, however, accompanied by a decrease in the price of gold in any way comparable to the fall in the price of silver which took place in the last three decades of the nineteenth century.

More recently, Cottrell (1992) has emphasized the relative stability of the metallic ratio before the 1870s, though he rightly adds that it came under severe pressure at times, pointing out that the upward pressure on the silver price resulting from the relative increase in gold supplies encouraged the formation of a silver-standard school in England long before 1870 and that support for them came from such luminaries as Cobden and Chevalier. He also suggests that France's continued adherence to a statutory (15.5:1) ratio during these years (the 1850s and 1860s) effectively forced that country on to a *de facto* gold standard: '[a] complete reversal of the situation which had prevailed since 1803, as during the first half of the nineteenth century, gold had been undervalued by the French mint ratio ... ' (ibid., p. 223).

Whether this should be seen as part of the normal working of a statutory bimetallic system (the view of the bimetallic school) or the inevitable and unfortunate tendency of bimetallism to revert to one or other form of monometallism (the gold-standard school) is not discussed by Cottrell, but these interpretations underpinned the debate which was to come to a head in Britain and elsewhere in the late nineteenth century.

But it is a matter of hard historical fact that after 1873 there began a decline in the gold price of silver which truly threatened the whole of the trading world. Indeed, one could argue that the fall of silver was the single most important economic fact of the period 1870–1900.

The great debate

As the decline in the price of silver gathered pace in the 1870s and 1880s, and as various nations demonetized silver, thereby accelerating its decline, a debate took place as to how to respond. This was not an

organized debate in any way. It consisted of contributions from a remarkably wide range of sources and took many different forms. It has
been pointed out that the issue spawned possibly more publications
than any other economic controversy in the whole of the nineteenth
century (Green, 1988). Pamphlets were written by thousands of interested organizations and individuals, ranging from lawyers and chartered
accountants in Lancashire cotton towns to Indian mill-managers and
Parsee businessmen, and from American academics to merchant bankers in London's Square Mile. The debate eventually centred around the
idea of replacing the gold standard with a bimetallic one, though in
parts of the world, notably the United States, the preference was often
for silver over gold. The contributions were many and varied because
the impact of the great monetary issue, which I have called the 'fall of
silver', was global and pervasive and recognized no national, social or
economic barriers. Indian plantation-owners were as wont as Lancashire cotton operatives or Oklahoma farmers to define the monetary
problem as a 'bread-and-butter' issue that ought to command the attention of everyone.

Thus we have seen that there were important write-in debates to *The
Times*, the most authoritative printed organ of the civilized world, as
early as 1889 (see Chapter Two). Monographs were written by experts,
self-appointed and otherwise, promoting various prescriptions or elabo-
rating upon some particular monetary nostrum. Green (1988) estimated
that even before the monetary controversy reached its peak (in the mid-
1890s) it was generating approximately one publication every two days
between 1881 and 1891. In a sense this is not surprising, for, as Green
(ibid., p. 590) points out, 'The central issue at stake in both the bimetallic and Indian currency debates was whether or not Britain should
retain the gold standard'.

Governments around the world set up committees of inquiry to look
into the matter, or existing committees (such as the British Royal Commission on Agricultural Depression) found themselves having to consider
monetary conditions in their findings and recommendations. World-
renowned experts such as Charles Dana-Horton and Francis Walker of
the United States, noted speakers on the subject, conducted international tours to spread the gospel of the dual standard, or to outline their
pet schemes or monetary philosophies. Businessmen and financiers sought
constantly to influence politicians and, at national elections, such as the
British General Elections of 1892 and 1895, local and national pressure
groups aimed to bring candidates 'up to speed' on the great monetary
issues of the day. Groups such as the City and the New York bankers
could expect to exert a direct influence over monetary outcomes, but
when they feared losing that influence they would resort to setting up

their own pressure groups to defend their position. Thus even the City was forced to respond to the bimetallic onslaught by setting up the Gold Standard Defence Association of 1894.

Long before then a bimetallic league had been set up, around 1881 to 1882 according to Cottrell, to argue in favour of radical monetary reform in Britain. This was supported early on by such groups as farmers and foreign merchants in the South American trade. Eventually it came to be dominated, as we shall see, by the Lancashire cotton merchants and was then widely supported by the cotton operatives' unions. Eventually its headquarters were located in Manchester, though there is some doubt about when it actually moved there (Wilson, 1990). Then at the highest level there were the international monetary conferences of the period: 1878, 1881, 1889 and 1892, all of which were convened in direct response to the silver crisis and the dislocation of the metallic ratio as a result of the fall of silver. Cottrell has recently dealt with these, arguing that the 1878 International Monetary Conference had led to some measures which had effectively lengthened the monetary life of silver. Germany proclaimed at the meeting that it would stop selling the silver it had received as an indemnity after the Franco-Prussian War of 1870–71, and Italy agreed to continue coining silver. The Americans had already agreed to purchase silver, despite being on a *de facto* gold standard. And it must be concluded that factors such as these eased the fall of silver in the absence of an effective French parachute. For most of these countries currency matters were a source of repeated concern in the nineteenth century. Social upheavals such as the Revolutions of 1848 had naturally tended to undermine currency systems and the existence of an ever-extending frontier in North America must have had much the same economic effects in the United States. Together with the Civil War of 1861–64, these were factors which continually threatened to puncture the course of monetary development in the new republic, for as we must appreciate, currency and sovereignty are always intimately bound together.

As we have seen in Chapter Two, Britain had been something of an exception here and presents us with an almost polar opposite of the American case, at least before 1880. Britain had settled down with the gold standard and was by and large comfortable with it. The Napoleonic Wars had necessarily driven Britain off the commodity standard and there had followed a series of debates about how resumption should be achieved. The debates over the Bullion Report are of great interest to historians and, if nothing else, show that support for the gold monometallism was not always as monolithic as is often assumed. However, these debates took place within very narrow social and political limits, and as Kindleberger (1984, p. 63) has concluded:

> In the long run, after recovery in 1824, resumption at the 1717
> price of gold rooted the gold standard deeply in the British eco-
> nomic habit system, defeating supporters of silver, bimetallism and
> inconvertibility and rejecting any, and all, adjustments proposed,
> to ease the transition.

One might go further than this and say that the British ultimately came
to see the gold standard as almost part of the natural order of things: if
free trade was accepted as an article of faith, then the gold standard was
part of the divine providence which accommodated it. Checkland (1957)
has shown that this monetary orthodoxy was rarely challenged by men
of the City even after the mid-century metal finds had threatened to
bring it down.

The real challenge to gold orthodoxy emerged much later in the
century and came to a head in the 1890s. Since it came to be dominated
by Lancashire we might refer to it as the Lancashire school of bimetallism, and what gave rise to it was the price mechanism. Since 1969,
when S. B. Saul wrote his short but highly influential volume on the
'Myth of the Great Depression, there has existed a virtual consensus
among economic historians that the years 1873 to 1896 should no
longer be regarded as a unitary period of British economic history. Saul
sought to deny the notion that there had been a prolonged depression in
these years by arguing that many of the characteristics of the period
were merely typical of the nineteenth century as a whole, if slightly
intensified. The tendency to follow Saul was probably increased by the
realization that the term 'Great Depression' perhaps ought to be reserved for the altogether more pervasive phenomenon that occurred in
the interwar years. At any rate, Saul's stricture has allowed some British
economic historians to fall in line with American colleagues, who of
course use the term to denote the 1930s. But even Saul had to admit
that in one respect there was good reason to pick out the years 1873–96
as exceptional: the 'drastic fall' in prices which 'for some commodities
and products continued unabated until the late 1890s' (ibid., p. 14).
Chief among these commodities was cotton, and indeed the price fall
for Lancashire cotton began even earlier than 1873, arguably in 1864
(though interrupted in 1869–72) and continued until 1898. Farnie (1979,
p. 171) has said that 'the gross volume of [Lancashire] cotton production contracted unsteadily as prices sank and did not surpass the peak
volumes attained in 1872 until 1904'.

Contemporaries blamed the cotton-price fall on a wide range of
factors. Farnie listed these as: overproduction, underconsumption, foreign competition, hostile tariffs and fluctuations in the price of silver.
Overproduction was often mentioned in the context of the massive
expansion in cotton capacity which had occurred during the peak of

1869–72 when many new mills had been added to the Lancashire skyline. Underconsumption (not a term used much before 1900) presumably referred to the fact that Britain had not succeeded in penetrating important markets such as China, whose population were thus 'underconsuming' cotton. Foreign competition was a constant feature of a period when Lancashire had eagerly supplied new producers with all the machinery they needed to compete against them, and this was used, predictably, as a means of import substitution of Lancashire exports. Lancashire traders were acutely aware at all times of the spread of tariffs by foreign countries as these were often directed against British cotton exports, but felt powerless to act. Tariffs might lead to higher prices in the countries concerned, but did nothing to raise the demand for Lancashire cotton exports, and thus lowered prices for foreign merchants in Manchester.

This left the silver question, which in turn was aggravated by the fact that in these years Lancashire was becoming more and more dependent on India as an export market for its goods. As we have seen in Chapter Four, India remained on a silver currency until the 1890s, yet Farnie (1979, p. 115) went so far as to say:

> Its [India's] influence raised the Lancashire cotton industry to the status of a world industry, averted a catastrophic decline in its rate of growth after the depression of 1837–42, and extended its lifespan for fifty years after it had reached its peak of importance in the British economy.

Predictably, then, Lancashire exporters were concerned about any developments which might threaten their position in their most important market. But there was a further element which raised their anxiety: India was itself developing a modern cotton-producing industry at precisely this time. Little wonder that Lancashire men saw the name of Ichabod ('the glory is departed') written bleakly over their horizons in the 1890s. The rise of the Bombay cotton industry was not a coincidence, however: the fall of silver and the consequent decline of the Indian rupee acted as a protective measure for nascent industries in India: imports were becoming more expensive and it was easier for India than for Lancashire to export to third markets which were still silver-using, such as China and Japan.

Conversely, the economic prospects of the Lancashire cotton industry had worsened significantly during the 1880s. Exports had remained stagnant and this was put down, by all sectors of the industry, to the problems of the 'eastern exchanges', that is, the state of the rupee. There can be little doubt that Lancashire had come to depend far too much on its oriental markets by this time, but given the failure of free trade elsewhere in the world, and the fact that textile manufacturers were naturally drawn towards markets containing large populations, this is understandable.

But in September 1891, Indian-produced cotton yarns began to reach Manchester warehouses for the first time. To say that this represented 'coals to Newcastle' would be to underwork the metaphor; it produced considerable alarm among cotton interests. 'Indian mills attack us on our own ground', reported one Manchester newspaper, 'several parcels of 16s [coarse grade yarns] have been sent here and disposed of at lower prices than we can produce them' (Wilson, 1990, p. 53). Depreciation of the rupee was taken to be the most important reason for the penetration of the Indian yarn, though the usual calls were also made for the extension of the British Factory Acts to India, to 'level the playing field', in modern parlance.

The Lancashire bimetallists

This widespread concern for the cotton industry's future even caused Lancashire men to doubt free trade, and it was in the context of Indian competition that the Manchester Chamber of Commerce once famously – or infamously – voted against the great liberal shibboleth in 1895 (Redford, 1956). There had also been some support for fair trade since the 1880s. Thanks largely to two men, however, the attention of the Lancashire public was turned towards the monetary issue and the notion of overturning the gold standard. One was the cotton manufacturer of Stockport, Sir William Houldsworth, and the other was the cotton trade union leader, James Mawdsley.

Houldsworth's name springs up at almost every turn in the progress of the monetary controversy in Britain, and he was also prominent on the international scene. Had he lived a generation earlier he might well have been involved with Cobden and Bright in the free trade campaign, since the motivation and rationale of the two movements were so similar, namely the recovery of the cotton industry on a sound international footing. But since free trade triumphed, at least for a while, and bimetallism ultimately failed, Houldsworth's name is not as well known as it should be. This is despite the fact that he made so many contributions in other spheres of activity – as churchman, engineer, statistician, temperance reformer, architectural sponsor, founder of Manchester University and, of course, entrepreneur (Howe, 1985). He was possibly the richest man in the north-west (though strictly speaking, his mills were in Cheshire rather than Lancashire) in the late nineteenth century.

Houldsworth was the nearest that the bimetallic movement came to having a single leader to parallel Cobden and Bright of free trade. He became a leading light of the Bimetallic League in the 1880s and, as MP for Stockport, the chairman of its parliamentary committee, a strategically important position for the movement. He published numerous articles on the subject and frequently made speeches outlining the aims of the League, both in Parliament and elsewhere. He sat on the Gold and Silver Commission, which reported in 1888, and represented Britain at the International Monetary Conferences of 1892 and 1895. As a prominent member of the Manchester Chamber of Commerce he and a coterie of accomplices attempted to shift opinion amongst the local business community in the direction of currency reform during the 1880s and 1890s. At a time when the Lancashire cotton industry was suffering contraction, if not extinction, Houldsworth's stance on industrial relations emphasized conciliation and moderation towards the trade unions, and this was essentially because he saw the problems of the industry as largely exogenous, or at any rate outside the Lancashire region. His general analysis was therefore little different from that of the trade unionists, who generally shared his Conservatism. The Cotton Spinners' Union was the best organized and probably the wealthiest of all trade unions in Britain, and probably the world, in the late nineteenth century.

No one represents the Conservatism, and conservatism, of the trade unionists better than James Mawdsley, General Secretary of the Amalgamated Association of Operative Cotton Spinners from 1878 to 1902. If there was a 'producers' alliance' of employers and operatives in late Victorian industrial Lancashire, Houldsworth and Mawdsley can be taken to be its twin leaders. Like Houldsworth, Mawdsley became a keen bimetallist during the 1880s depression. But whereas Houldsworth's fame is perhaps due to the neglect of historians, Mawdsley had only himself to blame for his subsequent anonymity. For Mawdsley was in many ways a low-profile character and not at all the kind of person one would expect to find leading a major trade union in any period. He was referred to by the biographer of James Macara (another cotton magnate) as 'definitely a man behind a mask', and it would seem that he became the union's leader by virtue of his intellectual abilities rather than any talent for oratory or rabble-rousing. In the late nineteenth century the cotton-spinners chose their officers by competitive written examinations, which included papers on rhetoric and dialectics as well as mathematics, which, 'in view of the extremely abstruse calculations by which Lancashire wages are calculated, was decidedly the major subject of the test', according to one commentator.[1]

Mawdsley's aptitude for mathematics, vital to the understanding of wage lists and the computation of wage rates for his members, must have held him in good stead in arriving at an understanding of the monetary issues of the day, and such matters as the Indian import duties controversy in which he also played a part (Wilson, 1990). Several accounts, however, suggest that he shunned publicity and, although in many ways he was the obvious choice as MP to represent the cotton interests on behalf of the operatives, it would seem that on at least one occasion he turned down the opportunity, though he succumbed in 1897 when he stood with Winston Churchill at a by-election in Oldham. However, his main claim to fame must be the part that he played, with Charles Macara, in the making of the Brooklands Agreement of March 1893. Mawdsley for the cotton-spinners and Macara for the employers brokered an agreement which ushered in a period of industrial peace and conciliation for the cotton industry at a difficult period in its history. Indeed, one might argue that it was this equipoise in industrial relations in Lancashire which allowed the two sides of industry to look for other solutions to the problems facing them.

Mawdsley had no doubt that the foreign-exchange situation with India was the most critical one for his industry, and he was able to promulgate his ideas by helping set up one of the world's first large-circulation workers' newspapers, the *Cotton Factory Times*, in 1885. Mawdsley wrote the keynote article for the newspaper in its first edition and continued to write leader articles through the 1880s and 1890s. Though many of these articles are anonymous, it is possible to detect his style and approach in many of these pieces. By the late 1880s the *Cotton Factory Times* was a thoroughly bimetallist organ, carrying literally hundreds of articles on the issue, including a didactic series in the early 1890s aimed at providing its readers with a full background and history to the currency issue (Wilson, 1990).

Many of these articles were aimed at the poor state of the cotton trade's exports to India. Often they were quite doom-laden and predicted the total collapse of the industry unless exports could be boosted in some way. However, the Lancashire trade unionists were always pragmatic and Mawdsley increasingly saw currency reform as a potential solution to cotton's travails. By the 1890s the *Cotton Factory Times* had a circulation of over 50,000 and, given the multiple readership of the period, must have been read by over 100,000 workers (and no doubt owners and managers) of the industry. Bimetallic reform was presented as a bread-and-butter issue in which all workers should take an interest. Remarkably, Mawdsley and his colleagues attempted to make bimetallism, famously one of the most arcane of all economic remedies, comprehensible to the man in the street. To the extent that it succeeded, this was probably the first real attempt to make the matter of currency a plebeian concern in modern British history. There has always been a tendency in Britain to regard currency as a matter for the experts, in strong contrast to the United States. Mawdsley and his associates were often derided for burdening the common man with abstruse economic ideas, but their aim was always elucidation in support of a specific programme of reform. As we shall see, to socialists such as Hyndman of the Social Democratic Federation, this kind of campaign was risible, but historians should take it more seriously.

Lancashire and India

Given the notion that trade has to benefit all parties to it in order for it to take place, it might be supposed that India had as much to lose from any hindrance to trade as Lancashire, and that therefore one might expect a similar response in India as in the metropolitan country. The reality was very different. The imperial connection must always be considered, and this meant that the deliberations of, for example, Indian administrators were not always motivated purely by the needs of India itself. This might be because the imperial agent was working consciously in the interests of the 'home country' or it could be, and in India often was, the result of ideology of some kind. In the case of India this was political economy, which was often imposed in a much less adulterated form than in Britain, where political pluralism could be inimical to economic principle. In two convincing volumes, Ambirijan (1978, 1984) has demonstrated the overriding importance of liberal economic thought in the governance of India in the nineteenth century. This meant that Britain and India could be governed by totally different economic principles, and we have noted the remarkable fact that the two countries found themselves on completely different commodity standards at the crucial hour of the nineteenth century. Furthermore, the governor-general, and later the viceroy, and their councils, were highly influential at all times, and although the queen's deputies were chosen from a very narrow social milieu, they varied widely in their economic thinking. Lord Ripon, for example (1880–84), was totally opposed to bimetallism for the subcontinent, despite the fact that his council were generally sympathetic towards it. Ripon's opposition, it seems, was based upon his reading of Henri Cernuschi, though it is remarkable that he even knew of Cernuschi. But Ripon's successor, Lord Dufferin (1884–88), was a convinced bimetallist and on one occasion wrote to Lord Cross, the then Secretary of State for India, as follows: 'All my financial advisors here [in India] are strong bimetallists ... I have no hesitation in announcing myself from an Indian point of view as a bimetallist' (Ambirijan, 1978, p. 128).

Dufferin was thus overtly adapting his beliefs to suit his position and office, though it is very unlikely that such a man would have questioned the gold standard in any way had he remained in Britain. Ambirijan reckoned that most civil servants in India were in fact in favour of bimetallism for India by the 1880s. If political economy is assumed to be consistent with the orthodox gold standard, this would have run counter to their Haileybury training.[2] They managed to conceal the fact, and two factors account for the Indian civil servants' attraction to bimetallism by the end of the nineteenth century. First there was the matter of their pensions. These were payable in rupees and exchange depreciation meant that the real value of their retirement earnings was being significantly reduced by the fall of the silver rupee. Hence their desire to tie the rupee to sterling by some mechanism and, short of introducing a gold standard in India, which was regarded as difficult, this meant bimetallism. Second it was recognized that India's balance-of-payments problems were becoming increasingly acute and that something had to be done to reduce the burden of the 'home charges' – the payments made by the Indian government to Britain to cover the costs of administration and defence of the subcontinent. This in turn would reduce the overall tax burden to the Indian taxpayer and thus moderate criticism of British rule, which was also mounting, especially in a period when famine was becoming more rather than less prevalent. It is no surprise to find that an increasing number of government officials, judges, army officers and civil servants were openly in favour of bimetallism for India by the 1890s (Ambirijan, 1978).

Yet Indian merchants and industrialists tended to be strongly supportive of the existing silver rupee. This is well illustrated by the Bombay Chamber of Commerce, the most powerful of its kind in India. Numerous utterances emanating from Bombay were picked up by the Lancashire newspapers, and the British bimetallists were able to make much use of them as propaganda. The Indian industrialists had enjoyed considerable expansion under a depreciating standard and had no wish to change the *status quo*. The Bombay cotton industry was threatening to displace Lancashire as the supplier of yarns not merely to sections of the Indian market but also to third markets such as the Far East. We have seen that India had even been able to send cheaper cotton yarns to Lancashire by the 1890s. Of course, the fact that the Bombay Chamber was conservative on the currency issue served to convince the Lancashire school that they were right: silver depreciation protected inefficient Indian manufacturers. This had been evident since the Bombay Chamber's resolution of 1886:

Any interference with the currency is to be deprecated, and while admitting the inconveniences of constant fluctuation [in the exchange rate], we are of the opinion, after considering the question from all sides, that the fall in the exchange leaves a balance of benefit to the commerce and the people of India, and we are in favour of allowing things to run their natural course.

(Wilson, 1990, p. 43)

What of the Indian economists who were making their mark by this stage? The evidence suggests that they were largely uninterested in currency reform. This is certainly true of the nascent nationalist school of Naoroji, Joshi and Dutt. It is not difficult to see why. Naoroji himself wrote: 'the fall in exchange [as a result of the fall of silver prices] would not matter much to India if her trade alone were concerned. She can control her wants by taking more or less' (Ambirijan, 1984, p. 134).

Naoroji recognized that the home charges were an enormous burden on the Indian economy and taxpayer, and indeed had been instrumental in drawing attention to them, but he was not interested in ameliorative measures to lessen the impact of the charges. He wanted complete abolition, arguing that the imperial power itself should pay for the administration and defence of its entire empire (Ganguli, 1965).

In relation to Britain and India in the 1890s and the question of currency reform, we are left with a curious but nice asymmetry. In Britain the bimetallic campaign drew its support largely from the 'productive classes' of agriculture and industry and from a section of the trade union movement; in India these same groups were generally opponents of reform. In Britain the administrative establishment, though often somewhat mute on the subject, was against changes to the gold standard; in India such groups were often overt supporters of bimetallism. Leading economists in Britain were usually quite open to the prospect of monetary reform, whereas the Indian economists had no time for it, consumed as they were by matters of nationalism. No better way of illustrating the great divergence of economic interest that existed between Britain and her great colony could be devised.

It has to be admitted that there were many exceptions to these generalizations. Nevertheless, the pattern of allegiance as outlined did not augur well for the successful prosecution of monetary reform at the end of the nineteenth century. We might conclude that it was much less likely that supranational or sub-imperial organizations might emerge from within the British group of nations. Thus there is little evidence of Lancashire bimetallists seeking union with like-minded people in India or elsewhere in the Empire: it would not have been easy for cotton union leaders to lie down with notoriously class-conscious Indian civil servants, much less their esteemed viceroy, however sympathetic to silver these people may have been. On the other hand, it is unlikely that Indian nationalists such as Naoroji would have wanted any congress with British Treasury officials or City financiers, but at least they had the *status quo* on their side.

At this point we have to return to the 'Great Depression' of 1873–96. It would seem that India did not suffer from this international phenomenon. The decades after 1873 were years of rapid economic and industrial expansion for India, albeit that this often consisted of 'enclave' industrialization characterized by heavy concentration in certain cities (Charlesworth, 1982), or the 'unbalanced growth' indicated by the dominance of 'export industries' such as jute and cotton (Kidron, 1965). Nevertheless, the absence of prolonged depression, which was the main impulse to currency reform in Europe and elsewhere, necessarily means that it would be more difficult for bimetallists in India to produce a convincing case. It is surprising in many ways that the arguments of the Indian nationalists that imperialism was 'draining' wealth away from the subcontinent were not more clearly linked to a call for currency revision, but the fact is that they saw this as tinkering with a rotten system. This in turn isolated the Indian civil servant who might have supported bimetallism (against his better judgement). He clearly stood to gain from it in a direct way but obviously was not in a position to enter fully into political debate in Britain, where ultimately all the important decisions about India would have to be made. If Indian civil servants had campaigned for a bimetallic rupee it would in any case have been seen merely as special pleading – as a pension-protection scheme. Thus it was left to the Lancashire bimetallists to make the running by themselves.

A north–south debate

The great currency debate threw up curious schisms and unusual patterns of allegiance. British bimetallists faced opposition from every possible source, including their direct counterparts in India. They also received vociferous condemnation from socialists within their own country, where City financiers were far from being the only group to criticize their stance. In characteristically tactless form and at the height of the bimetallic debate, H. M. Hyndman, Britain's foremost Marxist thinker and leader of the Social Democratic Federation, poured scorn on the very notion of a 'producers' alliance' and attacked the Lancashire school for entertaining their 'bimetallic balderdash' in the pages of *Justice* magazine:

We hear a great deal from time to time of the ability and vigour of the 'hard-headed men of the North', as contrasted with the softness and incapacity displayed by us inferior folk [the SDF]. But then we remember that somehow these stalwarts were once fools enough to follow the free trade red herring which Cobden, Bright, Villiers, Fox and Co. dragged across their pate to economic freedom ... Just imagine the London Trades Council voting a £10 note for bimetallism! The thing is inconceivable. London workers, whatever their shortcomings may be, know perfectly well that no amount of currency-juggling will relieve them of the wage slavery to which they are damned so long as capitalism exists ... What *are* the contentions of the bimetallists, as they foolishly call themselves?[3]

Hyndman had had many run-ins with the northern unionists in the past and hated them for their cautiousness and inertia in the face of the imminent collapse of the capitalist system. By the mid-1890s his power was perhaps on the wane, but he still commanded respect as a significant doctrinaire thinker of the major orthodox socialist party of his day. Furthermore he was an expert on Indian trade and finance, having published numerous articles and tracts on the subject and having worked in the City. Ironically he agreed with much that the bimetallists had to say about the essential problems of trade with India, and was quite ready to admit that India had indeed suffered from having a silver currency in an increasingly gold-monometallic world. He accepted the Sauerbeck index as a representative and accurate indicator of the state of the international economy, and had read Naoroji and agreed with his analysis of the 'great drain' – the annual 'tribute' which Britain received from India. Indeed, he met and welcomed the great Indian economist when he visited England in 1895. He even agreed that silver, 'used as it is by the majority of people of the planet, would be the best metal in which to estimate prices universally, leaving gold to be dealt in at its day-to-day price and to be used, as it always was in wealthy countries, as the most convenient means of balancing large transactions'.[4] The socialist Hyndman could be just as orientalist in his thinking on currency as the merchant banker. But where he differed fundamentally from the Lancashire bimetallists was in his analysis of the causes of the 'price shrinkage'. Like many contemporaries and later historians, Hyndman was convinced that the price fall of the late nineteenth century (and indeed of the century as a whole) was due wholly to general economic causes such as improvements in productive methods and the territorial expansion of agriculture. Monetary factors were an epiphenomenon just as much as they were for Lyon Playfair: for both the price fall of the 'Great Depression' was engendered by the onward march of progress.

Hyndman pinned his hopes on a very different political combination than the 'producers' alliance' which he saw in the Lancashire bimetallist campaign, which he despised and deprecated. He had set 1889 (the centenary of the French Revolution) as the date for 'the complete international social revolution' (causing his accomplice H. H. Champion to waste months drilling the unemployed in readiness for hostilities), and was still smarting from its non-appearance when the monetary debate broke out (Cole and Postgate, 1938). The cotton unionists had been somewhat more sanguine about the coming social revolution. At the International Trades Union Congress of 1886, Mawdsley (a Conservative in the 1890s) had admitted that he 'did not understand their (the European delegates') Socialism. He had not studied it as perhaps he ought to have done. The workmen of England were not so advanced as the workmen of the Continent ... Nevertheless, they possessed at least one clear conception; they realised that the actual producers did not obtain the share of the wealth they created', he added.[5] This was fighting talk for a man of Mawdsley's politics, though in 1886 he had been a Liberal rather than a Conservative (perhaps his meetings with European socialists were a formative experience for him). No doubt he was simply saying what he thought the assembled proletarians wanted him to say as the leader of the most highly organized group of workers in the world's most advanced industrial state.

In many ways Hyndman was merely reasserting the belief, widely held in Britain, that the setting up of a bimetallic system would result in inflation of a kind that would inevitably benefit the capitalists rather than the workers:

> If, as the bimetallists argue, the remonetisation of silver will raise prices at once 50%, then, manifestly, the purchasing power of wages which are now paid on a gold basis will be reduced by 33% at the same time. As this very reduction means of course increased profits to the capitalist class to begin with, it will still further enhance the 'boom' for the profit-mongers. But how about the wage-earners? If there is one point in economics which is more certain than any other it is that wages follow a rise of prices with comparative slowness ... The wage-earners of all gold-using countries would find the purchasing power of their wages cut down by one-third if silver were constituted the regulator of prices. Is this what our 'hard-headed men of the North' want to bring about? Why not give socialism a little consideration?[6]

For all their internationalism, nineteenth-century socialists could be decidedly racist when it came to people of the non-industrial, pre-proletarian world. A colleague of Hyndman's, A. P. Hazell, derided the use of silver as a habit of primitive peoples:

> The Bimetallists are anxious to monetise silver, which virtually means raising it to an artificial value. In India and Japan, owing to the peculiarly ancient customs and the low economic development

of these nations, silver has not yet conformed to the world's markets and fallen to its real value. Consequently goods manufactured in these countries are produced relatively cheaper [sic], supposing labour to be paid in silver there, than they are here where production is carried on a gold basis.[7]

As we have seen before, Hazell was perpetrating a form of orientalism which was far from uncommon even amongst informed opinion in the 'west' in the nineteenth century. But, like Hyndman, Hazell was certain that bimetallism would lead to inflation: 'A man paying his debts would be a fool to pay them in gold if he could pay them in silver and save the difference between the two. Prices would rise. Amongst the victims would be the workers, who have to take silver for their wages.[8]

SDF thinkers and socialists generally in the nineteenth century were faithful to the gold standard in Britain. Hyndman reckoned that gold had achieved its primary position in the industrial countries by the 1880s because it represented labour power more exactly than silver. If silver had fallen in value, as indubitably it had since the early 1870s, the labour theory of value insisted that it must be a reflection of the falling labour input. He rejected the theory that silver had fallen in value because of its demonetization and was certain that only supply-side explanations were admissible, thereby remaining consistent with the labour theory of value. Hazell, on the other hand, was sure in his conviction that 'money was gold and gold was money'.[9]

Monomaniac monometallists

Revolutionary socialists such as Hyndman and Hazell may not ultimately have had much influence over events in the world of money, at any rate unless or until they could persuade the labour movement generally to adopt a revolutionary consciousness and directly threaten the existing capitalist order. This was less likely in Britain, or should we say England, than in other European countries such as France or Germany. However, as we have seen in Chapter Five, working people, when they were as well focused in their aims as the Silverites of the United States, could come very close indeed to dictating the monetary ordering: had Bryan won the presidential election of 1896 there is little doubt that the United States would have adopted a silver currency (either de facto or de jure) there and then, and sought an international bimetallic agreement with even more vigour than William McKinlay, try though he did with the Wolcott Commission of 1896.

It was widely believed in the 1890s that the real decisions on monetary reform would have to come from Britain in the end, if only because the City of London was by then so strongly entrenched as the centre of world finance in all its many facets. If enough members of Britain's *haute finance* élite could ever be persuaded that specific things needed revising, then change would almost certainly become possible. But the impression given by students of the City, from Checkland and Cassis to Kynaston and Cain and Hopkins, is that the City was permanently locked into short-term thinking and virtually immune to reform of any kind. The City accepted the *status quo*, which happened to be gold, and rarely suggested any movement away from it. There were people in the City who were sympathetic to bimetallism because they dealt with countries still on silver currencies, but they were seemingly never in a position to influence the consensual view of the majority.

It is perhaps not surprising that the bimetallists tended to draw their inspiration from other countries just as the socialists, or the syndicalists, did a generation or so later. On a regular basis the Lancashire bimetallists reported that foreign movements or even parliaments were calling for change to the monetary system. It might be the silverites in the United States or the French Assembly or the German Reichstag. The *Cotton Factory Times* regularly reported debates from such sources, and when an international monetary conference was imminent, they could draw even greater encouragement.

But it might well be that all of this came to nothing because successive Chancellors of the Exchequer in Britain were devout supporters of the ancient British gold standard. It should be noted that before the First World War, Chancellors had rather more discretionary power than they have had in the twentieth century as a whole. This is true of members of the cabinet generally, who had greater power to act within their domains than in the modern era: just as Foreign Secretary Grey could be largely responsible for taking Britain to war in 1914, so contemporary Chancellors had the power to commit Britain to the gold standard. Two successive Chancellors in the 1890s, one Liberal and the other Conservative, were vehemently opposed to bimetallism and resented any criticism of the existing system. Sir William Harcourt (Liberal Chancellor from 1892 to 1895) and Sir Michael Hicks Beach (Conservative Chancellor from 1895 to 1902) were not to be turned on the issue.

Gladstone's Chancellor, Harcourt, is quoted as saying that 'a man who is not a monometallist is a monomaniac'. Yet when Gladstone came to power the Lancashire bimetallists had been hopeful of reform. They believed, probably wrongly, that the Grand Old Man had said some things in the past which had been sympathetic to the idea of a dual standard, and they hoped in 1892 that he would fly another Hawarden Kite in their favour (Wilson, 1990). Unfortunately for their cause, and for many others, Gladstone proved to be still obsessed with the Irish issue, and this crowded out most other things. In any case, it can be established that Gladstone was always a gold-standard man and later wrote to the Gold Standard Defence Organization that he could be relied upon to support their cause. True, he had in the past uttered such thoughts as 'Fluctuation is economically an evil', which caused 'inconvenience, and even distress in trade and industry.' But it is a telling fact about the state of knowledge, and of communications generally, at the end of the nineteenth century that the Bimetallic League in Manchester could be quite uncertain about the actual beliefs of an incoming prime minister on a vital issue of the day. They remained unsure well into his actual term of office.

Gladstone's Chancellor, Harcourt, evinced no such doubts about where he stood on bimetallist reform, and was clearly in a position of such power as to confidently hold it off, but even with him the Lancashire bimetallists were unsure. They did not know that when he took the Treasury job he wrote to his leader as follows:

> It is quite plain that he [Goschen, his Tory predecessor] found himself between the devil and the deep blue sea, with Salisbury, Balfour and Chaplin as bimetallists on the one side and his own monometallic convictions on the other, with a side-glance at the Manchester cheap-money men at the election.
> (Gardiner, 1923, p. 205)

Harcourt wanted nothing to do with the looming international monetary conference and, according to his biographer, he was instrumental in preventing the meeting taking place in London. This, he feared 'would give the impression that the country favoured bimetallism ... in these days of contagion I can't have London infected by an incursion of insane bimetallists. It would be too embarrassing to have to treat them as *compos mentis*' (ibid., p. 205).

The conference took place in Brussels, and Harcourt was determined to undermine it as much as possible. He packed the British delegation with gold-standard men, though he included Sir William Houldsworth as a sop to the Lancashire interests, to which he accorded some political clout, if little brain. Though he later denied hand-picking the delegates (a charge by Henry Chaplin), he wrote at the time that he had entrusted the conference to 'good men and true – what Gladstone calls "sane men"' (ibid., p. 205). But if there can be any remaining doubts about Harcourt's position on currency reform, we are told by his biographer that in February 1895 he wrote to the queen as follows:

> The object of the bimetallists is to change the simple gold standard of this country for a double standard of gold and silver. The gold standard was established in 1816 and has been firmly maintained by all English statesmen ever since. But a school has arisen which

> believes that it is possible to raise silver to its former price, which
> was double the value it now bears, by an international agreement
> ... they think that by this means they could create a superfluity of
> money and thus raise prices ... for the benefit of the agricultural
> interest.
>
> (Ibid., p. 378)

For some reason Harcourt did not mention the cotton interest. But it is
clear that he was deeply prejudiced against bimetallic reform and was
intent on keeping the gold standard. He possibly occupies an extreme
position on the issue: as certain as Robert Giffen but without the latter's
insight into and knowledge of monetary matters. Yet we can say that
during his period of office as Chancellor he was the most powerful man
in the world when it came to global monetary matters.

In October 1895, Harcourt thought that the bimetallic campaign was
'blowing over', but he was not entirely sure that his likely Conservative
successor would carry on the defence of gold, especially since leading
Tories such as Balfour and Salisbury were known to be sympathetic to
the currency-reform arguments. But his successor turned out to be Sir
Michael Hicks Beach, to whom Salisbury gave the job which might well
have gone to Goschen, who is thought to have moved in favour of
bimetallism, or Arthur Balfour, the prime minister's nephew, who had
long been associated with reform and was MP for East Manchester. The
new parliament had already voted in favour of a resolution 'to do all in
their power to secure a stable par of exchange between gold and silver'.
The resolution had been inspired by Lancashire bimetallist members
(Wilson, 1990).

But one of Hicks Beach's first statements to the new House was to the
effect that there would be no change of policy over the gold standard.
He opined:

> That standard had been the foundation of the great prosperity
> enjoyed by British trade and of the finest system of credit banking
> in the world ... the fall in prices is due to foreign competition,
> cheapened transport, improved communications and other changed
> conditions. There is no real scarcity of gold. On the contrary, the
> annual production has doubled since 1885, the stock in the banks
> has never been so large, nor the rate of discount so low.
>
> (Hicks Beach, 1932, p. 27)

He went on to argue that silver was 'capable of being produced in
almost limitless quantities'. His biographer and widow, Lady Hicks
Beach, recorded that all who listened to her husband's speech were
impressed by the mastery it deployed. Be that as it may, the former
Chancellor rose to his feet and paid tribute to 'a speech of which I will
say that I have never heard one which surpassed it in ability, in close-
ness of reasoning, and in frankness and downrightness of statement ...

a declaration on the part of the responsible government that England does not intend to part from its present monetary system' (ibid., p. 28).

Any bimetallist who witnessed this mutual sycophancy might have been excused for abandoning the cause there and then: the two men who represented the economic power of the two great parties of government were, it seems, as one in rejecting the slightest notion of monetary reform. Remarkably, Arthur Balfour was true to his beliefs and, though a cabinet colleague of Hicks Beach, spoke on the opposite side of the ensuing debate, declaring that 'the whole of civilised opinion is in the direction of the double standard' (Zebel, 1973). It seems scarcely credible that two men such as these could differ so fundamentally on one of the great economic issues of the day and yet remain together in the same cabinet, especially as Balfour kept his job as First Secretary to the Treasury in 1895.

None of this is meant to suggest that 'Chancellor monomania' in the 1890s, or at any other time, was in any way a matter of chance. Cassis (1984), in his study of the City of London in this period, came to the firm conclusion that only politicians who had the sympathy and support of the City of London were ever seriously considered for the post. Cassis thought it difficult to imagine Balfour ever occupying the Chancellorship. Indeed, he believed that Balfour 'knew that nothing was possible, in terms of currency reform or his own elevation to Chancellor, without converting the banking community to bimetallism, a gargantuan task in the circumstances' (ibid.). Balfour, of course, became prime minister after 1900, but only after the bimetallist controversy had entirely run its course. But in any case, his uncle's sympathy towards the double standard had not stopped him selecting the monomaniac Hicks Beach as his Chancellor. One wonders exactly how the City's massive political leverage was applied in these years, but sadly the recent excellent biography of Lord Salisbury scarcely mentions the bimetallist cause or his subject's precise attitude towards it (Roberts, 1999).

As we saw in Chapter Five, the Chancellor at the time of the American Wolcott Commission's visit in 1896 was Hicks Beach, and Cassis (1984) has no reservations about the true power of the City over the government at this juncture:

> At the highest levels of government there was always the consciousness that the prosperity of the country depended upon the supremacy of its commerce and banking structure, and therefore it was impossible to oppose, in a radical way, the monetary views of those who upheld this edifice.

Cassis has been supported in this view by Cain and Hopkins (1993), and it seems clear that retention of the gold standard was the *causa sine qua non* of all British Chancellors of this era. Little wonder, then, that this basic idea was carried over so strongly into the post-1918 years. We could stop the explanation of the course of the bimetallic controversy here and now. The simplest explanation runs as follows: some few million people in Arkansas, Paris and Manchester wanted to abandon the gold standard in the 1880s and 1890s, but the actual power to change direction lay with one man in the British government, and that man was always hand-picked by the City to remain steadfast to gold, even if his own prime minister was a closet bimetallist.

The problem of the ratio

The sheer scale of the political problems facing the bimetallic campaign in the 1890s was such that we can now say with some certainty that it never really stood any chance of success, but given the state of communications, and hence the poor intelligence of the movement, the bimetallists themselves were never in any position to know this. But as well as political and logistical problems there were obvious theoretical problems that they failed to come to terms with, and these vitiated the political context. There was always the problem of the desired ratio of exchange between gold and silver, perhaps the thorniest problem of all. As we have seen, in the period to *c.* 1873 both the market and the official ratio of exchange had remained remarkably stable and had hardly moved from the 15.5:1 set at the end of the Napoleonic Wars. Demonetization and/or depreciation of silver meant that its exchange rate against gold fell from this 'traditional' level to around 35:1 by the 1890s.

So the most important question for any monetary reformer in the period was what the ratio should be on return to a dual standard. It could be anything between 15.5:1 and 35:1. At any rate, no one ever seriously suggested a return outside these historical limits. The lower the ratio proposed, that is, the nearer to the pre-1873 level, the greater would be the inflationary effect of silver's rehabilitation. American silverites tended to be at this end of the scale, whereas British bimetallists, especially the academic ones, tended to be at the other, 'current ratio', end of 30–35:1. This would be a useful way of distinguishing between two (or more) very different theoretical positions in the period, but sadly the distinction was never clearly made in the nineteenth century, allowing Harcourt, the British Chancellor, and others, to lump all bimetallists together as an insane minority.

Alfred Marshall correctly predicted that the question of the ratio would be a great difficulty for the currency reformers. But it was probably a stickier one than even he expected. Political opponents of reform, such as the Gold Standard Defence Association, could easily exploit any uncertainty about the desired ratio if reformers deliberately chose not to identify one. Yet if they did propose one it could be shot at from all angles. The ratio of 15.5:1 could be, and was, regarded as recklessly pro-silver and risking worldwide inflation on an unprecedented scale; 35:1 could be regarded as meaningless unless accompanied by government guarantees to purchase and mint specific quantities of silver annually, which could be accomplished without ditching the gold standard. Even die-hard 'gold-bugs' would not deny any country minting silver at a current ratio as 35:1 would in itself not 'do anything for silver', to use the contemporary term. For these reasons there was a reluctance to advance a prescribed ratio alongside demands for bimetallism and the remonetization of silver; the Lancashire school, for example, never adopted one.

Bimetallists generally were chary on the issue, even though it is clear now that the question of the ratio was at least as important as the matter of remonetizing silver itself. An analogy might be drawn with other great currency deliberations such as the return to gold after the First World War. After 1918 the decision to return to gold at the historical ratio of $4.86 to the pound was swamped by the actual question of return itself, and Keynes, rightly or wrongly, made great play of this throughout the 1920s, though not always for the reasons one might expect from his post-1925 strictures.[10] At the start of the twenty-first century, British deliberations on whether or not the country should join the European single currency (shot through as they are with deep political misgivings and suspicions) are crowding out the issue of the ratio at which Britain should join the system if it ever does.

Yet the sober 'high-ratio' or 'current-ratio' bimetallists of the 1890s also tended to believe, in their very cautiousness, that the matter of the ratio ought to be decided not by any one group or even one country, but by a general agreement between representatives of the nations of the world. Although it was never actually said, this effectively meant the leading western nations (what we would now call the 'core countries') of the international economy, and their allies. There tended to be, therefore, a rough correspondence between 'current-ratio' bimetallism and the idea of international bimetallism. The high-ratio schools, such as Lancashire, wanted stability of exchange rates rather than the rehabilitation of silver as such. Thus they placed high hopes on the outcomes of the international monetary conferences of the period and remained optimistic about the 1892 conference, even though the three earlier ones had proved nugatory. In this they were very close in intention to the Republican administration of McKinlay, which wanted retention of the gold standard until an international agreement could come up with a better alternative which had a place for silver. For Harcourt and Hicks Beach, the international conference was a useful way of heading off bimetallic reform and at the same time satisfying the desire of the House of Commons that the government was working for a stable par of exchange.

But the failure of the Lancashire bimetallists and others to proffer a suitable working ratio left them open to charges of mendacity or deliberately seeking to mislead. In one sense such charges were well laid, since many bimetallists had talked openly about mild inflation and higher prices being a good thing, a stimulus to the economy and a way out of the chronic depression of over twenty years' duration. In a formal sense, the onus truly was upon them to advance a ratio as part of the call for a dual standard, if only so that their opponents knew the true nature of the arguments they were expected to deal with: to a demand for a piece of string one is entitled to ask, 'how long?'

In the 1890s the bimetallists frequently argued that the workers had nothing to lose from higher prices (not an argument easily accepted by a population long inculcated with free-trade propaganda, especially in Lancashire) and that the only people who stood to lose were the southern parasites in the City of London and elsewhere. They pointed out that the high-price/high-wage economies of the United States and Australia were veritable workers' paradises compared to Britain (Wilson, 1990). This could only mean that they were thinking of a lower ratio for silver than the current 35:1, but they never actually said as much. This is indicative of woolly thinking at best and considerable political naïvety or innocence at worst. Yet had they advocated a 'moderate' ratio of, say, 25:1, it could have been attacked (quite rightly?) as entirely arbitrary. Indeed, any ratio other than the current 30–35:1 or the historic 15.5:1 was essentially arbitrary. It could well be that it was this very same problem which allowed the Cunliffe Committee of 1919[11] to get away with its assumption of an eventual return to prewar parity with the dollar in the 1920s, though it is interesting to note that this was often predicated on guesses about future American prices (though this in itself does not mean that the decision to return at full parity was any more realistic than Keynes and McKenna always argued).[12] On the same point, it is also interesting to note that two of the most influential witnesses to the Cunliffe Committee in 1919 were none other than the two great bimetallist economists, Professors J. S. Nicholson and H. S. Foxwell. Nicholson, it seems, was an extremist on the crucial matter of the pace at which deflation should be allowed to accomplish adjustment, arguing that it ought to be allowed to begin 'as soon as peace is restored' (Moggridge, 1972).[13] Clearly bimetallists were of the view that currency was foremost and that wages and prices should adjust accordingly: in this they had their day in the 1920s.

All this serves to emphasize the fact that there were several schools of thought within bimetallism on such issues. American bimetallists, even including the Wolcott Commission, generally favoured a low, or historic, ratio for silver. British bimetallists generally favoured a high, or current, ratio for the remonetization of the metal. The two groups were miles apart in reality – further apart in some ways than the Lancashire school and the monometallists. Yet this was, naturally, always fudged: Manchester men could claim the support of the Americans but were not always arguing for the same thing. An exception to this rule might be Francis Walker, who would have been closer to the British bimetallists. Had the great bimetallic conversion got closer than it did to achievement, the gold-bugs could have had a field day with the 'confusion of the ratio', but in retrospect it seems unlikely that any international conference could ever have arrived at an agreed ratio, so far apart would the participants have been on the issue.

The more one considers the matter, the more one is convinced that the bimetallic movement was an impossibilist campaign and the greater the feeling that it never stood a chance of victory given the true state of affairs which opposed the reformers. And the clearer it becomes why the gold standard was able to survive the enormous theoretical onslaught of its detractors. There may have been many other reasons, as discussed in Chapter Six, why international bimetallism was never very close to its objectives.

Unilateral bimetallism?

However, some bimetallists believed that an international agreement was not a necessary condition for the restitution of a bimetallic world order. For example, Sir David Barbour, Financial Secretary to the Government of India in the 1880s, thought that such a thing had existed in the past quite adequately with only a few fully bimetallic countries, and therefore could do so again in the future. Barbour concentrated on the parachute effect of the French economy and its tendency, as we have seen in Chapters Three and Six, to absorb whichever of the two precious metals was in ready supply and thus depreciating. This 'unilateralist' or 'partialist' bimetallism thus rested upon recent empirical grounds and contained a practical advantage over international bimetallism: it did not need a universal agreement and could be achieved in a piecemeal fashion. The problem here is that this represented another split in the ranks of the bimetallists (though Barbour himself would have preferred an international agreement if it might prove possible). Inevitably, there would be 'high-ratio unilateralists' (the ratio would have to be close to the current one in order for one country to contemplate it) and 'high-ratio internationalists' as well as the 'low-ratio internationalists', such as the Wolcott Commission. But American silverites also occupied a 'low-ratio internationalist' position which was, arguably, theoretically unjustifiable.

Barbour (1886, p. 154) was unsure about what ratio should be adopted by the new monetary regimes to incorporate silver and act as a replacement parachute:

> There is no magic in the ratio of 1 to 15½ rather than 1 to 10 or 1 to 20. The loss of the old ratio was a terrible calamity, but the advantages of bimetallism will in the long run be obtained as satisfactorily under any other ratio which may be chosen by common consent ... The future ratio should be determined by the circumstances of the time; the benefits of the ratio, whatever it may be, will last for all time. The ratio of 1 to 15½ has tradition in its favour, and tradition is powerful in a matter of this kind, and ... it is probably the only ratio that would be accepted by nations such as France, which hold a large amount of silver valued above the present market rate. I do not deny that the adoption of the ratio of 1 to 15½ instead of the present market ratio of 1 to 19 or 20 [in 1886] would involve loss to some and gain to others ... On the other hand, it must be admitted that arguments of great weight can be advanced either for adopting the present market ratio as the future legal ratio, or for adopting a ratio somewhat higher than the present market ratio, but not so high as the old ratio of 1 to 15½.

Barbour (ibid., p. 155) then made the mistake common to many of his colleagues in the movement:

> The problem [of the ratio] must, if a satisfactory solution is to be found, be approached in a spirit of conciliation, and the future welfare of the world depends very much more on the adoption of some fixed ratio rather than on the adoption of any particular ratio.

In other words, he was saying that virtually any old ratio would do, so long as we have a ratio. Barbour clearly had much faith in the economies of the world to adjust quickly and easily to any stipulated new value for its major currencies. As well as being naïve in the extreme, this position would inevitably have been quite unacceptable for holders of gold, not least the men of the City, who would have had to sustain a totally unknowable loss at the onset of any such regime. Little wonder, then, that the City came to oppose bimetallism so vigorously.

Further problems

There were yet other problems facing the would-be reformers. The 'entrepreneurial argument' advanced by such as Lyon Playfair, outlined in Chapter Two, aimed to explain the Great Depression and falling prices by reference to the expansion of labour-saving technology of various kinds and superior organization of trade and industry. In the late nineteenth century this became a popular argument in Britain, perhaps because it seemed to excuse industrialists from blame for the depression, or at any rate show that they were merely the victims of their own success. In this explanation a regime of falling prices could be seen as the culmination of the Victorian programme of political economy, which always emphasized cheapness and competitiveness. Many entrepreneurs and businessmen fully accepted the argument because they were keen to emphasize their own sense of progressiveness: the Whiggish view of history accorded with their own self-esteem in many ways. Even hard-headed Lancashire millowners and managers came to accept it, and this is expressed clearly through the newspapers which represented them. Green was quite wrong to argue that Lancashire in the 1890s stood 'four-square' behind the bimetallic position. Most of the millowners and certainly the 'Oldham Limiteds', which expanded rapidly in these years, were totally against monetary reform (Wilson, 1990). It is clear that the readers of such newspapers as the (Manchester-based) *Textile Mercury* and *Textile Manufacturer* accepted the 'entrepreneurial view' and were simply uninterested in the matter. They saw no reason to intervene in the market to reintroduce silver at an artificial level of scarcity, though they obviously drew the line at the Indian import duties when they were reintroduced in the 1890s, but this is because they saw this as an unwonted incursion by other vested interests (such as the Indian government and the Indian cotton interests). Ironically, such groups must be counted among the manufacturing interests who went over to tariff reform in the next decade. In the mid-1890s, the anti-bimetallist *Textile Mercury* was clearly drifting this way and began to challenge the wisdom of free trade:

> Retaliation ... must eventually become an important idea in the political programme of the manufacturing districts ... the Free Trade organs will have to modify their views and acknowledge that while Cobden's idea of universal Free Trade was a glorious one, the present system of untaxed imports here and taxed exports in every other civilised country is not to the advantage of England.
> (Wilson, 1990, p. 179)

Quite obviously, this group posed a formidable opposition to the bimetallists even within Lancashire: there was never a chance that they would support the trade unions or Sir William Houldsworth and his group on the matter of currency changes. When the two manufacturers' newspapers did deign to discuss bimetallism, it was to ridicule and oppose it. The 'producers' alliance' of which Green and others have spoken was much narrower than they supposed.

Lastly, bimetallism could always be seen as special pleading by all opponents so long as its main centres of support were restricted to Lancashire cotton and English agriculture, but it seems not to have spread across Britain from these centres.[14] True, there was support from Dundee and the jute interest, and bimetallism found favour with a number of important chambers of commerce, including even Birmingham's, but it seems not to have become a major movement amongst the industrial classes outside of Lancashire (Wilson, 1990). If the bimetallic movement depended, as it surely did, upon a bandwagon effect, the geographical and structural limitations of its expansion have to be recognized. As we have always argued that Britain was the key country in terms of the international bimetallic campaign, this might well have been its most critical limitation.

The new gold and the demise of bimetallism

What finally killed off bimetallism, however, was the change (or perceived change) in the relative supply of the precious metals towards the end of the 1890s, in Britain and elsewhere. Ironically, it was the currency reformers themselves who had predicted that new supplies of gold would eventually be found and that the seemingly limitless expansion of silver would one day be checked. We have seen that in this they differed from Keynes and others who believed that gold discoveries were largely accidental, yet this was not a necessary condition for their case for they also believed that the main reason for silver's loss of value was its demonetization rather than its excess supply. We have seen that there was always much to commend this viewpoint, which is now generally accepted by economic historians who have considered the reasons for the 'fall of silver'. What we can be sure of is that much new gold was discovered in the mid- to late 1890s, with major finds in Colorado (from 1890 onwards), Mexico (1894), the Klondike (1896) and South Africa (small finds in the 1880s but large-scale production from the mid-1890s, then interrupted by the Boer War). To say the least, these were sufficient to dispel any feelings that gold would again become so scarce as to make the gold standard unworkable in any sense. Historians such as Clapham and Ashworth claimed that the new gold destroyed the position of the bimetallists. Whether or not this is true is still debatable, but what is important is that contemporaries perceived it to be the case. Many bimetallists changed their views as a result of the new gold, often because they believed it would have the same effect as bimetallic reform; perhaps they were right. Many bimetallists gave up the chase without publicizing the fact, and virtually forgot that they had ever been interested: what is the value in admitting to a credo which has had its day? They were as content as the monometallists to allow the matter to drift out of public sight and the consciousness of individuals, though the Bimetallic League was still being recorded as a Manchester society as late as 1910. Adherents such as Arthur Balfour preferred to banish it from their memoirs if not to suppress it from their memories. Even the great bimetallist himself, William Jennings Bryan, whilst reproducing his famous 'Cross of Gold' speech, otherwise failed to mention it in his autobiography. If ever an idea had its time, it was bimetallism in the Great Depression of 1873 to 1896.

Notes

1. Haslam Mills, *Sir Charles Macara, Bart., A Study of Modern Lancashire*, 1917.
2. Haileybury College was set up by Thomas Malthus to train recruits to the Indian Civil Service.
3. *Justice*, leader, 19 January 1895.
4. Ibid.
5. International Trades Union Congress, 1886, Minutes.
6. *Justice*, January 1895.
7. *Justice*, December 1894.
8. Ibid.
9. Ibid.
10. See Moggridge (1972). Moggridge shows that Keynes in 1924 was predicting that placing the sovereign at pre-1914 parity would, thanks to inevitable American inflation, result in massive imports of gold into Britain and thus inflation. He therefore recommended that the British authorities retain the power to close the mint or lower the price of gold to prevent these inflationary pressures.
11. Committee on Currency and Foreign Exchanges after the War, 1919 (Cunliffe Committee).
12. See Moggridge (1972).
13. Moggridge reckoned that the evidence given by Nicholson and Foxwell was the most interesting of all the memoranda received by the Commission.
14. See Cain and Hopkins (1993).

References

Ambirijan, S. (1978), *Political Economy and British Policy in India*, Madras.
———— (1984), *Political Economy and Monetary Management: India, 1766–1914*, Madras.
Artis, M. and Lewis, M. (1991), *Money in Britain. Monetary Policy, Innovation and Europe*, London and New York.
Barbour, Sir D. (1886), *The Theory of Bimetallism and the Effects of the Partial Demonetisation of Silver on England and India*, London, Melbourne, New York and Paris.
Blainey, G. (1970), 'A Theory of Mineral Discovery: Australia in the Nineteenth Century', *Economic History Review*, 2nd series, 23.
Bordo, M. D. and Rockoff, H. (1996), 'The Gold Standard as Good Housekeeping Seal of Approval', *Journal of Economic History 56*, no. 2.
Brogan, H. (1985), *The Penguin History of the United States of America*, London.
Bryan, William Jennings and Bryan, Mary Baird (1925), *The Memoirs of William Jennings Bryan*, New York.
Cain, P. J. and Hopkins, A. G. (1993), *British Imperialism. Vol 1, Innovation and Expansion, 1688–1914*, Harlow, Essex.
Canovan, M. (1981), *Populism*, London.
Cassis, Y. (1984), *Les Banquiers de la City à l'époque Edourdienne*, Geneva.
de Cecco, M. (1974), *Money and Empire*, London and Oxford.
Chandavarkar, A. (1989), *Keynes and India*, London.
Charlesworth, N. (1982), *British Rule and the Indian Economy, 1800–1914*, London and Basingstoke.
Checkland, S. G. (1948), 'The Birmingham Economists, 1815–1850', *Economic History Review*, 2nd series, 1, pp. 1–19.
Checkland, S. G. (1957), 'The Mind of the City, 1870–1914', *Oxford Economic Papers*, new series, 9, no. 3, October.
Chevalier, M. (1857), 'On the probable fall in the value of gold, the commercial and social consequences which may ensue', Manchester.
Chown, J. F. (1994), *A History of Money, from AD 800*, London.
Clapham, J. H. (1921), *Economic Development of France and Germany, 1815–1914*, Cambridge.
Cole, G. D. H. and Postgate, R. (1938), *The Common People, 1746–1946*, London.
Connor, R. D. (1987), *The Weights and Measures of England*, London.

Cottrell, P. (1992), 'Silver, gold and the international monetary order, 1851–1896', in S. N. Broadberry and N. F. R. Crafts: *Britain in the International Economy, 1870–1939*, Cambridge.

Crouzet, F. (1982), *The Victorian Economy*, London.

Darwin, L. (1987), *A Summary of the Arguments for and against a Bimetallic System of Currency*, London.

Deane, P. (1965), *The First Industrial Nation*, London.

Eichengreen, B. (1996), *Globalizing Capital. A History of the International Monetary System*, Princeton, NJ.

Ensor, Sir R. (1936), *England, 1870–1914*, Oxford History of England, Oxford.

Farnie, D. (1979), *The English Cotton Industry and the World Market, 1815–1896*, Oxford.

Fetter, F. W. (1965), *Development of British Monetary Orthodoxy, 1797–1875*, Cambridge, MA.

—— and Gregory, D. (1973), *Monetary and Financial Policy in Nneteenth Century Britain*, London.

Flandreau, M. (1995), 'Was the Latin Monetary Union a Franc Zone?', in J. Reiss (ed), *International Monetary Systems in Historical Perspective*, London.

Foreman-Peck, J. (1983), *A History of the World Economy. International Monetary Relations Since 1850*, Totawa, NJ.

Frank Baum, L. (1900), *The Wonderful Wizard of Oz*, New York.

—— (1904), *The Marvelous Land of Oz*, New York.

Friedman, M. (1990), 'The Crime of 1873', *Journal of Political Economy* 98, no. 6.

—— (1992), *Money Mischief: Episodes in Monetary History*, Orlando, FL.

—— and Schwartz, A. J. (1963), *A Monetary History of the United States*, Princeton, NJ.

Gallarotti, G. M. (1994), 'The scramble for gold: monetary regime transformation in the 1870s', in M. J. Bordo and F. Capie (eds), *Monetary Regimes in Transition*, Cambridge.

Ganguli, B. N. (1965), *Dadabhai Naoroji and the Drain Theory*, Calcutta.

Gardiner, A. G. (1923), *The Life of Sir William Harcourt*, 2 vols, London.

Gleeson, J. (1999), *The Arcanum*, London.

Green, E. H. H. (1988), 'Rentiers versus Producers? The Political Economy of the Bimetallic Controversy, c1880–1898', *English Historical Review* 408, July.

Hackett Fischer, D. (1996), *The Great Wave. Price Revolutions and the Rhythm of History*, New York.

Hicks Beach, Lady Victoria (1932), *Life of Sir Michael Hicks Beach*, London.

Howe, A. C. (1985), 'Sir William Houldsworth', in D. Jeremy (ed.), *Dictionary of Business Biography*, Cambridge.

Howse, D. (1980), *Greenwich Mean Time and the Discovery of Longitude*, London.

Hudson, P. (1992), *The Industrial Revolution*, London.

Hutt, W. H. (1979), *The Keynesian Episode. A Reassessment*, Indianapolis.

Hyde, F. E. (1973), *Far Eastern Trade, 1860–1914*, London.

Kannangara, A. P. (1968), 'Indian Millowners and Nationalism before 1914', *Past and Present* 40, July.

Kemp, J. and Wilson, T. (1999), 'Monetary Regime Transformation: the scramble to gold in the late nineteenth century', *Review of Political Economy* 11, no. 2.

Kidron, M. (1965), *Foreign Investment in India*, London.

Kindleberger, C. P. (1984), *A Financial History of Western Europe*, London.

Kulke, H. and Rothermund, D. (1986), *A History of India*, London.

Kumar, D. (ed) (1983), *Cambridge Economic History of India, Vol. 2*, Cambridge.

Kynaston, D. (1994), *The City of London, Vol 1, A World of Its Own, 1815–1890*, London.

Laughlin, J. L. (1919), *Money and Prices*, London.

Lawson, P. (1993), *The East India Company. A History*, Harlow, Essex.

MacKay, R. F. (1985), *Balfour, Intellectual Statesman*, Oxford.

Mantoux, P. (1928), *The Industrial Revolution in the Eighteenth Century*, London.

Martín-Aceña, P. (1994), 'Spain during the classical gold standard years, 1880–1914', in M. D. Bordo and F. Capie (eds), *Monetary Regimes in Transition*, Cambridge.

Mathias, P. (1969), *The First Industrial Nation*, London.

Miller, R. (1993), *Britain and Latin America in the Nineteenth and Twentieth Centuries*, Harlow, Essex.

Mitchell, A. (1979), *The German Influence in France after 1870. The Formation of the French Republic*, London.

Moggridge, D. (1972), *British Monetary Policy, 1924–1931*, Cambridge.

Nevin, E. (1964), *Textbook of Economic Analysis*, London.

Nicholson, J. S. (1908), entry on bimetallism in *Chambers Encyclopaedia*, London.

Panić, M. (1992), *European Monetary Union. Lessons from the Classical Gold Standard*, Basingstoke and London.

Quigley, C. (1961), *The Evolution of Civilizations*, New York.

Redford, A. (1956), *Manchester Merchants and Foreign Trade*, Manchester.

Redish, A. (1990), 'The Evolution of the Gold Standard in England', *Journal of Economic History* 50, no. 4, December.

—— (1994), 'The Latin Monetary Union and the emergence of the gold standard', in M. D. Bordo and F. Capie, *Monetary Regimes in Transition*, Cambridge.

Ridley, M. (1996), *The Origins of Virtue*, Harmondsworth.

Ritter, G. (1997), *Goldbugs and Greenbacks. The Antimonopoly Tradition and the Politics of Finance in America*, Cambridge.

Roberts, A. (1999), *Salisbury. Victorian Titan*, London.

Rockoff, H. (1990), 'The "Wizard of Oz" as a Monetary Allegory', *Journal of Political Economy*, August.

Rostow, W. W. (1960), *The Stages of Economic Growth: A Non-Communist Manifesto*, Cambridge.

Russell, H. B. (1898), *International Monetary Conferences, Their Purposes, Character and Results*, New York and London.

Said, E. (1978), *Orientalism*, London.

Saul, S. B. (1969), *The Myth of the Great Depression, 1873–1896*, London.

Sayers, S. (1935), 'The Question of the Standard', *Economic History* 3, February.

Seaby, P. (1985), *The Story of British Coinage*, London.

Smiles, S. (1847), *Boulton and Watt*, London.

Stern, F. (1977), *Gold and Iron. Bismarck, Bleichröder and the Building of the German Empire*, Harmondsworth.

Tomlinson, J. D. (1979), 'The First World War and British cotton piece exports to India', *Economic History Review* 32, no. 4, November.

Vilar, P. (1976), *A History of Gold and Money, 1450–1920*, London.

Walker, F. (1898), *International Bimetallism*, London.

Watson, A. M. (1967), 'Back to Gold and Silver', *Economic History Review* 2nd series, 20.

Weber, E. (1980), *Peasants into Frenchmen*, London.

Wilson, E. R. (1990), 'Lancashire Cotton and the Bimetallist Controversy of the 1890s', M.Soc. Sci. dissertation, University of Birmingham.

Zebel, S. H. (1973), *Balfour. A Political Biography*, Cambridge.

Index

Industrial Revolution 24, 27, 35,
116–19, 121
Information Revolution 113, 143
Innocent IV, Pope 41
interest rates 87, 95, 139, 140, 142,
153
l'interlope 45
International Geodesic Conference
(Rome, 1883) 57
International Geographical Congress
Antwerp (1871) 56
Venice (1881) 57
International Meridian Conference
(1884) 57–8
International Monetary Conferences
15
(1867) 16, 34, 97, 130–32
(1878) 33, 34, 96–100, 126, 148,
159
(1889) 16, 34, 159
(1892) 16, 34, 83–4, 159, 163,
173, 177
(1895) 163
International Prototype Metre 59
International Statistics Congress
(1867) 51–2
International Trades Union Congress
(1886) 170
Irish exchange rate 25–6
Irish question 13, 173
Italy
company law in 61
and international bimetallism 100,
159
in Latin Monetary Union 51, 53,
100
token silver coins introduced in
(1862) 49

Jackson, Andrew 134
Jaget Sheth (Fatehchand) 68
Japan, silver–gold ratio in 149–50
Jevons, S. 53, 79, 130
Johnson, Matthey and Co. 59
journal 59
Junkers 123
Justice 168–9
jute trade 82, 83, 89, 101, 168, 182

Kannangara, A.P. 79, 81
Kemp, J. 146

Keynes, J.M. 10, 36, 67, 71, 87–9,
114–15, 177, 178, 182
Indian Currency and Finance 67,
87–8
Kidron, M. 168
Kindleberger, C.P. 8, 16, 41, 42, 44,
123, 127, 155n., 156, 159–60
Kipling, Rudyard 147
kitemark, gold standard as 137–43,
147, 149
Klondike, gold discoveries in 103,
147, 182
Kondratieff, N.D. 153, 154
Kondratieff Cycle 151
Küchler, Conrad 25
Kulke, H. 68
Kumaon Ironworks 80
Kumar, D. 69
Kuznets cycles 151
Kynaston, D. 27, 28, 149, 150, 172

labour theory of value 171
Lagrange, Joseph Louis de 58
Lancashire cotton industry
bimetallism supported by 16, 38–9,
65–7, 111, 159, 160–68, 181–2
Indian gold standard supported by
78
protest against Indian tariffs by 80
Landes region 59
Laplace, Pierre Simon, Marquis de
58
Latin America, gold standard in 140,
141–2
Latin Monetary Union (1865) 29, 34,
51–5, 62, 100, 130
Laughlin, J.L. 115
Lavelaye, Émile de 47
Law, John 12, 42–4
law, standardization of 60–61
Law of 7 Germinal (1803) 46, 60,
127, 133
Lawson, P. 74, 89n.
lead, as money 2–3
Lease, Mary Elizabeth 101–2
Lewis, M. 6
liards 60
ligne 58–9
Lindsay, A.M. 85
Lindsay scheme 85–6, 87
liquidity, definition of 1